Thank you for the ark in which to write. Andrew

For Jim & Janice —

My Diva

Thanks for
hosting our
writers' retreat.
You are patrons
of the arts!

Your home and
surroundings worked
as a wonderful muse.
Thanks for the gift
Erik

Thank you for
letting us stay in
your beautiful home.
We had a lovely weekend!
Patrick

Thanks for the
inspiring weekend.
Best wishes,
Lewis

My Diva

65 Gay Men on the Women Who Inspire Them

Edited by

Michael Montlack

TERRACE BOOKS

A TRADE IMPRINT OF THE UNIVERSITY OF WISCONSIN PRESS

Terrace Books
A trade imprint of the University of Wisconsin Press
1930 Monroe Street, 3rd Floor
Madison, Wisconsin 53711-2059

3 Henrietta Street
London WC2E 8LU, England

1   3   5   4   2

Printed in the United States of America

Library of Congress Cataloging-in-Publication Data
My diva : 65 gay men on the women who inspire them /
edited by Michael Montlack.
p.   cm.
ISBN 978-0-299-23120-0 (hardcover: alk. paper)
1. Gay men—Identity.   2. Gay men—Relations with heterosexual women.
3. Gay men—Biography.   4. Gay men—Anecdotes.   I. Montlack, Michael.
HQ76.M892   2009
306.76′620922—dc22
2008043125

"Grace Paley: O Stone! O Steel!" by Mark Doty is reprinted by permission
from *The Massachusetts Review* 49, no. 4 (Winter 2008).

This book is dedicated
to the memory of my father
HOWARD MONTLACK
who believed in this project,
and in me.

Venus doesn't glitter when she stands next to you . . .
Stevie Nicks, "Garbo" (1983)

Contents

Contents

Contents

Contents

Contents

Contents

Acknowledgments

I would like to acknowledge the following individuals and organizations for their generous support: Marilyn Nelson and Soul Mountain Retreat, Charles Flowers and Lambda Literary Foundation, Virginia Center for the Creative Arts, Ucross Foundation, and Berkeley College.

Thanks to all the contributors for their wonderful essays, enthusiasm, and professionalism. Special thanks to D. A. Powell (for being first to sign on); Mark Bibbins (for all the introductions); and Jim Elledge, Michael Klein, Christopher Lee Nutter, and David Trinidad (for their advice).

Also to David Groff (for the encouragement to start), Richard Schneider, Jr. and *The Gay & Lesbian Review* (for publishing the call for submissions), Raphael Kadushin (for recognizing the book's potential), and my agent Maya Rock (for finding me in *Cimarron Review*).

Thanks to my friends: Will Baker, Kerry Carnahan, Rebecca Curtiss, Warren Davidson, Ivan de Petrovsky, Ellen First, Michael Frew, Marty Garcia, Mary Gilhooly, Vicki Hallas, Tonya Hegamin, Lori Jacobs, Candi Jiosne, Lisa Karakas, Pam Kaskel, Sian Killingsworth, Chip Livingston, Molly McCloy, Susan Miller,

James Pacello, Pat Patterson, Bill Peters, Gerri Reinberg, Eric Sasson, Steve Streeter, and Stephen Wolf.

Also to Nicolas Arellano, Nik Velasquez, and Liz Yozzo (for their photographs), Julia Markus (for all her insight and wisdom), and Stephanie Fairyington (for pushing me to write the essay that began this project).

Love and affection to my mother, Claire; my sisters, Michele and Pam; my niece, Kimberly; and my brother-in-law, Joe.

And finally my deep respect and gratitude to Stevie Nicks and all the women featured in this book. As well as to the others whom I wish appeared and admire greatly: Elizabeth Bishop, Frida Kahlo, and Gertrude Stein.

Acknowledgments

My Diva

Introduction

Diva Complex

Michael Montlack

As soon as I started telling people about this project, the response was almost always the same: "Why hasn't this been done before?"

The book just seemed to make sense on so many levels. Gay men and divas—like Gertrude and Alice, smoke and mirrors, Patsy and Edina. It was sure to be organic, not to mention fun, even campy, and undoubtedly glamorous.

But the momentum was there from the beginning. When I approached writers for submissions, I could see I had tapped into something deeper than any campy stereotype; this was a book that had been waiting (and no longer patiently) to be written. The guys seemed genuinely delighted to participate. Their excitement and pride sometimes felt tangible, as if they had been finally assigned the roles they had been preparing for all their lives: acting as representatives for the women they adored, revered, worshiped. They all had stories to tell. And I have been lucky enough to collect them for you here.

In less than two weeks I had forty contributors on board, with submissions arriving daily. The idea had materialized into something concrete alarmingly fast. And not only was everyone saying yes, but they were offering the names of other accomplished writers who were sure to be interested. I was overwhelmed: Their gushing was sweet. Charming. Many were downright boyishly enthusiastic—yes, these award-winning, socially conscious professorial poets and writers, all showing up for the game, smiling, ready to play.

Included are gay men of various ages (twenty-something to eighty-something), places (England to Ghana, New York to California) and backgrounds, but they all share something in common—this special kind of love or connection (or relationship, if you will) to women they have never (for the most part) even met, women who have shaped their lives, inspired them to come out, given them strength, acted as role models for them, or just plain made them laugh.

This momentum, of course, was reinforcing. I just hadn't expected it to be so consistently strong. I mean, after contacting fifty writers, nearly no one had said no—with the exception of a couple guys whose divas had already been reserved.

Yes, that was one of the few guidelines: *No duplicates. One man per diva.*

"I'm sorry. I just couldn't imagine writing on anyone else," someone e-mailed.

"It's *her* or no one, I'm afraid," another said. "Tell me if the other guy drops out."

Such fidelity. Such jealousy. I loved it.

But even more surprising was the diversity of divas.

To be honest, I had expected, and even feared, a barrage of Barbras, Madonnas, and Judys. What would I have done with that? Yet, as you will see, those names aren't even on the final roster. How'd that happen? I don't know. Sure, there are plenty of standards (Cher, Bette Midler, Miss Ross, Liz Taylor) but there are plenty more surprises (Björk, Princess Leia, Julia Child, Queen Elizabeth I), which is what I had been hoping for both as an editor and as a gay man. I wanted the book to explore this bond in the broadest way possible, to illustrate how although there are common threads among us, there are even more threads that make us each unique. After all, what was perceived as my own "individuality" is what put me on the path to this book in the first place.

With events like Night of a Thousand Stevies, a large-scale drag club night held annually in New York City (and copycatted in cities around the country—for example, The Bella Donna Ball in San Francisco), it may not seem so strange to think of Ms. Nicks as a bona fide diva, but when I first came out fifteen years ago, the idea met with a lot of resistance, namely in the form of my first gay friend, Evan, who thought Stevie was, like my ponytail and sideburns, too rock and roll to be appreciated as a queer icon. We bickered playfully about it, but it was enough to make me reflect on questions that became the seeds for this anthology, questions that I myself posed to the contributors:

Who is this woman to you?
Why are you attracted to her?
What about her speaks to your being gay?
How has she influenced your life?

Judy Garland is perhaps the first figure to come to mind when thinking of gay icons or divas, and why not? Her death was a catalyst for Stonewall, what would become the start of the gay liberation movement as we know it in America. Her vulnerability, her suffering (substance abuse, failed relationships . . .), and her strength to withstand it all are qualities that many people can identify with, but especially people who have been historically oppressed. Plus, her role in *The Wizard of Oz* as Dorothy—the small-town misfit who finds herself in an enormous magical city, where there is diversity, color, and opportunity to pursue whatever one needs or desires—would certainly appeal to us as a community. Only, we're not all from Kansas.

Obviously, we have different styles, aesthetics, and interests, as it should be. Yet there seems still to be a particular type of fandom, or devotion, that only gay guys can deliver, the *Gay Following* if you will. Whether it be for Deborah Harry or Bea Arthur, Britney Spears or Frida Kahlo, we show up for the ladies like no one else and usually stick with them for life. I know I did. And do. Why is that?

As I discuss in my own entry, Stevie was a fairy godmother while I was growing up. Like Judy (or Dorothy), Stevie transported me to other (better) places in her songs with references to mythological witches or gypsies or dreams. Places more welcoming than the sometimes hostile and always homogeneous suburbs where I was raised. It might sound corny, but I have to say it: Stevie very well may have saved me in a sense, or at least spared me a good deal of pain. Later, when I might have been tempted to turn to drugs or alcohol to deal with homophobia and the fears of coming out, I could turn to her. Her music. Her own public battles with drugs and loneliness. Even her struggles as a woman in a male-dominated music industry would inspire me to never limit myself because of societal role restrictions.

So my friend Evan did me a favor those years ago when he teased that I couldn't "do any gay thing right," including picking a diva, because he caused me to investigate this bond, first in myself and now in others. And though there are some unifying themes, every man has his own diva experience with his own reasons for the attachment, whether it be emotional, social, psychological, cultural, or intellectual. The diva phenomenon is, as I point out in the title of this introduction, not simple but *complex*.

These singers, actresses, writers, politicians, chefs, and comediennes have, without a doubt, risen to the top of their fields and left their marks on society. But in the process they have also managed unknowingly to make an impact on the gay community, as well as on individual gay men and the closeted boys they once were. This book explores just how these women have helped to forge the identities and spirits of these men, in essays that are honest, poignant, and witty.

You will witness moments when our divas bring us back to the boyhoods we never could fully enjoy under the weight of our secrets. Jeff Oaks points out that we were not alone, though, that even "Wonder Woman had a secret identity." And there was company to be had, if we looked, such as in Julia Child, whom Bill Fogle refers to as "our favorite babysitter . . . a part of what it felt like to be at home." Luckily, John Dimes reminds us, we can even reclaim some of our youth as adults through spritely divas like Björk whose "childlike forces resonate with me as a queer gent because I recognize that . . . within myself."

Far off and seemingly out of reach, these women were still able to guide us through our difficult self-discoveries and insecurities, as seen when Jim Elledge says, "I never wanted to be [Tina Turner]; I just wanted her strength, her self-assuredness, and a body I wasn't ashamed of." Or when Walter Holland, upon first hearing Marlene Dietrich sing "I was made that way," realizes "exactly which 'way' that was . . . the life she was preparing me for." Forrest Hamer says about Mahalia Jackson, "I was listening in her voice for some sense of who I would finally be." So in these women, we were able to find our true selves and ultimately accept them.

But our divas would even be like older sisters too, when it was time for us to learn about love: how to survive it and how to live without it. In referring to Mary J. Blige, Jeffery Conway says, "In my despair, there she was. My sober black sister who, apparently, had been seeing the exact same type of man. . . . Together we made it through." But Edith Piaf would show a young, closeted Gregory Woods that "in the meantime, the emotional intensity

7

of the music fed the intensity of [his] sense of unsatisfied—and unsatisfiable—desire."

Often we found our political and artistic heroes in these women, which paved the way for the development of our own voices and visions. As Alfred Corn reminds us, in discussing the music of Billie Holiday, we "see an equivalent to racial discrimination in society's apparently ineradicable homophobia. But it's also possible to claim that gay males were, traditionally, followers of the arts to the point that they perfected their taste and were able to recognize excellence." This recognition of excellence is echoed on a more personal level when Regie Cabico admits, "While my poetry-writing Muse of my youth may have been a good-looking, dark-haired, exotic man, my poetry-writing Muse of adulthood is Nina Simone." But then Reginald Shepherd explains, while considering Kate Bush, that he has always "identified with female voices . . . because however idolized, they are also marginalized, as women speaking out of turn, speaking too much, making their presence too known."

Sam J. Miller well summarizes both the political and artistic influence divas have had on us in his essay on Bessie Smith: "The gay community also has lots to learn from women who seize hold of the oppression they face and turn it into something revolutionary, something beautiful, something fabulous." This creative and healing impulse seems to be what Edward Field is getting at in his examination of Gloria Swanson: "There is something about these larger-than-life movie stars that represents our yearnings for vindication, in which we see ourselves transcending the difficulties a gay man faces in this world."

But whatever the role the divas have played for us individually or communally—muse, goddess, sister, pioneer, survivor, alter ego, fairy godmother—they have protected us, guided us, and delighted us. They do this, they have done this, and they will continue to do this, as Rigoberto González points out in his essay on the late Rocío Dúrcal: "Even in death she is always there, faithful as oxygen." I guess a diva's job is never done. And so we owe them a great debt, which we seem to happily pay with our unending devotion and fierce love. This book is just another installment in the payment plan, I suppose. But I feel richer for having done it. In fact, Joseph Campana is right when he touches on this feeling in his essay on Audrey Hepburn: "The desire for icons is not the desire to become an icon but rather the need to create from nothing a source of nourishing love."

Perhaps in loving our divas, we have found a way in this world to love our selves.

Thank you, Ladies.

Sappho

Love, I Implore You in Polyester Lapels

Michael Broder

I guess you grow up knowing the name Sappho. Maybe it's got some vague associations in your mind with poetry and love and lesbians, and maybe not—it's too long ago to remember for sure. But after college I learned ancient Greek and then I began a doctorate in classics, and in 1986 I took Professor Stern's Greek poetry survey and that's when I read the famous fragments of Sappho, including the one that begins: *Not an army is it on horseback or of foot soldiers or a fleet of sailing ships that on the black earth is the most beautiful thing but rather whatever someone loves* (Sappho, fragment 16; all Sappho translations are by the author, based on the Greek text in *If Not, Winter: Fragments of Sappho,* trans. Anne Carson [New York: Knopf, 2002]). I was twenty-five years old then and falling for my first great love. He was a boy in my class. We sat across from each other in libraries and cafeterias and deserted classrooms and translated Sappho, and he passed me a note that said, "I'm stoned right now." A few months later he broke up with his boyfriend and made love to me, and a few months after that he vowed never to see me or speak to me again because he was so ashamed of how he'd led me on. Now he's dead, but I've still got the empty Cuervo Gold bottle from that bitter cold night in Coney Island. And I've still got Sappho.

When I first read Sappho, the space between language and experience disappeared, and where that space had been there was poetry and love, which are nearly the same thing, one being desire, the other being the voice of desire, its melody, its song, its prayer. The boldness of her conception filled me like sails on a windy sea—*That man seems to me to be equal to the gods, he who sits opposite you and up close hears your sweet words and pleasant laughter . . . for when I see you, no voice is left me, I go blind, deaf and dumb, I sweat, I tremble, and I am all but dead* (Sappho, fragment 31). Her thoughts and feelings came in a flood and she poured their full torrent through a finely turned spout of rhythmic language, which is to say music. She prayed, she praised, she pleaded, she lamented, she empathized—*But I say the most beautiful thing is whatever one loves; for Helen, who surpassed all in beauty, left her fine husband behind and went sailing to Troy with no thought for her children or beloved parents, compelled by desire* (Sappho, fragment 16). This was what I wanted from poetry, not so much imagery and symbols as what Gregory Orr, in his "Four Temperaments and the Forms of Poetry," calls "abstract imagination" (*Poets Teaching Poets: Self and the World,* ed. Gregory Orr and Ellen Bryant Voight [Ann Arbor: University of Michigan Press, 1996], 275), a poetry of ideas and emotions, what the ancient Greeks called *sophia,* the wisdom of poets, urgent, soaring, easy to see and hear but impossible to catch, like a squadron of fighter jets on evasive maneuvers.

I came oddly late to poetry. As a boy I loved stories, and that meant prose fiction. When I got older I studied poetry as literature but I didn't really love it the way I once loved *A Wrinkle in Time* or *The Lion, the Witch and the Wardrobe.* For a long time my only voice was academic, and when I first renewed my creative license, it was for short stories about secret loves and hopeless adolescent longings. My adult narrator—ironic, detached—looked back with wry self-compassion on his own gay coming of age. But I grew impatient with the narrative arc and I yearned for a language of pure climax. In time, my narrative voice became a lyric persona of its own accord, and I transitioned from fiction writer to poet. As I found that new mode, the model I echoed, the chanteuse, as it were, whose stylings I imitated, was Sappho. *Before you say a word, I am yours. Take without asking. Don't explore; don't discover. Make use—make me do it.* In recent work, I've poked fun at my own Sapphic investiture—*What about a good old-fashioned* ich-du *type poem, like the old days, Budweisers and brown paper bags, high school sweethearts and gym-class heartthrobs, the bad skin, bad teeth, never saying, always doing, the art of the locker room drive-by . . .*

To be sure, when I perform Sappho on the papyrus scroll of my imagination, she comes onstage first in corduroy jeans and polyester lapels, a boy who wanders down the halls of his high school afraid another boy will catch him checking out his crotch. After a smoky set of steamy numbers in hendecasyllables and Adonics, followed by a brief intermission, I return to the stage all grown up and this time it is *my* package on display in tight, faded Levis. In my first set I ache with regret, but in the second set my full truth emerges—yes, my heart is mastered by desire . . . by the unattainable Bay Ridge jocks and Bensonhurst hitters of adolescence; by Randy Snyder, with Liddell & Scott's *Greek-English Lexicon* tucked under one arm, a stack of Elton John records under the other, and a bottle of Cuervo Gold tucked away in his knapsack

13

on a night many years later, bitter cold and bittersweet (it was Sappho who first called love "bittersweet"). Yes, my heart is mastered by desire, but I have a sort of mastery now, too, because in the years between my first set and my second set, the space between language and experience has collapsed, and where that space had been, there is poetry—which is nearly the same thing as love, for love is desire, and poetry is the voice of desire, my melody, my song, my prayer.

This essay is dedicated to the memory of Rand Snyder (1960–1996), classicist, AIDS activist, Sappho queen, and diva.

Queen Elizabeth I

Heart of a King

Patrick Letellier

*Y*ou're a depression freak," my friend Jocelyn said one night over dinner. I had just told her that in the nine months since the sudden death of my close friend Darrel, I'd become so gloomy and morose that the only things I enjoyed were weight lifting and long-distance running.

"Most depressed people sleep all day, binge on chocolate, or can't get off the couch," Jocelyn said. "You work out and run marathons? I love you, darling, you know that. But you're a freak."

I knew she was right. I also knew I couldn't outrun my grief. After being so close to Darrel for thirteen years, it was hard to imagine my life without him. As soulful as he was playful, with a mischievous twinkle in his eye, he had moved through the world with incredible grace and humor. For Christmas the year I met him, he gave me a rubber chicken. "I just thought you needed one," he said. He never lost his wit or optimism, even through the grueling illness and death of two lovers to AIDS. "There's always a solution," he'd say, about any hardship, "you just might not see it yet." I trusted him. Loved him. Needed him. And almost a year after his death, I was still fumbling in the dark for solutions.

What I hadn't told Jocelyn was that the only *other* pleasure that sustained me during that long, overcast year was my unwavering obsession with Queen Elizabeth I. Never mind that she's been dead for four hundred years. I credit the crusty, white-faced Gloriana, as she was called late in her reign—aglitter with jewels, her regal head propped up proudly by those enormous, absurd, puffy collars of the day—with giving me the steely tenacity I needed to pull myself together and face life again, sans Darrel. Forget Judy or Madonna or Diana Ross. I needed a force-to-be-reckoned-with diva, and with Elizabeth, I got all that and more.

She's best known, of course, as the daughter of Henry VIII and his second wife, Anne Boleyn. To marry Anne, Henry had to divorce his first wife, and in doing so he defied the pope, split with the Catholic Church, and made himself head of the new Church of England. But when Anne failed to produce a son, giving birth instead to a wily, red-headed daughter, Elizabeth, Henry had Anne beheaded, and moved on to find a woman who would bear him a son. Twenty-five years later, after the death of Henry and the brief, tragic reigns of his other two children, Edward (who succumbed to tuberculosis) and Mary (who historians believe died of uterine cancer), Elizabeth was anointed queen. She reigned over England for the next forty-five years and is considered one of the greatest rulers of all time.

That said, I grant you she is undeniably a nerd's diva. In fact, she's a perfect storm of nerdy divadom, mixing European history and religious strife with geo- and gender politics at the end of the

Middle Ages. She was the kind of person who translated Italian poetry into Latin—*for fun.*

But she also had a penchant for handsome young men, often commenting on the big legs of those she admired. And she enjoyed a long affair with a married man who, before she lauded him with titles, had been master of her horses. She was famously outspoken, had a fiery temper, and was better educated than most men of her day. All the while ruling as a single woman who refused to marry, a radical stance for any female ruler of that time, she traipsed about the country adorned in a thousand yards of silk bearing a huge, shimmering crown. Like me, her subjects wildly adored her. I mean seriously, what gay geek can resist her? She's all the glamour of Audrey Hepburn plus all the fun of a Renaissance Faire!

But that's not what draws me to her. Though Elizabeth and I share two common bonds—we both lost our mothers young *and* both grew up wanting to become sovereign of a small island kingdom (I've always felt I should be king of someplace—Hawaii maybe, or Catalina; even Alcatraz would do)—what draws me back to her again and again, and what has propelled me through a slew of books and films about her, is her seemingly boundless strength and humanity. No matter how bleak the horizon, she refused to succumb to the twin demons of despair and self-pity. And at various times during her reign she had good cause to. Her cousin, Mary Queen of Scots, plotted relentlessly to overthrow and kill her. The pope, calling her a "heretic bastard," declared a holy war against her. Meanwhile, the formidable Spanish Armada attacked England. But Elizabeth remained unshakable. Determined. Proud.

"I have the body of a weak and feeble woman," she famously quipped, "but I have the heart and stomach of a king!"

She delivered that line in a speech I watched at least ten times in the HBO version of her life, with Helen Mirren playing the gutsy, resolute queen. And hokey as it may sound, I told myself that if Elizabeth could withstand the Spanish invasion with grace and grit, surely I could survive the loss of a dear friend. If she could shrug off papal death threats, perhaps I could put down my own grief, even if briefly.

If she can, I can. Isn't that how divas work? Like the tragic heroes of ancient Greek dramas, through their glory and fortitude and the heights from which they fall, they remind us all of our fragility. And if one so great can be humbled and rise again, perhaps we, too, can do the same.

It's been eighteen months since Darrel died. I still run and work out religiously. But the aching sorrow of his loss has passed. And like Elizabeth after the loss of her dear love, the Earl of Leicester, I'm determined to live out the rest of my reign in glory and style. Like a proper queen should.

Virginia Woolf

This Perpetual Revision of Thought

Brian Teare

—*h*esitant, I write a sentence, erase it, then hesitate, hover above my thoughts about her, unsure where to begin, and begin again. To write about her directly seems impossible. To begin anywhere, to choose any one detail with which to introduce her biography, would give her away too cheaply, oversimplify her, though were I to choose one story to tell, I'd dramatize the dichotomy between the "Virginia Woolf" of the public eye and Woolf's own interior experience of being a writer. Perhaps it's that I've been thinking about her life and work for over a decade; perhaps it's that I've read almost everything she lived to publish in addition to the writing her relatives released posthumously—her habit of thought no longer seems separate from mine. Within my own life, she continues to live a life that, though dependent on mine, nonetheless seems independent of it.

"I am interested in how Virginia Woolf's image generates custody battles over who gets to define her meaning," writes Brenda R. Silver in her marvelous study *Virginia Woolf Icon* (Chicago: University of Chicago Press, 1999). "This includes . . . those who insist on . . . an 'authentic,' legitimate Virginia Woolf to whom, they assert, they have a direct line" (5). And if Woolf is iconic it's because that to those who adore her, a diva is always already an icon in the senses the etymology of *eikon* suggests. Greek for "likeness, image, similitude," *eikon* later came to be *ikon,* a highly stylized image of an Orthodox saint or holy figure, and also *icon,* a rhetorical term for simile. A diva is foremost a simile: a goddess in the way that *diva* is Latin for "goddess."

To suggest, however, that my attraction to and respect for her work is solely a form of worship would be misleading: first, it would diminish her role in my intellectual and emotional life by couching it in a too-reductive metaphor; second, I'm interested in her as much for our commonalities as for our differences. And if I see myself in her, isn't that because a simile is a kind of mirror, a likeness? After all, she was the one to write, "All interesting people are egoists, perhaps; but it is not in itself desirable"; it was Wayne Koestenbaum—a gay man—who wrote, "Narcissism doesn't seem silly when a diva practices it" (*The Queen's Throat: Opera, Homosexuality, & the Mystery of Desire* [New York: Poseidon Press, 1993], 86).

Were I forced to introduce her biography, I might make a point of saying that, as a woman born in 1882 to the educated middle class, she was denied access to the formal education her brothers, Thoby and Adrian, were given. As the daughter of literary Victorian Sir Leslie Stephen, editor of *Dictionary of National Biography* and friend to Henry James and other luminaries, she was given private lessons and access to her father's books, both of which served as her writer's education; however, as a privately and, she thought, quite imperfectly educated "educated man's daughter," as a younger sister trying to keep up with her older brother Thoby's classical education, she was highly sensitized to the fact a private education taught her to read not only books, but the world itself, and that the lesson she learned was a gendered one invisible to the men around her.

Wednesday, October 23rd, 1929
    I will here sum up my impressions before publishing *A Room of One's Own* . . . there is a shrill feminine tone in it which my intimate friends will dislike. I forecast, then, that I shall get no criticism, except of the evasive, jocular kind . . . also I shall be attacked for a feminist and hinted at for a Sapphist . . . (Virginia Woolf, *A Writer's Diary* [London: Hogarth Press, 1965], 148)

And if I had to risk one metaphor with which to inscribe our relationship, it would be this: she has over time become my teacher, a role not incompatible with that of the diva whose voice "sets up vibrations and resonances in the listener's body," Koestenbaum writes in *The Queen's Throat.* "Listening, your heart is in your throat" (42). What he means, I think, is that a diva teaches by presenting herself as both goad and goal; by example her words lure my own to the brink of a similar risk: that they always flirt with the intonations of song, that they risk nothing less than mastery, control, and virtuosity. What I most admire about her pedagogy is that, while her public performances are matchless, her rehearsals reveal technique to be as much endeavor as inspiration, as much difficulty as ease, as anxious as it is relaxed. If the seemingly effortless eloquence of her nonfiction and novels tends to produce in me emotions closer to awe and veneration, it's in the practice room of her diary I learn most readily from her example as a working writer, for it's there I feel closest to being a fellow artist.

"WOMAN STARTS NEW SEX-WAR," claims the May 29 banner headlines of *The Sunday Referee,* "Says Men's Clothes are 'Barbarous.'" This is how a portion of the British popular press chose to frame the 1938 publication of Woolf's antiwar treatise, *Three Guineas* (New York: Harcourt Brace & Company, 1936), and in doing so underscored one of her most important achievements: she imbues with ideological import the phenomenal world, makes visible the invisible taken-for-granted power relations that render the domestic a truly fraught and social sphere for women of all classes. So Clarissa Dalloway goes out to buy flowers; and Lily Briscoe, alone with her vision, paints a portrait she thinks will likely sit in the attic forever; and Mrs. Ramsay, at a cost to her own sense of self, tends to her husband and children before she dies, too young, in her prime; so what? "The majority of women are neither harlots nor courtesans," Woolf writes in *A Room of One's Own,* "and the novels, without meaning to, inevitably lie." Because of this, the ordinary lives of women,

> these infinitely obscure lives[,] remain to be recorded I said . . . and went on in thought through the streets of London feeling in imagination the pressure of dumbness, the accumulation of unrecorded life . . . Above all, you must illumine your own soul with its profundities and shallows . . . and say what . . . is your relation to the everchanging and

turning world of gloves and shoes and stuffs. (*A Room of One's Own* [New York: Harcourt Brace & Company, 1989], 89–90)

In placing emphasis—*you must!*—upon the "world of gloves and shoes and stuffs," Woolf subtly rebels against what literary men have claimed make the novel Important; she would remind us that such Importance, without meaning to, "inevitably lie[s]." Deliberately undermining what have falsely constituted the novelist's proper methods, she reveals within our seemingly trivial intimacies with the material world the presence of the immaterial schemata (gender, class, nation) we live by and struggle against, and which bring us into relationships fruitful and painful, vital and disappointing, just and unjust.

—but I've hardly begun, have only gestured toward the role she's so far played in my life, and perhaps in some essential way this is as it should be, for it's in the shape of my sentences and the trajectory my thinking follows that I find her lambent voice and habits of mind limning my own. It's only when I suspect myself of inadvertently quoting her that I stop and take down from the shelf one of her books in which, the way a child sees himself of a sudden in his mother's profile, I find the intimate gesture I'd thought wholly my own.

Margaret Dumont

Duchess of Dignity

Christopher Murray

Margaret Dumont was called "the fifth Marx Brother" by
Groucho, appearing in seven of their films. In each, she played the
comic foil: a stately society matron who was a perfect target for
the boys' insults and jibes. Unlike some other divas, she was not a
subject of adulation, but rather has become someone for whom I
have empathy. She played the role of an often-oblivious woman
whose only purpose was to be made fun of. This is a lesser-known
kind of diva, but an important one. As much as gay men identify
with the glamour of a screen siren or disco diva, we also have always been drawn to tragic figures of ridicule. Monica Lewinsky is

a recent inheritor of this mantle, a society woman who becomes a target for widespread sexualized derision. It takes the special perspective of the homosexual male to rescue her, to reverse the prevailing attitude, and to put her on a pedestal as a survivor, a person worthy of dignity.

Dumont was also the still center around which comic chaos revolved. Without her, the Marx Brothers' madness had no form, no structure. I imagine the never-seen internal experience of her character and a growing rage toward her tormentors. This parallels the gay man's anger at being a target of bullies and demagogues. Certainly, she was ridiculous: pompous, hefty, and self-important. Her flaws rationalize the enmity directed at her, but don't excuse it. The viciousness of humor operates in opposition to the human necessity for tolerance and understanding. In our fantasies, like our comedies, we take delight in behaviors that wouldn't be acceptable in our real lives. The sadism shown toward Dumont is the sublimation of those darker impulses toward misogyny and even rape in the deepest reaches of the male psyche. Dumont is punished by the Marx Brothers for no longer being sexually attractive and for representing the power found in social position and money. For this, she must undergo humiliation. If she isn't destroyed, she may become the castrator.

This weak stab at Freudian interpretation aside, my attempt to imagine Dumont's pain is analogous to any gay man's attempt to connect with the glamour and emotional freedom of a more conventional diva. In fact, my groping toward empathy for Dumont embodies that creative leap from observation to identification that is the hallmark of the gay man's love of his diva. That it can be applied not only to the victorious siren and femme fatale, but to the forlorn, forgotten, fat, and fatuous as well, is, to me, moving and transformative.

I never thought the Marx Brothers were all that funny. They were barbarians and bullies, stupid and self-aggrandizing. But something in me responded to their cruelty. When I was in fourth grade, with my parents involved in a bitter separation, I took my confusion and hurt to the schoolyard. There by the tree next to the swing set, I became one of the Marx clan and mercilessly teased and taunted an outcast, a boy named Mark with a round face and funny square glasses who spoke in a stilted, strangled voice. I made him my bitch, calling him names and pushing him in the dirt. I relished in making him cry, tears drawing a path down his face toward his mouth open in a round howl of surprise and pain.

My favorite teacher, Mrs. Brady, witnessed my torture of Mark, and I'll never forget her confusion and dismay as she asked me why, why had I targeted this poor boy with such ferocity? And then I felt flooded with shame, felt it rising in my throat like bile. It was my first and maybe still my most intense experience of being ashamed, greater than any based on my latent sexuality. I had become my disapproving father, my rough brother. After that, I knew somehow that I couldn't live my life managing my own pain and fear by transforming into an aggressor. It felt too terrible to have a person I admired like Mrs. Brady show me to myself as a bully.

Eventually, I tried to make amends to Mark, befriended him. At first he was wary and uncertain, but after a while I learned his solitary games, began to share his complex inner world of dreams and fantasies. For the rest of my life, I would carry with me a special sympathy for the underdog, the misunderstood and the maligned. I make no claims to perfection in this; I'm still too aware of the seductive pleasure of sadism, the glee and sexual thrill of kicking someone when he's down, but I know I am unable to sustain that mode of being in the world.

Gay men get a lot of labels and proclivities slapped on them. At worst we are vain, shallow, obsessed with image and externals, sex-crazed drug addicts. At best, we are image-makers, czars of style, and wielders of wickedly delightful wit. But in my personal experience, we are most often alternating between a trio of roles: the outcast feeling fat and excluded by the cool disdainful beauties, the tormentor who cackles "Get *her*!" and points toward the frump sitting on the barstool across the room, and the rescuer who recognizes the beauty and dignity of the maligned.

It's so hard not to keep seeing other gay men as a united front of unapproachable, shirtless clones. The challenge is to reach into that swirling mass of bodies and recognize a person who you can cultivate as an individual with his own secret history of pain and resilience. At best, gay men are ultimately kind because they understand derision firsthand and know at their core what it is like to be excluded. Margaret Dumont wore her ridicule on her face for all of us to see, with only bemusement and faked obliviousness as her protection.

There was a myth about Dumont, promulgated by Groucho, that she never even got all the jokes and insults targeted toward her. That was a fib. "I'm a straight lady, the best in Hollywood," she later said. "There's an art to playing the straight role. You must build up your man but never top him, never steal the laughs." Dumont played the dupe, but it was an act, a role that showed us the power of punny punctures that the Marx Brothers used to deflate pomposity. But for me she will always remain a duchess of dignity in the face of ridicule, only her eyes secretly communicating the diva's ultimate message, "I will survive."

Bessie Smith

Empty Bed Blues

Sam J. Miller

Sometimes, gay men idolize divas who are always defiant, strong, and dominant. Ladies like Grace Jones or Mae West or Marlene Dietrich: we value them for their strength, for their uncompromising resistance to patriarchy and conservative morality. More often, however, the women who the gay community celebrates are more complex: they balance the strong and the weak, the defiant and the dominated. Madonna can be a gutsy kick-ass woman who shocks prudish male culture-makers and empowers her female listeners—but also a helpless little thing who sings of being "down on my knees," reduced by lust and need to abject helplessness. In *The Wizard of Oz* Judy Garland is "Dorothy Gale, small and meek"—but also plucky, brave, and fully capable of bitch-slapping a lion who threatens her loved ones. One of the reasons that "I Will Survive" has become *the* gay anthem is that so many gay men identify with the process of going from "at first I was afraid, I was petrified" to being proud and strong enough to say: "go on now go, walk out the door, just turn around now, you're not welcome anymore."

The "Empress of the Blues," Bessie Smith, stands as popular culture's first expression of that dynamic. Her songs constantly straddle the line between oppression and empowerment. In "Aggravatin' Papa," Bessie sings:

If you stay out with a high-brown baby,
I'll smack you down, and I don't mean maybe!

But in the very next line:

Aggravatin' Papa, I'll do anything you say . . .

At once demanding and desperate, powerful and powerless, this persona has particular resonance with gay men who can identify with the sensation of victimization by patriarchy, and who can spend a lifetime developing a strong, gutsy, take-no-shit attitude in spite of it.

Another element of Bessie's appeal to gay men is her fierce front-and-center sex life. Her songs are full of lewd innuendo and frank explorations of the joys and miseries of sex. She revels in the fact that she owns her sexuality—

I need a little sugar in my bowl, I need a little hot dog on my roll.

—but lust has also brought her low; in many of her songs she warns young women of the pain that sex and love and loneliness can engender.

Like her mentor Ma Rainey, Bessie was bisexual. Both singers were quite radical by mainstream cultural standards of the 1920s, because they treated queerness as a normal part of life (Ma Rainey sings of losing her man to a sissy, and of dressing up like a man and going out with "women, 'cause I don't like no mens"). And while Bessie has been hugely influential, and has a significant gay following, she has never been one of the Absolute Essentials that stir up tingly excitement in the gay community. She's no Cher, no Donna Summer, no Bette Davis. The reason for this has a lot to do with the history of American racism and the way that American racism gets mirrored even within anti-oppression struggles like the gay liberation movement.

In *A Room of One's Own,* another fab dyke diva, Virginia Woolf, asks us to imagine if Shakespeare had an equally talented sister. Imagine how, while William tramped off for London to hustle around his plays and become an actor and set up a theater company, his sister was prevented from receiving an education, forced into an unhappy marriage, trapped in the domestic world, and unable even to travel on her own. For Shakespeare's sister, madness and invisibility were the only options for artistic expression. While Bessie's afterlife in the blues pantheon is secure, in life she was "invisible" to white mainstream culture, which puts her off the radar to this day.

A useful comparison, to show just how thoroughly racism contributed to Bessie's being shunted off to the sidelines of both gay *and* mainstream culture, is with Mae West, only fourteen months younger than Bessie. Both were big, proud, bawdy ladies. Both saw the stage as a way out of childhood poverty. And in the 1920s both became superstars in separate vaudeville worlds: Mae West scandalizing Broadway with her smutty plays and voluptuous Diamond Lil persona, and Bessie dominating the chitlin' circuit and becoming the highest-paid black entertainer of the decade.

With the advent of the talking motion picture, vaudeville suffered a blow from which it would never recover. And while Mae West could pack up and head to Hollywood and take her craft to new heights and massive new audiences and a comfortable lifestyle, such an option was not available to dynamic, raunchy black ladies like Bessie. She never stopped performing, but the Depression hit her hard, and after 1929 she would only record once more, in 1933. In 1937, after a car accident, she died in a segregated Mississippi hospital. Mae West kept on making movies into her eighties—in her last film, *Sextette,* made when she was eighty-five, she sings one of her standards, "After You've Gone," a song made famous by Bessie Smith.

But the matter is not as simple as "racism destroyed Bessie while Mae went on to superstardom." Mae West did not just passively benefit from Hollywood's hostility to blacks; she exploited it. She borrowed heavily from black performers, and did nothing to create space for them within her movies—with the exception of her maids, at whose expense she makes racist jokes. If some elements of Mae West's screen and stage persona employ "a subversive parody of white genteel norms" (Leslie Fishbein, review of Jill Watts, *Mae West: An Icon in Black and White* in *Journal of American History* 89, no. 3 [2002]: 1103), in other places she plays into one of the most genteel white norms of all—the appropriation and exploitation of black culture and the black experience. Today, some scholars conjecture that West was of mixed race, and that her onscreen appropriations of blackness were the acting out of a conflicted racial identity—but this, like rumors in the '30s and '40s that she was actually a man, is pure speculation.

Bessie and Mae were not the same; each was a dazzling, inspiring artist who has earned her own separate space in our collective memory. Queers have done a ton of work digging up and dusting off gay artists like Walt Whitman, but hardly anything of the sort has been attempted with Bessie or the equally inspiring Ma Rainey. In her brilliant book *Blues Legacies and Black Feminism* (New York: Pantheon, 1998), Black Panther and feminist Angela Y. Davis stresses that Bessie "demonstrates an emerging model for the working woman—one who is sexually independent, self-sufficient, creative, and trend-setting" (10). The gay community also has lots to learn from women who seize hold of the oppression they face and turn it into something revolutionary, something beautiful, something fabulous.

Claude Cahun

Masks, Makeup, Meaning

Peter Dubé

$\mathscr{I}$ saw her for the first time at a dressing table; it was set up for a lady's toilette. The woman who owned this particular table was a friend of mine, and we were preparing for an evening out. I have long forgotten what our plans for the evening were; the force of my encounter has displaced all that. My friend left the room for a moment. Being a typical young fag of the time, I immediately went to the table to play with her cosmetics, to pick up and examine all those shiny little jars. There were small pots of powder and liquid in gold and violet, ecru and rose; tubes of lipstick in dark reds and pinks; and elaborate vials of perfume. And there was a mirror too, a tall one, which is where our gazes met.

She was taped in a corner: Claude Cahun, alongside Garbo (I think), a pop star who made a good deal of noise at the time, and a couple of fashion images whose slick perfection meant nothing beside Cahun's visage. She was blisteringly white, topped with an intricate coif; painted hearts ornamented her snowy cheekbones, and her lips were drawn together in a tight, dark *moue.* She was grotesque, gorgeous, and glowering at me through heavily made-up eyes whose expression married defiance and amusement in equal proportions.

Stunned, and jumping up from the table as my friend reentered the room, I asked, "Who is that in the white clown makeup?" She answered simply, "Claude Cahun . . . an artist from the '30s."

Although that first encounter is, retrospectively, a little too perfect—after all it took place among jars of makeup, and makeup was central in a lot of Cahun's self-portraits—it is still a slight enough beginning for a relationship that would become anything but. Claude Cahun's image, her work, her memory hit me hard and—let's just say—took hold.

My friend's introduction was only half-right; Cahun was a writer *and* an artist, having received attention for her literary work before her photography. Born Lucy Schwob (the niece of turn-of-the-century author Marcel Schwob), her life was a busy one; she was an active participant in a variety of avant-garde groups through the '20s and '30s, holding her own with such powerful personalities as André Breton and Georges Bataille, and contributed to multiple little magazines and exhibitions. During the war she and her partner, Suzanne Malherbe, would live on the island of Jersey, where they undertook a risky form of creative political resistance to the occupying Nazis. In 1929/30 she published a book called *Aveux non avenus* (the title is a tricky bit of French, and the book has recently appeared in English as *Disavowals*). She created numerous photomontages and surrealist objects, but despite so large and so various a body of work, produced in so short a time, it is her self-portraits that linger. Provocative, baroque, *so deliberate*—they spoke to me with overwhelming force, suggesting a delirious world of possibilities.

The following trio of photographs, all created in 1928, might provide a sense of the tempest they stirred up.

First, Cahun standing before a mirror, shorthaired, without apparent makeup, dressed in a harlequin-patterned shirt. She looks fairly butch in the shot. Her face is pressed, almost, against the glass but is turned from it, away from her own reflection and looking back at us. The game of self-representation is unavoidable but no less subtle for it. Her clothing references a tradition of performance; the glass reminds us of the game of gazes. She knows we're looking and she tells us in no uncertain terms that she is playing with her own appearance, but because she is not looking at herself, she underlines that she is doing it—in some ways at least—for us, or *to us . . .*

Then there is another, entitled *What Do You Want From Me?* Her head is shaved, though one should say "heads" because two of them seem to grow from a single torso. The monstrous pair is covered in white makeup, blurring the details of skin and features. One head faces the viewer, but is half-turned away; the other has its back to us, but half-turns toward our gaze. Or maybe, on the other hand, it is turned to whisper in the ear of the first. There is no way to know—anything—for certain.

Finally—a third: as purposeful as it is ambiguous. Against a fabric background (A curtain? A bedspread? Is she standing erect or lying down?) a female figure, nude as far as we can see, holds up her hands, touches her shoulders in a gesture that suggests modesty and self-pleasure all at once. The upper part of her face is covered with a black-and-white mask through the eye openings of which appear no eyes, merely blank, white spaces. Both her gaze and ours is thwarted in a *photograph,* that most direct invitation to look—hers by the covering of the eyes, ours by the mask. Here is the image of a face that is not one, the look that can never occur.

And that thought reminds me of another of her images, one of the photomontages that were part of her book *Aveux non avenus*. A line of text snakes across a page littered with heads and faces. It reads, in French, "Under this mask another mask. I shall never finish stripping away all these faces."

It is that phrase, coupled with Cahun's endless proliferation of self-portraits, that always reminds me of why I love her work, her figure, her inexhaustible impossibility so much. Those words call back precisely why she remains so constant a touchstone for me. At the bottom of all the paradox, Cahun's work is about its own incongruity; it is about costume, cross-dressing, roles and playing them, the contradiction of full self-consciousness and utter sincerity. I mentioned earlier, in confessing my quick rummage through my friend's cosmetics, that I was a keen young homo then, so there had already been some diva worship in my trajectory at that point, of course . . . Dietrich most of all, but the Liza of *Cabaret* for sure, and a couple of more contemporary ones: literary women like Angela Carter, *chanteuses* like Diamanda Galas, but somehow or other I found Cahun at exactly the right time. The truth is, despite being at the start of my proverbial journey, I had figured out that I was heading for full-on "art-faggotry," and Cahun had a lot to teach me about that.

Her images of herself are an unparalleled example of the power of masks to tell the truth, of how the embrace of artifice with enough commitment will make it a new kind of authenticity by sheer force of will. And although I had already caught a whiff of that in Wilde, her pictures took it up a notch for me. She showed me just how powerful making an image of yourself can be and why that can matter . . . for yourself and the whole damn world.

Her work is about claiming the power to *create one's own life outside the space of normalization,* which, let's face it, makes it both *queer* and *art*. Decades before Stonewall, she did what so many of us (the sensitive and creative ones at least) have to learn to do just to survive sometimes. She had the balls to willfully construct her freakhood and to make it beautiful. That was magnificent and I owe her for it. Big time.

Gracie Allen

Comic Muse

Lloyd Schwartz

I first discovered Gracie Allen listening to the *Burns & Allen* show on the radio. It was love at first sound—the lilting, silvery twinkle of her voice. But even more, I found her slippery use of words, taking them more literally than they were intended, hilarious and irresistible and mind bending. Playing with words amused me from my earliest childhood. I remember howling at the joke:

> "Whatever happened to your get up and go?"
> "It got up and went."

Comedy, irony, turning things inside out became my defense against not fitting in. In high school the tough kids disliked me because I was a good student. But when I acted in plays or invented comic pantomimes for school assemblies and amateur contests, even the scary tough guys got a kick out of my willingness to make a fool of myself in public. Kids who once threatened me suddenly adopted me as a mascot. It was cool to like me, because I made them laugh, because I didn't seem to be taking myself as seriously as they thought I would, because I didn't think I was better or smarter than they were.

Something similar was true about my love for poetry. I knew there was beauty in the world—I saw it, I read it. But I didn't feel I was part of it. I loved Keats not only because his poems were so beautiful, but also because that beauty had meaning. And since I never thought I could reproduce that beauty, I tried to turn that beauty inside out, create something that was something like the opposite side of the same coin—something that had meaning because it was the opposite of beauty, the inversion of it. My first poem was called "Moonlight and Garbage."

Did this have something to do with being gay? With a sense that I "didn't fit in?" Well, probably—though I see this explanation now only in retrospect. And because the question this book poses has forced me to think about it. Of course, this answer is too simple. After all, not all comedians are homosexual (and yet they don't call homosexuals "gay" for nothing). Isn't all comedy a good way of defending oneself against a hostile world?

Eventually, I started writing poems in the voices of other people, other characters—often quite the opposite of myself (although we shared significant qualities). It was like being an actor (one of my most serious ambitions)—both escaping from qualities in myself I didn't especially like or want and extending my own range of possibilities. My first book, *These People,* was essentially a collection of dramatic monologues. After that book was (finally) published, I didn't want to repeat myself. I wanted to move away from simple monologues toward something more narrative, in which more than one voice would come into play. In Boston a local UHF TV station was playing ancient repeats of the *Burns & Allen* show, and all of a sudden my childhood delight in Gracie Allen overwhelmed me. I was tickled, teased, titillated. Bewitched and bothered. I wanted to kiss her and strangle her. Her modesty and generosity and affection (like my mother's!) were remarkably touching. Yet her ineptitude was causing real damage. But wasn't that also her source of power?

And what could be funnier? When Gracie hears that one of her friends has to choose between spending money on a face-lift "or the Bahamas," she thinks her friend should get the face-lift first, and then deal with her "Bahamas" later.

Seeing these shows again inspired me to write a poem—half comedy, half elegy. I couldn't figure out how to use that last joke (it was too simply a joke), but other Gracie-isms seemed more profound, more poetic—more *my* kind of poetry. When I was assembling the poems for my second book and looking for a title, *Goodnight, Gracie* seemed the inevitable choice. Wasn't her embodiment of inversion, of turning things on their heads, my own response to the world, to the world of poetry? Hadn't she always been my real Muse?

Lotte Lenya

Divine *Weltschmerz*

David Bergman

We always gathered at Mary's house because hers was biggest and her mother only came back to make dinner and her father was never home. The place resonated with defiance, for here her brother had done what to us appeared unimaginable: thrown his Princeton diploma in his parents' faces, saying, *This is what you wanted.* What *he* wanted I hoped was someone like me, because in the pictures he was beautiful and Mary loved him.

We were teenagers in the mid-'60s, and our afternoons had their rituals. First we listened to the Velvet Underground and the Fugs, who felt, as we did, like "homemade shit." We were teenagers after all and felt required to be unhappy. Then Mary played a one-handed version of Debussy's "Blanc et Noir" on the baby grand. It was the only thing she seemed to know, and she played it beautifully. I would watch her reflection in the smoky-mirrored back wall, her eyes half closed. Then Wendy, her best friend, whose face was covered with a fine coating of hair and who would become a lesbian (we all knew she was in love with Mary; we all were), then Wendy would put a joint out in the ashtray and say, "Lotte Lenya, it's time for Lotte Lenya." The LP would be changed, and we waited for our lesson in the fate of incommensurable passion.

We preferred the recordings in German. We were all Jewish, and German was the forbidden language, and we felt that anger, weariness, and defeat—emotions we were also forbidden since we were supposed to be nice, well-adjusted children—could be sung only in German. We sensed that we held within ourselves something forbidden. It was true that some of us were *A* students, and that we always went to class and didn't get into "trouble." But we liked to think we were only good because we had found no one yet worthy to lead us to the bad, the bad that Lenya seemed to hold like a high note. Certainly, we had found no one who loved us with the desire we yearned for, no Surabaya Johnny. (If only we could be used for money!) Yet it was important to know the irrationality, the helplessness, the completeness of loving that we heard somewhere lodged between the coarsely worn timbre of her voice and its naïve purity. Lenya had the world-weariness we aspired to, and the innocence we were stuck with, and she made the former seem possible and the latter less embarrassing. "Yes, the sea is blue, so blue," she sang as if she had never noticed it before and it might suddenly be taken from her. How I loved the way she pronounced *blau,* with the mouth opening up as if to take a bite out of it. Lenya sang with her teeth.

That was part of the steely toughness that I knew I would never have. Her cold vengeance seemed to me then exclusively feminine, which is why it was so frightening and so fascinating. I never imagined I could send a lover to walk the plank on a black-masted ship.

41

I would never be a Pirate Jenny for whom the only port was the one she was leaving. I feared, instead, that I might always be stuck at home. She had the exile's iciness, the survivor's ruthlessness. She and the world moved on. I stood still.

We couldn't tell when she stopped singing and the record began scratching in its perpetual groove. The two gritty, gravelly sounds seemed strangely alike. But at some point Mary would stand up, her thin arms in the air, too much lipstick on her puckered lips. "Hoopla!" she shouted, imitating the flat, dull, unforgiving voice of Lenya's unremitting but indispensable love. And then it was time to do homework.

Gloria Swanson

Sunset Boulevard

Edward Field

$\mathcal{I}$ grew up during the era when the movie studios built up their movie stars into gods and goddesses—but especially, for me, the goddesses, figures like Bette Davis, Joan Crawford, Rita Hayworth, Ava Gardner, Ingrid Bergman, Greta Garbo, and of course, Judy—a pantheon that dominated the fantasy lives of the whole country. The plots of their movies were inextricably part of the legends of these ladies, as well as their social and love lives, including their marriages, most of which were largely invented for them by the studios' publicity departments. It was a world of supreme fiction that engaged the imagination totally.

As a child, I wasn't allowed to go to the movies, and still I was captivated. My friends and I endlessly played the game of giving each other initials and we had to guess the names of movie stars. Of course, as soon as I got a paper route and earned some money, I haunted the movies, where the sexual possibilities in the darkness became an equal attraction. It's all mixed together in my mind. And in my book of movie poems, *Variety Photoplays,* I recreated memorable movies in the form they became in our subconscious minds—American legends.

The movie goddess with her grandiose fantasies was epitomized for me in *Sunset Boulevard* (1950), which brought out of retirement the very much out-of-this-world actress Gloria Swanson, star of the '20s, the "real life" embodiment of the heroine of the movie, who, when she said, "We didn't need voices, we had faces," was perfectly believable. If this was acting, it was like a time machine had restored to life a historic, even mummified, actress to the screen.

I had barely been aware of her. Perhaps I'd heard her name as just another silent movie star of yesteryear. It was as if she emerged from the remote past where she'd been relegated to an L.A. bungalow colony and card games with old cronies, waiting for the call from the studios. In an age of naturalistic action with Marlon Brando and The Method, her style of acting was tinged with silent movie exaggeration—I knew it well from silent films at the Museum of Modern Art where the audience sometimes broke the worshipful atmosphere and laughed—which made Gloria Swanson, in her comeback movie *Sunset Boulevard,* an absolutely believable heroine. But still she made me uncomfortable, at first, with her mannerisms, her affectations.

After she made this comeback, I saw her on a TV talk show where she behaved in the same unreal manner, with that affected voice, discussing her obsession with health food to stay young, and when a handsome young actor joined the panel, she ran her forefinger around his manly jaw in admiration, and you could see her as the man eater she probably was—she'd gobble him up in a minute! A true sign of the diva! I was certain that all through the years of neglect, she'd watched her own movies over and over again and had completely identified with her performances on screen. So *Sunset Boulevard* was perfect typecasting.

A poem I wrote called "Whatever Happened to May Caspar?" is about a similar over-the-hill movie star, who lived in a shabby hotel off Times Square, living out her leftover tawdry life after the public had turned away from her and the studios dropped her, which robbed her of her glamour, for her magic depended on the worship of the fans, just as gods lose their power when the worshipers no longer believe in them. But in the case of stars, if they fall out of sight, there is always the possible miracle of the "comeback." May Caspar, in my poem, is rediscovered, as Gloria Swanson was in real life, but for May it was too late—too late for the miracle of plastic surgery and pills to restore her to the perfection the camera demands. And when a close-up is called for, with the merciless camera thrust in her face, she collapses.

In a later poem of mine, "Comeback," the Gloria Swanson figure I call Connie is closely based on *Sunset Boulevard,* but I simply leave out the William Holden character, the hustler stud, as peripheral to the greater drama of the plot: the star's dream of a comeback in which she has the complicity of her faithful servant/ ex-director Erich von Stroheim. In the movie, the struggle of the star to remain young, to preserve her glamour, is portrayed as ludicrous, not to say grotesque. But the truth of this relationship is not so far from my own life. My partner, whom I met nearly fifty years ago, had remarkably indestructible looks and grace, and I've found myself living out the adoring, faithful Erich von Stroheim part, devoting myself to keeping his illusions of his youth and beauty intact. As Tennyson says, "Though much is taken, much abides," and in the von Stroheim role, I preserve my own illusions, seeing him as he always was. He is all the more touching and dear to me as the years go on.

You didn't have to be gay to worship the legendary screen goddesses, but they had special relevance for gay men. There is something about these larger-than-life movie stars that represents our yearnings for vindication, in which we see ourselves transcending the difficulties a gay man faces in this world. They act out our dreams for us, even if, as in Gloria Swanson's case in *Sunset Boulevard,* it is delusional. Never mind, she pursues her ambition to the end and goes down in a glorious denouement with the cameras on her, recording her greatest performance. That alone is her justification. For us, she acts out our struggles, our yearnings, our heroism on the screen in front of the world, and the world no longer sneers, but weeps for us.

Marlene Dietrich

Falling in Love Again

Walter Holland

$\mathcal{I}$ was drawn to things German from an early age. My family had German heritage, but my real attraction was something more mired in the tragedy of World War II. The decadence and brilliance of the '20s in Germany always held my interest. In the von Sternberg films with Marlene Dietrich, I got a taste of the deep, shadowy, restless world where beauty flirted with criminality, where life and death, goodness and sin were depicted in glittering silver and black. I knew the Weimar years had held "depravity," "sexual depravity," that was legend in the books my father bought about the prewar years.

Dietrich seemed to represent the mysterious European glamour I had read about, the romanticized concoction of artists such as Kafka, Mann, Lang, or Murnau. She carried a world-weariness on her young shoulders, and in her husky voice and cabaret ballads, I detected the allure of stranger things to come, my own inevitable collision with troubling desires and conflicting wishes.

The Blue Angel, which I saw on late-night TV, suggested a sadness that made love appear dangerous, foolish, and humiliating. I intuited even then that I felt little attraction to women, but I knew Dietrich wouldn't care. She would recognize me, shrug me off with just a stare and a knowing smile. It made no difference in the game of survival and hers had been a life of live-and-let-live.

Recently I started reading Marlene's autobiography in German and found my fascination with her renewed by her impassive tone of voice and her insistence that she was "made" and "created" solely by the vision of one man, Joseph von Sternberg, never a love interest, but a man who found her a medium for his ideas. She has reminded me of that unique relationship between gay men and female actresses as well as the female characters they have created to represent their innermost desires and thoughts.

Marlene, herself, was known for her bisexuality, and in that I found a clue to her allure for me. In *Morocco,* when she stoops to kiss a young, pretty woman on the lips, tipping her silken top hat, her outfit that of a dandy, I remember feeling a moment's shock as I stood, a young boy of twelve, in the basement of our house in Lynchburg, Virginia. How could a woman do that to another woman? What did it mean? Hers was a sophistication far beyond my upbringing in the American South, tied up in exotic locales, cabaret bars far beyond Monument Terrace in Lynchburg with its confederate statue and tobacco warehouse.

From the moment I heard the famous lyrics to her song in *The Blue Angel*—"Falling in love again / Never wanted to. / What am I to do? / Can't help it"—I knew that they were meant for me, for the young man who late on a winter's night would walk across a three-mile campus in upstate New York to spend ten minutes groping a fellow male student in the quiet of his room, our underwear pulled to our ankles, fear and elation trembling through our bodies as I exploded on his knee, and then barely look back as he implored me to stay and have some tea. I knew that the love she sang about was dangerous. I knew it would be, after my Catholic upbringing, a compulsion. And, as Dietrich sang "I was made that way" later in the song, I knew exactly which "way" that was. I knew the life she was preparing me for.

Marlene struggled with her home country, a country ruled by conservative forces. She took the side of the Allies during World War II, was called a traitor by Germany, and dealt with ill feelings in her native Berlin, but she returned anyway to show her solidarity, not with the fascist Nazi forces but with the suffering people. This sense of divided allegiance and betrayal in the face of great intolerance and violence, I felt, somehow related to my own experience many years later during the Reagan years in the United States and the advent of the AIDS epidemic. It took a certain courage for Dietrich, who became an American citizen, to renounce the political policies of her former country but not its people. I was made to find distant parallels as I witnessed many of my gay activist friends turn against the Reagan government, the NIH, and the pharmaceutical companies as well as the Moral Majority, often at great personal cost, dividing their families and breaking their hometown bonds. Anti-Semitism, intolerance, and fear Dietrich met with outspoken frankness. Gay men with AIDS faced the same costly prejudices, and she seemed someone who would have understood all that.

She never lost sight of her roots, her working-class beginnings, and the basic dignity of the studio workers around her, from hairdressers to makeup artists to lighting technicians. She saw Hollywood and Paramount as a factory of dreams, and in typical cynical Berlin fashion, she saw herself its gossamer product—not only product but factory worker as well, up on the set at 6 a.m., ready to be assembled, pushed, pulled, molded out of lights and lenses.

Loyal to the end, generous to and protective of her mother and her assistants, humble about her good luck, Dietrich was buried near her mother in Berlin, the city she retained fondness for and loved so well.

Joan Crawford versus *Bette Davis*

"But ya AHHH, Blanche!"

David Trinidad

$\mathscr{I}$ think I have more questions about Joan Crawford and Bette Davis, and their legendary feud (as over-dramatized now as it was then), than I have statements to make. Why have I always been drawn to them? Why are most (if not all?) gay men, sooner or later, attracted to them? Something in our blood, our DNA? Rare is the homosexual who can resist their theatricality. Perhaps that fascination is acquired, passed one to the other? How else does one learn at which altar to worship? Once converted, there's no turning back—you're as zealous as the rest of them, screaming "But ya AHHH, Blanche!" at the annual female-impersonated re-enactment of *What Ever Happened to Baby Jane?*

Perhaps it's all about the catfight: the oh-so-cultured Blanche receiving (deservedly?) the full brunt of Jane's alcoholic ferocity, or over-the-hill Helen Lawson pounding on the stall door as Neely O'Hara flushes her wig down the toilet. (One of the things that makes the latter camp is Susan Hayward's beautiful head of white hair; why should she be ashamed, try to hide *that*?) And if the catfight takes place in a secluded Hollywood mansion, or a posh powder room, all the better. Bachelard wrote about "the power of attraction of all the domains of intimacy." And what space could be more intimate than a closed movie set, where (we imagine) the real Davis and Crawford duke it out? "Straight men like catfights too," Elaine Equi told me, when I discussed this with her. "On that, all men agree: catfights are good." So we (the gay), it turns out, don't have exclusive rights? Does it work for straight men when the women involved *aren't* buxom babes? When they're two past-their-prime divas desperately fanning the embers of their careers (beneath the Oscars on their mantels)—same appeal?

In my early teens, my mother drove me to Topanga Plaza (the closest mall) in the West San Fernando Valley, where at Pickwick Books I bought (with money I'd earned mowing neighbors' lawns) *The Films of Joan Crawford* and *The Films of Bette Davis*. They were the most important actresses (to my mind) in the "films of" series, though I owned others: Judy Garland, Marilyn Monroe, Katharine Hepburn, Greta Garbo. I also owned Robert Osborne's *Academy Awards Illustrated* (the title imprinted in gold on the white cover), which then only went up to 1967 (the year of *The Graduate* and *Bonnie and Clyde*). These books were my lifeline: I pored over them repeatedly, memorizing much of their contents. Now, no one came up to me and said: *You're a young fag, so you have to idolize Bette Davis and Joan Crawford.* I simply gravitated toward them on my own. I saw *The Nanny* at a Saturday matinee when I was eleven. I'm not sure I had connected, yet, with Davis, as thoroughly as I later would. I only remember being traumatized by her drab, murderous portrayal, and by her pitiless bug-eyed stare. A couple years later, when I went to see Crawford in *Berserk!* at a local theater, not only was I primed for the performance of a diva, I was ready for the gore.

Somewhere between *The Nanny* and *Berserk!* (and must I state the obvious, that this was puberty) I bought into the notion of Davis and Crawford as great stars who, in order to survive, had taken to tawdry, low-budget horror; the notion that they were so tough and seasoned, they'd do whatever was necessary to stay on top; that no one was going to keep them down (i.e., off the silver screen). True beacons during a lonely, closeted adolescence. I knew (and loved) the Davis of *All About Eve* and the Crawford of *Mildred Pierce,* but I reveled in the ghoulish stuff. On late-night TV I watched *Dead Ringer, Hush . . . Hush, Sweet Charlotte,* and (most exciting of all) *What Ever Happened to Baby Jane?,* which paired these two indomitable actresses, and which I viewed (sorry to say) with a total lack of irony. This was serious (I was serious!) Oscar-nominated fare. I felt I was being let in on something important, that through their demeanor (as actors and as characters) I was being shown the dark (and therefore true) side of stardom, of what comes from that glittering thing (fame) I, a child of my time, had been mesmerized by for as long as I could remember. Small wonder I was thereafter drawn to *Whatever Became of . . . ?,* Richard Lamparski's series of books about celebrities who'd faded into obscurity. The washed-up have their own special glamour: strands of sloughed-off tinsel glinting in a moonlit gutter.

So when did something so serious become camp? An invisible line, but at some point I crossed it. When I finally made gay friends? When I saw, for the first time, a female impersonator impersonating Bette impersonating Joan's affected mannerisms: *Oh really, did she like it?* A mystery, the mix of pleasure and repulsion such moments afford. When I read what Lee Israel wrote about

53

Tallulah Bankhead's makeup, that "[h]er lip-line had ceased . . . to have anything to do with the shape of her mouth," I equated it with Davis and Crawford; it seemed to solve a piece of that mystery. Clown mouths. These aging actresses are "about glamour rather than glamorous." This applies more to Crawford than to Davis. Unwilling to relinquish her sexual allure, Crawford broadcast the idea (versus the thing itself) of youthful femininity, perfected an exaggeration of the persona she'd basked in, in the 1930s, the height of her status as glamorous movie star. Unafraid to look the frump, Davis insisted on her own integrity as an actress, dedication to her craft. But she was always mugging for that third Oscar. Everything got too big, too loud: the waving of the cigarette, the downing of the martini, the tossing of the hair. Oh, and the hand on the hip. Of course she took it, intentionally, to the ultimate extreme in *Baby Jane,* though the fact that she cried when she saw herself in rushes I find particularly poignant.

I'm the only homosexual I know who doesn't consider the two women in the documentary *Grey Gardens* hilariously funny. I'm actually repelled by their delusional, symbiotic relationship. But maybe that relationship (and our reaction to it) mirrors the dynamic between Crawford and Davis? We're asked to share in a pathology; at the same time we see the horror of it, and laugh in spite of ourselves? Why then do we relish it, love to mimic it? And what does any of this have to do with men having sex with each other? A few days ago, on the phone with Jeffery Conway, I whined about having to write this. "I don't know *why* I'm attracted to Bette and Joan." His response made me laugh: "Why do birds fly south? They don't know. They just go." I suppose that was his way of saying: *But ya AHHH!*

Lucille Ball

Flaming Redhead

Lawrence Applebaum

It's a helluva start, being able to recognize what makes you happy.

Lucille Désirée Ball, on being gay

On April 26, 1989, Lucy died. I was working as a coat-check clerk at the newly opened gay bar the Townhouse on 59th Street, just nine blocks away from where the Ricardos lived in the Mertz's fictitious apartment building at 623 East 68th Street.

It was the first time I ever cried for a famous person. That afternoon I bought all the newspapers I could. The world had lost a muse—or at least I had. As a descendant of Holocaust survivors, I grew up with an atmosphere of death in our household. So it's not so surprising that as a child, I told my mother if I were ever to fall into a coma, I wanted to hear *I Love Lucy* episodes playing in my hospital room. Watching her was so life affirming.

I Love Lucy fired up my inquisitiveness, which led to many of my firsts. At three, I went off with her (through the magic of television) to Florida, California, Paris, Italy, Cuba, even Japan. At twelve, I purchased my first bottle of Egyptian henna rinse (brown, not red—I would go red at fifteen). Then I wanted to go "Downtown" (even before Petula Clark) to see Lucy's Manhattan playground. To eat bacon and eggs at a drugstore counter that unfortunately doesn't exist anymore—now we grab Power Bars at Duane Reade. Or to go to the top of the Empire State Building, see a Broadway show, take a dance class, ride the subway to Brooklyn with a veiled loving cup on my head (all right, minus the cup and veil). I did a lot of those things as soon as I could. Lucy's inhibitions turned mundane daily living into an amazing adventure (or when I was lucky, a hilarious fiasco).

Lucy Ricardo broadened my thinking. She would try anything, like delivering Aunt Martha's salad dressing on roller skates or sneaking into the Tropicana. She introduced me to (seemingly) gay characters by having a séance with Mr. Maryweather in the "Ethel to Tillie" episode, or singing "I tippy tippy toe through my garden" with the English tutor Percy Livermore. I didn't know what a homosexual was, but these performances piqued my curiosity and made me feel less alone, because Lucy liked these flamboyant men even though they were ridiculed by the rest of the characters.

I would mimic her too. If there was something I wanted to do or have, and I didn't get my way, I'd warn my mother, "I'll shave my head! I'll wear a mask!" Lines from Lucy's "Italian Movie" episode—when her skin turns blue after that fight in the vat of grapes she was stomping. If I really wanted to press it, I'd add, "Couldn't I say I'm an American tourist who is homesick? And that's why I'm blue?" It never worked, but I felt good saying it. I repeated this so often, my mother would tell people, "Just ignore him."

Even her Max Factor makeup fascinated me. I didn't know what "drag" was, but Lucy was always dressing up as someone else. The Queen of the Gypsies, Superman, even the first Drag King on television (singing in that barbershop quartet). Somehow Lucy managed to be glamorous frozen in a freezer with icicle eyelashes! I was in love. And not just with her. There was also the importance of being Ethel! She and Lucy became one of my first models for friendship and fun. Looking back, it seems Ethel was the first fag hag of the '50s: Lucy's slightly overweight sidekick, always ready with a campy one-liner.

When I was five, my brother, David, who was fourteen, had a job delivering groceries in our Bronx neighborhood. He came home one day and announced that he had just delivered to Lucy's mother-in-law and that he had seen Lucy's wedding pictures (this was her second marriage, not to Desi, but still). I figured he was teasing and never believed him. Years later, I met her daughter, Lucie Arnaz, at an American Theater Wing seminar and mentioned my brother's story, asking if it could be true. She said, "Oh yes, Grandma Morton lived in the Bronx. We all used to visit her there."

Recently I met a neighbor from my old building, Barbara, who said, "I remember seeing Lucy once, walking down Lydic Avenue, passing all the stores and bakeries, with that carrot hair and wearing an impeccable pantsuit with piping. She was smiling at everyone and I thought 'Am I dreaming? Lucy on Pelham Parkway by the bagel shop?'" Yes, it is hard to picture Lucy as fully real, and doing those boring everyday things we all do, at least not without imagining her getting into some sort of trouble before inevitably getting herself out of it.

But then my big break came and I had the chance to see her in

Lucille Ball

person when I lived in a dorm on 23rd Street. I saw a sign in the window of the Red Apple Supermarket: *Lucille Ball will be filming here next Wednesday night.* And went in to ask the manager about it. He said, "She wants people in the neighborhood to know she's coming." So that Wednesday I found a spot in the crowd and got a glimpse as she pushed a grocery cart along the sidewalk—her hair a mess, her face filthy, but those blue eyes still radiant. I saw a technical person (standing beside, of all things, a "Gaylord Productions" sign) and asked about the film. "*Stone Pillow,*" he said. "About a homeless woman named Florabel." So the first diva of television was still taking chances, even in her seventies.

But back to that night in 1989: in the Townhouse coat check, where I was arranging the candle I'd snatched from the bar so that her photo (now captioned "1911–1989") would be easily seen in an appropriate flickering glow. People stopped on their way to the restroom to pay their respects, maybe sharing a favorite moment or two from the show. Though none of those mourners is as memorable as that man, maybe thirty-five, from a small Midwestern town, who said, "Seeing her, as a boy, in all those New York scenes is what made me want to run away to the city. She's why I'm here." I handed him a tissue and thought: *He's right.* So many gay kids felt the need to escape to the big cities, where they could live anonymously if not freely. And Lucy was there in our living rooms, showing us what fun (and trouble) there'd be for us when we arrived.

At the end of the night, alone again in the nearly empty coatroom, I opened one of the newspapers to a quote from her: "I was never funny. What I am is brave." Maybe that was what I and so many other gay people appreciated most about her. Though we would certainly need a sense of humor, what would really get us through the tough days and nights was a little Lucy-like fearlessness.

Mahalia Jackson

Divine One

Forrest Hamer

Studs Terkel describes that when he first heard Mahalia Jackson sing (a record store in Chicago happened to be playing her 1946 Apollo recording of "I'm Gonna Tell God All About It"), he was reminded of Enrico Caruso, for both of them continuously exceeded imagined limits of the human voice. The comparison is apt, for Jackson's voice was operatic, an "uncommonly large" voice (according to biographer Jules Schwerin in *Got to Tell It: Mahalia Jackson, Queen of Gospel* [New York: Oxford University Press, 1992]), and one prone to render epic the gospel songs she performed.

I have listened to her all of my life. Growing up in a very religious family, we listened to recordings of her voice in North Carolina on my grandfather's Victrola (which played 78s); we listened in Germany, where my father was stationed in the late 1950s and then again several years later; and then throughout the rest of my childhood stateside. Her voice not only helped my family locate home in each new place, it made each place a possible new home. And because ours was sometimes the first black family in a neighborhood, being able to feel at home was crucial to our being able to thrive in not-such-promised lands.

Mahalia's singing was the unacknowledged other half to Martin Luther King Jr.'s "I Have a Dream" speech at the 1963 March on Washington. Jackson had preceded his speech with a few songs, among them the spiritual "I Been 'Buked and I Been Scorned," and she had requested that King forego another prepared speech to give this one. The speech completed a narrative arc set up by this particular spiritual—from an acknowledgement of deep, long-lived pain to astounding hope—and this arc characterized her performance of many of the songs she sang generally. It was an extraordinary confluence of an artist's gifts with the historical moment. How appropriate it would also be that she would sing at King's funeral some five years later.

To the extent that a people and a self can be described separately, her voice also transcended any definition of particular identity. It was, of course, a unique voice—exceptionally controlled and unbounded, joyful and mournful, individual and cumulative; it was also one that could transcend itself by reaching far beyond what we were typically listening to hear. It was a voice I would be personally receptive to when, after spending most of my Sundays in church (morning, afternoon, *and* evening services), I was overwhelmed by gospel music and sermons, and simply wanted silence; and even later when I came to reject much of the religious teachings of my upbringing. What I heard went beyond the limits of specific religious teaching: I heard in her voice the chance for ordinary grace and the promises of extraordinary transformation through devotional action.

At the annual assembly of churches in the eastern part of North Carolina—the black half of the Church of Christ, Disciples of Christ denomination—several vendors sold sheet music on the grounds, and some of the most popular featured songs were written by Thomas A. Dorsey as sung by Mahalia Jackson. By the late 1960s the moniker "Queen of Gospel" was undisputed, and stories of prima donna behavior—occasional irascibility, refusals to sing until she'd been paid her high fees in cash, the dropping of her long-time accompanist Mildred Falls because Falls asked to be paid more, gaudy displays of her considerable wealth (her vigorous skin-lightening efforts late in her life, among them)—did little to tarnish the regard with which so many held her. She was *Mahalia*, after all, and her talents and causes suggested to us that her own relationship to her gifts was probably complicated and sometimes a little too much to bear.

I did not know who or what I was going to be. As a young child, I suspected I would become an adult someday, and a man at that. This also meant I would not become a woman, despite my love of and for women and my awe of them. Mahalia's powerful voice necessitated that I find some way of aspiring toward her emotional power while accepting I would never be someone who would sing the way she did (I didn't know that being a woman was not enough to make this possible.) I knew I was sometimes different from other boys—quieter, comfortable with girls and with so-called feminine things—but I did not know what this difference might come to mean when I would grow up, when I would be a man. I was listening in her voice for some sense of who I would finally be. I had already heard there the possibility of transcending all I thought I could know. I suppose, these years later, in some manner more important than I could construe, I still listen for the same.

Julia Child

Life's Ingredients

Bill Fogle

Celebrity has the habit of being highly selective. Fame assigns a set of familiar, beloved features that calcify into statues, leaving us with the beauty but also the smaller dimensions of the gallery.

Julia Child has been served but also restricted by her adoring public, and she is forever fifty, unintimidated by cholesterol, dropping turkeys (she didn't, actually), and crowned everlastingly in a brown helmet of bedroom hair.

Everything I've read about her indicates that despite her sang-froid and semi-noble birth, she struggled with life much as we all do, perhaps more so for the added burden of expectation that comes with her social class. For this reader, her life story is a series of false starts: an early attempt as a writer, a very brief career as an advertising copywriter, and a few years in civil service. Not failures, certainly, yet each has the quality of a search. It's irresistible to picture Julia Child as a novelist or bureaucrat, or a bright, too-ambitious presence at the table during an office meeting. Thankfully, that's not how it went.

What seems to have been swept under the table with the turkey is a very passionate woman, a good mixture of just enough objectivity with an abundance of Epicureanism. Julia seems to have been the exception to the rule of fame for divas such as Maria Callas and Madonna. It was from within her priorities as a private individual that her stature was given birth. One truly doubts that her early ambition outlasted her harmonious marriage, and when celebrity found Julia Child it never deserted her simply, it would seem, because it was never *sought*. Yet she was no less of a performer for being a long-lasting one.

Those who search more deeply into the documentation will, at some point, discover a dichotomy between the exacting, peevish author and the theatrical gestures and rounded-off measurements of the television pioneer. Compare any recipe you find in *Mastering the Art of French Cooking* with the same dish as prepared by Julia on television and you will discover a genius of adaptation, a circumstantial inventor. When it came to the intimacy of television, the trust with which she gained admittance into so many homes, Julia Child was not above frozen phyllo dough.

If Judy Garland is every gay man's dream of a best friend or clubbing partner, Julia Child is our favorite babysitter. In fact, for many of us she kept just the right hours, bringing her copper pots and carbon steel knives into our lives just after school let out. Maybe others saw her only on sick days, or at holidays or during the summer. In any case she was a part of what it felt like to be at home.

Yet she outpaced Mary Poppins, in the same humble couture, with a startling polymorphism. For here was the glamour of La

Belle France, a table of impractical refinement prepared in the solid, unaffordable cookware of the elite. What she did with eggs was *elegant.* Thus she was a wolf in sheep's clothing, of our home but oh so far beyond it. So it was that we all began clarifying butter.

Like everyone, for Julia Child, too, the confident focus of early life gave way to the shapeless universality, the hesitant humility of intellect that characterizes vast experience. Her last major cookbook declared, "It's not all about French cooking anymore." Were these the words of a woman who had lived outside Provence too long? More likely, they were the result of such thorough study that the similarities of national dishes outweighed any disparity.

Late in life Julia herself traded on an acquired commodity: her personal celebrity. Not even Tammy Faye Bakker could escape the socio-sexual leveling ground of media exposure, and Julia was no exception. So she could construct her anecdotes, telling us how hard it was for a woman of her height (six feet two) to shop for clothes on a budget: "I had to elbow drag queens out of the way to grab the last blouse in my size."

All those years, I think she knew we were watching.

Billie Holiday

Lady Day

Alfred Corn

The first time I heard Billie Holiday's voice was during a dinner party at Edmund White's apartment on West 13th Street in New York. This would have been in 1968, I think, roughly about two years into our friendship. In those days he liked to advocate for artists he'd discovered—the novels of Colette, Victoria De Los Angeles's recording of Canteloube's *Les Chansons d'Auvergne,* the paintings of Ludwig Kirchner, or the *Pillow Book* by the Japanese noblewoman and Heian court diarist Sei Shonagon. None of Ed's proselytizing ever failed with me; in fact, I still like all of those figures.

That evening he played the last album Holiday recorded, the one titled *Lady in Satin*. Its cover photograph shows the singer toward the end of her life, dressed, as a matter of fact, in a low-cut satin evening dress, her hair severely pulled back in a ponytail, an enigmatic half-smile contradicting and complementing the lines that pain and fatigue have inscribed among her beautiful features. Discographers rate the cuts in this album as not even close to the best that Holiday ever recorded. By that time her voice had eroded considerably, the inevitable result of decades of performance in smoky dives on 52nd Street or in Greenwich Village, the tempestuous love affairs that often ended in black eyes and sore ribs, the heroin use, and the time done behind bars for drug convictions. But magic is magic, even when glimpsed through a glass darkly. I became a fan immediately. Ed and I swooned and laughed over faintly camp numbers like "You Gave Me Violets for My Furs" and fell silent at the evident pain behind "I'm a Fool to Want You," pain so little fought off it registered as the unoptimistic calm of the survivor who has seen it all, the scapegoat who will never again be shocked by injustice and cruelty.

I remember that Ed loved Billie's way of delivering lyrics of loss and abandonment in a perfectly cheerful tone. The lover may be callous, he may leave you without a second thought, but he's still "My Man." You certainly get that with the late recordings. But, as I was about to learn, there is more to Holiday, beginning with the puttin'-on-the-ritz sass of "Miss Brown to You," the amused self-vaunting of "Gee, Baby, Ain't I Good to You," or the eerily ironic indictment of racism and lynch law in "Strange Fruit." And sometimes loss was put across as just that, with no window dressing of comedy or irony, in songs like the Ellington classic "In My Solitude," sung with unforgettable plangency in more than one version. (Actually, Holiday's several renditions of her signature numbers always vary in fascinating ways. She once said, "I never sing a song the same way twice, because that ain't music.") She didn't have a voice as honeyed as Ella Fitzgerald's or as pyrotechnic as

Sarah Vaughan's, but her timing and phrasing, her inventively added or revised notes, her skill at injecting extra meaning into a simple lyric, outdistanced all her contemporaries. How many different things she did with that voice! Besides that, she lived a life that had the makings of legend, and I'm not referring to trivial details such as her habit of performing with a lush gardenia pinned to the side of her head or her preference for a drink she called a "White Cadillac" (two parts milk to one part scotch).

Some time in the late '60s WBAI–Pacifica Radio in New York began broadcasting readings from Holiday's ghostwritten autobiography *Lady Sings the Blues*. Gripped by what I heard, I got my hands on a copy of the book and read it through without stopping. Even though dictated and edited, the text gives the rhythm and intonation made familiar from the vocal recordings. And it has an unforgettable opening: "Mom and Pop were just kids when they got married. He was sixteen and she was fifteen. I was two." I'm not sure at what point I read Frank O'Hara's most famous poem, "The Day Lady Died," but it seemed to endorse my emotional involvement with "Lady Day," as her fans called her, and beyond that confirmed the tentative friendship I'd begun feeling for O'Hara's poetry.

Why have gay males (including the classical composer Ned Rorem) always idolized Billie? Because they've often been dumped themselves and need the musical antidote to pain that Holiday offers, obviously; and they see an equivalent to racial discrimination in society's apparently ineradicable homophobia. But it's also possible to claim that gay males were, traditionally, followers of the arts to the point that they perfected their taste and were able to recognize excellence wherever they encountered it. I can see, though, that the queer demographic is no longer as devoted to fine art as was once true. The new generation knows almost nothing about Billie Holiday; she doesn't count for them in the way that, say, Erykah Badu does, or Christina Aguilera, or Beyoncé, or Kelly Clarkson. To understand her artistry requires an effort, partly historical, partly imaginative, and partly aesthetic—less than what's required for understanding Mozart opera, but still. It occurs to me that the above paragraphs may sound like an infomercial for the value of getting to know Billie Holiday. Well, *yes,* it is.

Edith Piaf

A Share of Pain

Gregory Woods

𝓜y mother owned a small collection of records to play on her deep-throated Black Box gramophone. We lived in a characterless modern villa near the mouth of a brown river that flowed into the Gulf of Guinea from the heart of darkness. Our large garden, although not really wild, made gestures toward exoticism: mango and banana trees, pineapples, large red land crabs, the occasional black mamba that had slithered in from the bush. We kept pet cats, but these disappeared from time to time.

Unlike many colonials, we did not have a radio on which to listen to the BBC World Service. My parents had left England because they wanted to leave it, so there was little point in pining for its distant voice. But they had left England for Egypt, not Ghana, and, through the spectacular incompetence of British foreign policy during the Suez crisis of 1956, we had been thrown out of Egypt. So Ghana was a kind of exile after all. Neither of my parents liked it much. It had none of the sophistication and few of the amusements of Cairo. Although already a great port, Takoradi could not compare with Alexandria—or Alex, as the British affectionately called it.

Some books, but not many, brought a touch of refinement to that bleak, concrete functionary's house. And then there was that music collection: some popular classics (Beatrice Lillie's narration of *The Carnival of the Animals*), a little trad jazz (Louis Armstrong, Jack Teagarten), two musicals (*Oklahoma!* and *Annie Get Your Gun*), a couple of Sinatra albums, some Bing Crosby, Eartha Kitt, *Noel Coward in Las Vegas* and *Noel Coward in New York*— and an album of Edith Piaf. If this were a man's collection it would look distinctly queer, but as a woman's it was not so far off the mainstream.

There were three of us children—I have an elder brother and sister—but I do not recall being significantly different from the others in my tastes. We could all sing along to many of the songs my mother played. I was no more likely than my brother—who is heterosexual—to ask for Piaf or Kitt. Nor, when either of these women was singing, did I ever feel I wanted to be her. My main difference from my siblings was my shyness. I followed the others. If taken on an adventure by them, I was adventurous. Only when reading books, I think, was I fully independent. I do not believe my interest in Piaf was yet at all queer.

If there was a particular moment when this changed, I cannot place it precisely. It recurs in my memory of an image in black and white. I was watching a television documentary about Piaf in my early teens—which would place us in the 1960s. My father had retired and we had moved home to England. At some point in the telling of her life story, Piaf appeared with one of her husbands or lovers: much taller, much younger, and wearing only swimming trunks. This is my moment.

It is at this point that I start to connect the Little Sparrow's life—and her myth—with my enjoyment of her work, which then intensifies as a result. Pricking up my ears, I hear about her addictions, and these I connect with what I have already deduced from her voicing of the songs: her loneliness. Our lives as colonial children had involved frequent changes of school, with consequent changes of friends; and my brother and I were now being sent to a Roman Catholic boarding school near Oxford, with the consequence that we had no friends around us when we went home to the south coast for the holidays. Add to this my growing sense of myself as becoming both bookish and "queer," and you can see that I was involuntarily making a major personal investment in loneliness.

The square-cut swimming trunks of Piaf's young man were iconic. I kept thinking back to them. Even if I never wanted to be the singer, I did rather want to have what she had. Although every note of her music made it clear that men were trouble, such men as this were beginning to seem a trouble worth taking. But it would be years before I dared take such a risk. In the meantime, the emotional intensity of the music fed the intensity of my sense of unsatisfied—and unsatisfiable—desire.

In the gay liberationist period of the 1970s, when I came out, I never felt, as some doctrinaire activists did, that thinking positively about one's gayness required a constant affirmation of happiness in one's love life. My conviction that "gay is good" (as our convenient but crass slogan had it) never undermined my understanding that love involves waves and cycles of less positive emotions such as doubt, disappointment, guilt, fear, anger, and sheer boredom. Love was not love without its share of pain. If I ever needed reminding of this, Piaf did the trick—perhaps not so much in her lyrics as in the plangency of her voice.

My love of the Little Sparrow has one other dimension. For me, she is quintessentially French. Her songs have always seemed to offer something more human than the dry pathology of Anglo-Saxon Protestantism. Hers was a Mediterranean voice, eroded by age and tobacco and dried out in the sun, full of wine and garlic and olive oil. It reeks of what Donald Rumsfeld so contemptuously dismissed as "Old Europe." So much the better.

Evita Perón

Santa with a Soundtrack

Guillermo Castro

With her iconic chignon in place, Evita beamed from a postcard taped just above the windshield inside the cabin of my uncle's 1937 Chevrolet truck. I spent many hours under her gaze pretending I was driving through the Alps, possibly transporting Juan Perón's Nazi treasure to a secure Swiss vault (or so legend has it.) Actually, the only treasure in the cargo cage was my uncle's fresh fruit and produce business. For supplies he'd go into the Abasto Produce Market and let me tag along. I'd stay in the truck though, ostensibly to "help" load the crates that Tío and his usual—hands down, my favorite—helper, Jara, would carry back from the market on very able shoulders. Jara was the kind of poor, dark-skinned fellow for whom Evita fought so much. While waiting for Uncle's return, through the slats between the boards encasing the cargo bed, I'd catch glimpses of penises belonging to the men pissing beside the truck. Fresh fruit indeed.

Uncle was only a boy when Evita came to the barrio dispensing gifts like a fairy godmother; he received a bicycle (to think that he gave me my first bicycle on my tenth birthday, and helped me ride it). Despite his family—single mom and two brothers— never getting a free, furnished residence in the housing project so demurely called Ciudad Evita, a bond was forged between them and the lady with the blonde locks and elaborate hats.

But it wasn't only devotion that María Eva Duarte de Perón inspired long after her death in 1952 from cervical cancer. In a zealous attempt at suppressing her memory from Argentine audiences over a quarter century later, anti-Peronist military censors excised a few seconds from a scene in *Superman II* that showed an ad for the musical *Evita* on the side of a bus. How ironic that this movie's three vinyl-clad villains—led by a general, no less!—reflected their three real-life counterparts, the heads of an authoritarian regime hell-bent on erasing their adversaries by any means necessary.

During this period I'd gotten my hands on a smuggled cassette of Lloyd Webber's *Evita: An Opera Based on the Life of Eva Perón*. I was serving in the army when, in April of 1982, a war broke out with Great Britain after Argentina's invasion of the Falkland Islands. And here I was listening to *la música del enemigo*! About a woman whose husband had had few friends in the armed forces. But I was hooked on something other than the music.

Private Rodríguez. He'd been the one who got me the English *Evita,* and that alone was reason enough to fall in love with him. And the fact we took showers together—and he seemed to prefer it that way—didn't hurt either. He also gave away mix tapes featuring the material banned by government censors. To my eyes that was badass, with a touch of Robin Hood (again the English!). Sitting on his bunk bed, we'd try our hand at translating the lyrics

74

to "Oh, What a Circus," "High Flying, Adored," and, naturally, "Don't Cry for Me, Argentina." (Quick side note: When I first moved to the United States someone asked me if this song was Argentina's national anthem. I swear this is true. I answered, "No, 'La Bamba' is.")

My love for Rodríguez was never consummated, much less expressed. I kept my queerness deep inside a closet that not even a whole army of juntas could pry open, a closet a whole nation seemed to have retreated into. It was one more thing, sexuality, I—we—learned you had to be quiet about if you valued your life. Not that it was safe otherwise: you could still get sent to a war.

Speaking of the unspoken, my parents and I knew to leave politics out of the conversation whenever visiting with Uncle. He would not tolerate disparaging comments directed at Juan Perón or Eva. Not that he would ever get physical and throw you out of his house. As a former boxer he certainly had, so to speak, the upper hand. But he was too sweet a person to do that. Instead he would just get upset, turning his anger inward, perhaps even cry (but not before gobbling up another empanada!). Yet many years later he'd remain perfectly indifferent to Madonna's presence in Buenos Aires during the making of *Evita*. While the rest of the country was in uproar—or at least those who'd been prodded by old guard Peronistas—my uncle responded to my question (and I dared raised that *subject*) with a simple and firm, "Who cares?" Tío would always remain loyal to the Peronist Party. Almost a decade after its leader had passed in 1974, he cast his vote for the new Peronista candidate as one for "Perón" and, of course, "Evita."

Grace Paley

O Stone! O Steel!

Mark Doty

Sometime in the mid-'90s, Grace Paley and I gathered with lots of other people in a small square at the foot of the Brooklyn Bridge, on a flawless June day, just a few happy-looking clouds out over the river. We were there for the Bridge Walk that Poets' House sponsors each year, a celebration of poetry and of New York City that ends at Fulton's Landing, where the ferry used to dock in Walt Whitman's day. Access to the bridge isn't especially pedestrian-friendly; you have to cross a busy street, a highway really, and then curve around onto the pedestrian pathway. It's thrilling, approaching the first tower with its beautiful harp-strings that seem to shift their pattern in mathematical precision as you get closer and then move away. As you move out onto the span of the bridge, you find yourself up above the traffic coursing below; you can look down on the cars that are rumbling past at what seems an inadvisable rate of speed. It ought to be quiet, suspended in the air over the river, but it's anything but; somehow I just hadn't imagined all those tires on the rough surface of the bridge, all buzzing and rattling at once. And therefore when we stopped at the top, where Grace was to read Marianne Moore's "To Brooklyn Bridge," I wondered if anybody in the assembled gathering would be able to hear her. I should have known better. Grace was a short woman, but she was a dynamo, and when she got to the exclamatory middle of the poem—"O stone! O steel!"—that voice rang out, in all the glory of its proud New York City vowels, firm enough to rise right above the unceasing action of the traffic.

It was a few years later, in the middle of summer, when Grace came to Provincetown with her daughter and her grandson, a handsome dark-skinned boy who was then perhaps five years old. We used to see them regularly at a café called Tofu A Go Go, an outdoor place on a roof deck, where you'd order your food and then sit and watch the world go by on the street below until they'd call your name and you could hop up and claim your tempeh reuben or your spirulina drink. Sometime that summer, Grace's grandson took to delivering the orders himself; he'd balance plates piled high with brown rice and miso'd onions and the most delicious roasted corn. Before long he was behind the counter; there was something slightly surreal about approaching the counter and finding there a child whose head barely cleared the glass case with its whipped tofu pie and vegan cookies. Since there was no place else in the busy town that offered a similar menu, the café was always busy, and ordering could be a bit of a trial; the line inevitably included at least one person who'd slow things up with many questions concerning salt, soy milk, yeast, wheat, and anything else one might worry about eating. The boy was cool, professional, and unfazed. He seemed to have found a calling, or at least a kind of real work, which must have been the most satisfying thing his child-self could desire: to be necessary, involved, of use.

While he was working, Grace used to sit at a favorite table, her legs spread wide as they often were when she was seated, usually a woolen bag full of student stories and flyers and letters and notebooks around her someplace. What I find hard to describe is her demeanor, the pleasure she took in her brilliant grandson's work. It was a mixture of admiration, a sly bit of humor, and absolute matter-of-factness lit with just a trace of surprise that this moment, this odd scene, had somehow issued from Grace: that was her beautiful grandson, fulfilling himself in this unlikely way, and everyone else was enjoying it, too.

I thought about that scene when Grace and I read together, in Amherst, just a couple of months before her death. It must have been one of her final readings, and she kept saying, "I'm going to read a story, but first some poems." She was clearly enjoying delivering the poems, and every now and then would remember that she had planned to read a story, and would say she'd get to it in a bit, but never did. That evening I understood Grace's poems better than I ever did, their humanity and clarity and the huge sense of warmth that seemed to radiate out from them. There were people in the audience who were unhappy because they wanted prose, and because the reading was long, but I couldn't have enjoyed it more. Here are the opening stanzas of "Here," one of the poems she read that night, one of her most memorable.

> *Here I am in the garden laughing*
> *an old woman with heavy breasts*
> *and a nicely mapped face*
>
> *how did this happen*
> *well that's who I wanted to be*
>
> *at last a woman*
> *in the old style sitting*

stout thighs apart under
a big skirt grandchild sliding
on off my lap a pleasant
summer perspiration

Those lines take me back to that Provincetown summer, to the presence of "a woman / in the old style," and her wonder at what her own body had brought forth, and who she'd become. Walt Whitman writes, in his great poem of crossing the ferry over the East River where Grace and I walked, "I too received identity of my body." Grace takes that notion a step further; if our bodies confer identity upon us, then are we brought new selves, as time moves on? Don't we all shake our heads, contemplating the transformation time brings, and ask, "How did this happen"? The poem allows me to sit, in that wide-legged old woman body, mildly hot in the sun, familiar little boy sliding off my lap, my own gender and age cast aside, for a moment, as poems allow us to do.

Ava Gardner

Small-Town Girl

C. Cleo Creech

$\mathcal{A}$va Gardner was from my hometown. Well, not exactly my hometown; it's always hard to explain to anyone just where my hometown is. You have to really know rural North Carolina to have ever heard of Stancil's Chapel or Shoeheel. So I generally have to start with a bigger city, like, "I'm from Raleigh." If people know that, I can add, "So maybe you know Johnston County?" If that gets an okay, then maybe they've heard of little places like Crocker's Nub, Middlesex, or my neck of the woods—Stancil's Chapel or Shoeheel.

So when I say Ava Gardner was from my hometown, it's sort of like in horseshoes and hand grenades—close enough to count. Our county seat is Smithfield, known mostly for being "no, not the one the hams come from." It is actually famous for two things though. First it has the Ava Gardner museum (more on that later), and then it was home to the last standing "Welcome to KKK Country" billboard in the nation.

I mention the KKK sign to give you a bit of a feel for the place. We're talking serious southern small-town living here. Oddly enough though, it would be wrong to pin everyone as hood-wearing rednecks. Yeah, we had a pretty high-class bunch of Klansmen, for the most part educated lawyers, business people, probably even a judge or two. This is an area of proper southern culture and deep-rooted prejudices and religious beliefs. It's also an area rife with ironies, like small Baptist churches where the preachers spew fire and brimstone but at the same time most every church organist is an effeminate pastel-wearing homosexual. He's also usually best friends with the minister's wife and also doubles as the congregation's wedding planner.

When I veered off the straight jock, marry-the-local-girl track, it didn't take long to realize that it wasn't a very good place to be homosexual. Not that I ever got beaten up or arrested, or had a cross burning in my yard, but I knew. I just knew.

So enter into this fairly bleak landscape Ava Gardner.

Ava Gardner is famous for a whole string of glamorous, big-studio productions. She worked her way up (some would say slept her way up) through years of B-movie studio fare. Finally though, she featured in dozens of now-classic movies, including such faves as *Mogambo, Bhowana Junction, The Barefoot Contessa,* and *Night of the Iguana.* She even showed up in the '70s disaster flick *Earthquake,* doing her own stunts.

Plus, she has one of those miracle Hollywood stories of how she got discovered. She went to visit her sister in New York. Her brother-in-law just happened to own a photography studio and asked if he could take some pictures of her as samples for his storefront. A movie agent walked by and—Voilà!—she's on her path to stardom.

She became one of the first real tabloid queens, even before the tabloids were big news. It's said she kept the studio publicity and damage control people fairly busy. Ava loved partying and dancing all night, and she was not shy about liking men. She did manage, though, to have three high-profile marriages, to Mickey Rooney, Artie Shaw, and most famously Frank Sinatra. Frank is billed as the love of her life. They had a hot on-again/off-again, stormy, intense romance. She even had an abortion with their child (since he was still married at the time, I guess it seemed the thing to do). Back then, this was pretty heavy-duty gossip column material. There was probably much more that was not printed, just said in whispers.

That too seemed to be the thing people in Johnston County couldn't abide. Maybe they could have overlooked the partying, sexcapades, and fast living. However, an affair with a married man AND an abortion—well, that pretty much made it open season for the local blue-hairs to tear her apart.

When a lifelong friend and supporter wanted to share his collection of substantial memorabilia and celebrate the area's most famous resident, apparently the locals wanted nothing to do with it, nothing to do with celebrating the life of this brazen hussy, home-wrecker, and fallen woman. The white-gloved, blue-haired church ladies put out the word that she wasn't exactly the type of woman they should be celebrating. So plans for her museum languished for years.

It didn't help that on her many summer visits to the area to visit family, she made a bit of a spectacle of herself. The local Cadillac dealership would give her a loaner every summer she was there, a practice that they ended up terminating because of her drinking. There were also complaints that her car needed a lot of "servicing," and these strapping young local mechanics would often have to spend all afternoon "fixing" her car. I wonder if many of these boys even knew who she was.

But back to why I love her: Imagine my surprise to find that such a famous, glamorous, and scandalous movie star had grown up on a rural tobacco farm—just like me! It actually took some time to process, but turned out to be a ray of hope for a small-town gayling like me.

If a small-town tobacco farm girl like Ava Gardner can become a big-studio movie star, marry some of the most celebrated men of her time, travel the world, and end up living in Hollywood, New York, and London, maybe there was hope for me yet. Not that I was even dreaming that big. However, it certainly made my more modest hopes of moving to the big city (Atlanta) and becoming something as unheard of as a writer, poet, and artist—well, maybe not so out there after all.

She gives me hope even now, as I get older. She did have this great love of her life, Frank Sinatra. He had a full-size statue of her in his backyard. One that he kept long after they'd split up. He only had it taken out after a new wife complained, and then only with a fight. Ava also traveled, living in Spain for years and bedding matadors left and right, living the life of a lavish bohemian expatriate. Later she lived quietly in a posh London apartment. So it seemed possible to live a full, rich life. It's funny how our priorities change, from fame and fortune as we're younger to love, travel, and fullness as we age.

The diva/hero worship can go both ways though. There is the "maybe there's a dream for me too" angle, seeing how someone you can identify with has blazed a trail, making your way a bit easier. But there's also the way divas can be surprisingly human, coming down to our level. When talking to a staffer at the North Carolina State Tobacco Museum (our other great cultural institution), she had all sorts of stories about Ava. However, probably the most telling comment was, "You know though, when you saw her on the street without her makeup in just jeans—she looked just like anyone else!"

So divas give us something to look up to, but also, when we're luckier, they offer a look at how they can be just like us. In the end, that's why she's my hero. She reminds us that even old Hollywood stars can live full, ripe lives. That we should go for it, live for the moment, and without regrets. That even small-town girls from rural tobacco farms like her (and me) can make it big and dream big-town dreams.

Aurora de Albornoz

Tía Divina

Scott Hightower

$\mathcal{I}$n the first grade, when my central Texas public school teacher asked what I "wanted to be" when I grew up, about the only professional (not a preacher, teacher, or rancher) that I could conjure up was . . . a Lottie Moon missionary. That did not come from a fervent religiosity, but from the notion that missionaries traveled to foreign countries and took photographs of their travels. They stood with other people in the world as witnesses to other places. At that time, that was about as "sophisticated" a version of an international, cosmopolitan life as my little imagination could muster up.

Years later, with my high school Spanish, the reading of my liberal arts education, and one seven-month's "bachelor's journey" to India under my belt, I took up a domestic life with a partner in New York City. Such innocent steps toward the unforeseen life ahead.

My "unblessed" union brought me onto the unaccepting slopes of a taciturn Republican Spanish family living in Puerto Rico. While all of my beloved's immediate family had misgivings, I heard stories of his aunt—his mother's sister. She was reportedly playful and sophisticated. Something of a scholar, poet, and literary figure in Madrid. Someone who had played "Auntie Mame" to my lover's "Patrick"—a diva who reportedly brought an infectious joie de vivre to the table!

Oddly, I don't recall the exact first moments of our meeting. Though we rather quickly settled into a loving conspiracy of three. When Aurora came to town, she stayed with her close friend, José Olivio Jiménez, a celebrated Cuban American literary critic and professor at City University of New York. The apartment—on West 90th Street—was a large two-bedroom with a long, high-ceilinged salon. Artifacts from José Olivio's travels in the Americas peppered the room: that coffee table fashioned out of a wagon wheel and a circle of glass, or the modestly framed, glee-filled, bacchanalia Picasso print. When Aurora came to town, there were parties of writers, academics, and bon vivants much like those I had only experienced somewhere along the way on screen with Holly Golightly. There were mixed drinks and naughty stories. A profound embrace of Freedom swirled around the room like expensive cologne. Tío Olivio's hybrid "American European sensibility" set the stage, and Aurora's extravagantly generous theatrical nature held center. I knew little and understood less. I developed a taste for olives and goat cheese, for sangria and Russian vodka.

Aurora's chestnut hair was bobbed and parted on one side, her cheek touched by one distinct auburn spit curl. She often wore strands of beads that she liked to fidget through her fingers. Part flapper, she could wrap her lovely figure up in her long brown mink or coat of lynx. Her cigarette was always held at bay from the tangerine or pink gloss of her lips by the dark span of a cigarette holder. Part Grande Dame, she could converse in four languages and muddle along joyfully in several others if put to the task. Part martini-drinking, cosmopolitan sophisticate, she was pro-youth, pro-sex, pro-tolerance. She wore Chanel-inspired suits, and while effusive, she was never vulgar. Quite the contrary. She was stylish. Everyone who knew Aurora knew that she refused to accept quiet desperation and used imagination and style to create a life worth living.

One night in Madrid she insisted we take in a screening of Visconti's rereleased film *Gattopardo* (*The Leopard*). The movie was in Italian and the subtitles were in Spanish . . . but what a classy count Burt Lancaster made—and what a waltz! (Years later, I purchased the DVD. On my own, I would go on to discover *The Damned, Death in Venice, The Garden of the Finzi-Continis,* and I would go on to research the Night of the Long Knives and see parallels to events in the Spanish Civil War.)

Another time, we dined at Café Gijón then sipped Calvados with friends at the speakeasy Oliver. And on another one of our days out-and-about, we sipped broth and savored petite sandwiches and toasted croquettes at (one of "our Patrick's" favorite places) the lovely storefront parlor of Lhardy's. She bought a small box of candied violets in a customized Lhardy's box as we left.

One weekend Aurora took us for an overnight trip to Toledo. We stayed in a hotel near the Alcazar in rooms with balconies that overlooked the city and visited the tomb of the historical archbishop Cardinal de Albornoz. That trip we dined at the Parador with the stately Severo Ochoa de Albornoz and his lovely wife, Carmen, who, like us, happened to be visiting the lovely historical city.

In time, I became more aware of Aurora's literary stature. The newspaper in Madrid often sought her out for her perspective on the literary legacy of Antonio Machado, on her recall of Juan Ramón Jiménez, on her insights into a wide variety of Spanish authors. She was called upon to introduce, preside, or read with emerging Spanish voices.

Years later, long after the parties at Tío Olivio's Upper West Side apartment had ceased, long after the late-night dinners in Madrid, I took up the task of wading as a translator into the eleven books of Aurora's poetry. First, I found her to be an innovative poet who incorporated prose poems, collage, and other modernistic techniques into her work. Unbeknownst to me, I had already begun to also wade into the uncollected biography of a figure on which I only had a slight grasp. In my own lack of facility, I had originally reduced Aurora to a dashing familial figure without any sense of the real legacies that she inhabited.

I began filling in parts of her biography by the work ancillary to the task of translating her poems. As a youth, she lived in Luarca, a small town in northern Spain. She lived there for the duration of the Spanish Civil War—1936 to 1939, a period that informed the youthful writer, her poetry, and her approach to the creatures of the world, for the rest of her life.

Her family was a noted family of poets; her grandfather and father were well known locally. But with the war, her family became marked for political and—due to timing—scientific accomplishments. Her father's uncle, Álvaro de Albornoz, was the minister of the Department of Justice of the Republican government of Spain until the civil war. Eventually, he became the president of the Republican government of Spain in exile in Paris that was superseded by Franco's dictatorship. (Álvaro de Albornoz eventually fled with his family to Mexico, where his children continued teaching and writing about constitutional law even after their father's death in exile.) In 1959 her uncle Severo Ochoa de Albornoz (who had fled Spain on a Republican passport), while living and working in the United States, was awarded a Nobel Prize in Medicine for deciphering RNA. (This was the gentleman with whom we had dined in the Parador in Toledo. By the time I met him, Severo Ochoa was one of the most celebrated personalities in all of Spain—and indeed, around the world.)

But Aurora's past was not only a familial claim of pedigree and academic accomplishment. Aurora was a young, self-possessed woman who attempted to make calculated forays into a slippery world. In August 1950 she married the handsome and dashing Jorge Enjuto Bernal, who, like Aurora, was from a Republican-affiliated family living outside of Spain. Jorge's father, Federico Enjuto Ferrán, was the Republican magistrate of justice who prosecuted General José Antonio Primo de Rivera, the founder of the Falange, the Fascist party in Spain. In other words, a relative of one of the most marked Republican families in Spain married the son of another high-profile Republican family: notoriety exponentially magnified. Aurora was not going to be living a life marked by low-profile safety. A radical world required a radical sense of one's duty . . . and even perhaps of one's destiny.

By 1967 some things were going well, some things were not. After living together in Puerto Rico, a short time in Kansas, and Paris, Aurora and Jorge amicably divorced.

Besides professor and poet, Aurora was a celebrated scholar. Throughout Spain—and in America, as well—she taught courses, participated in congresses, colloquiums, and writer's meetings; she collaborated toward cultural activities that dealt with scholarship and writing. These were the days that would lead to the festive parties at Tío Olivio's.

Was the last place we dined Toffaneti, Casa Patas, or Pepe Botella? Hontanares, Los Palos? Aurora was struck down by a cerebral hemorrhage. She died on June 6, 1990, in Madrid, just sixty-four years old.

Amazing how little we may know of the actual biography of a person in our own personal sphere . . . of the legacy we are taking on. Ahead would be my discovery of her poetry and the poems I would compose to commemorate those nights.

Ahead would be a trip to the beautiful city of Granada. . . . And on the arm of Aurora's own beloved nephew, who had learned her lessons in imagination and style. We would walk the streets with Álvaro (a poet friend I was introduced to by Aurora), and Pepa (his beloved). Álvaro, Pepa, José, and I talked of important factors that seemed to be trying to keep the world from tearing apart that summer of 2006. That same afternoon we had visited the Alhambra and Huerta Vicente, the pastoral home of the famous Andalusian poet García Lorca—where the four of us had stood quietly together and looked at the palm just outside the poet's bedroom window.

Joan Sutherland

Dame Joan and I

Gary Ljungquist

$\mathcal{M}$y earliest acquaintance with Joan Sutherland occurred via recordings. In the '60s, while the normal young people were participating in the youth revolution with its own music, I was discovering baroque music and growing enamored of the music of Handel.

It is in the context of Handel that I first heard Joan Sutherland. At that time there were very few recordings of Handel operas and oratorios, but two remain fixed in my memory: *Acis and Galatea* and *Alcina*. In the former Joan sang the role of an innocent who is lusted after by the giant Polyphemus. The purity of her tone, the sheer beauty of the sound that she made, and her obvious devotion to the lovely music made me play the recording over and over. In *Alcina* she played an evil sorceress who turned men into pigs. Perhaps I can blame Joan for some of my own early piggishness?

As Alcina, Joan got to sing more florid and emotive music. The aria "Tornami a Vagheggiar" knocked me out of my chair because of Joan's ability to do coloratura accurately and musically. Her embellishment of the repeat sent her voice into the stratosphere and me with it. Subsequently I have learned that this aria was not even written for her character and was appropriated by Joan, and who was I to quibble? She was the star and would have disappointed her fans if she had not chosen to "steal" the big number. Subsequent recordings of *Alcina* have restored that aria to its rightful owner, but no one has captured the excitement that Joan instilled in it. Maybe that's part of my attraction to her: everything she has done has a sense of occasion and commitment.

As time passed I discovered that there were other gays who liked good music and appreciated Joan's singing. As my musical tastes grew more catholic, I heard Joan do operas and arias from the bel canto repertory. While I didn't really love the music, I did love anything sung by Joan. I have grown to appreciate Maria Callas's fervor and dramatic intensity, but no one can compare to the sheer beauty and bravura of Sutherland in this repertory.

I only saw Joan Sutherland live once, in a concert performance at Carnegie Hall of Haydn's *Orfeo ed Euridice.* This was an unknown opera at the time, so I tracked down a recording and listened. It is rather nice, but there was a problem. Sutherland was to sing the role of Euridice, the tragic heroine, but the big coloratura showpiece was for the character of a genie. My worries were unfounded: At the moment that the big number began, Miss Sutherland walked out, the singer of the genie role disappeared, and Joan sang the number. It was a concert performance, no one complained at all, and I found myself cheering as part of a chorus of adoring males, who all seemed to be accompanied by other males. My partner whispered, "Now you've caught it. You're officially an opera queen." It was a magical moment, like watching a tightrope walker and wondering if she could do it. Recordings are one thing, but a live performance can't be done over.

That night at the opera helped me to understand the possibility of being publicly gay as part of a collective of other gay men who were all seeking the same thing: a transcendent experience. This was right around the time of Stonewall, and somehow for me being part of a group of opera fanatics marked a turning point in the long process of coming out. There would be no turning back—I was and would remain a publicly acknowledged gay man.

Two of Joan's last recordings seem symbolic for me. In the role of Puccini's Turandot, Joan Sutherland entered new territory at a time when other singers might be seeking to limit their repertory. Her voice was big and she endowed the selfish Chinese princess with a beauty of tone that somehow made her seem more human. On a recording of Handel's *Athalia,* Joan played the evil queen of Israel. Her tone was no longer as pure. This was obviously not the voice of innocence, but her dramatic commitment was palpable. To me it seemed appropriate that Joan should close her career with Handel, albeit in a historically correct performance with period instruments and performance practices. Making these two recordings took courage.

My love affair with Joan Sutherland focuses on her voice. Unlike Callas, whose physical being, facial expression, and body language were part of her allure, Joan's voice was the focus of my attraction; the sheer physical sound penetrated me in a place that is rarely touched. Now that Miss Sutherland is retired, I thank her for many hours of joy, of passionate musicianship, and I thank Nature for having created such a perfect instrument.

Eartha Kitt

Purrrfectly Detached

D. A. Powell

Someone is singing at the bottom of a swimming pool. Drowning. It's the worst rendition of "Smoke Gets in Your Eyes" I've ever heard. It's intoxicating.

The good thing about Eartha Kitt is that most people I grew up with didn't know her by her name. I'd have to say, "She was Catwoman on the Batman TV series. The third Catwoman. The black Catwoman." They would nod in vague recognition and move on.

I collected such celebrities. If anyone asked me the name of my favorite actress (not that anyone ever *did,* but they *might*), I'd have an arsenal of names to throw at them: Conchata Ferrell. Lynne Thigpen. Fay Bainter. Spring Byington. Barbara Harris. Lucille Bremer. Argentina Brunetti. Sally Kellerman. Rita Tushingham. Not stars. Artists who worked at the fringe of the curtain, who supported, who were characters, whose movies were not blockbusters, whose faces you might recognize but whose names you couldn't quite pinpoint.

In the clubs, late '70s and early '80s, minor players took center stage. Vicki Sue Robinson might have had only one hit in her career, but for the queer audience, she was a big name. Part of her stardom was the fact that she would deign to play the gay and lesbian version of the chitlin' circuit. As would Viola Wills. Debbie Jacobs. Claudja Barry. Jeannie Tracy. Sharon Redd. If someone asked me who my favorite singer was—not that anyone ever did—I'd answer, "Carol Jiani." If the person knew who Carol Jiani was, then he too was—like me—a child of the shadows, who watched the background players, the second- and third-tier SAG members, the working girls, the back-up singers who—only in the realm of other peripheral lives—got to step out into the spotlight.

$\mathcal{E}$artha Kitt was never a star of high magnitude. She worked steadily and had some successes. Broadway plays, cabaret performances, a few films. Most of her notoriety came from some novelty recordings: a song of existential ennui aptly entitled "Monotonous." A sultry Christmas ditty called "Santa Baby." "Uska Dara," which may have been the only song in Turkish ever to garner attention from American listeners. And a sexy, worldly, femme-fatale number, "C'est Si Bon," in which she mercilessly rolled every "r."

She was certainly better known than most of the women I've previously mentioned. But at the height of what fame she achieved, she crossed swords with the First Lady, Lady Bird Johnson, over Lyndon Johnson's domestic and foreign policies, and she was promptly shown out of the White House luncheon she had been attending. By Eartha's own account, this led to years of ostracization, and she had to move to Europe in order to find employment. The entertainment industry had blacklisted her.

*B*y the mid-1980s disco music had waned in popularity. But in gay clubs, there was still a body culture that desired a danceable beat, and labels like Rams Horn, Prelude, and Emergency Records were still turning out high-energy productions. Jacques Morali, the man behind the Village People, and his longtime collaborator, Henri Belolo, brought Eartha into a studio to produce a short album containing six songs, two of which—"Where Is My Man" and "I Love Men"—would become anthems of the era. "Where Is My Man" repeated one of Eartha's greatest tropes: the gold-digger, searching for a man with a "big, big, big, big yacht." And "I Love Men" underscored the high-risk sexual behavior that fueled the AIDS pandemic, with its all too poignant lines "I love men, what can I do? / I love men: they're no good for you."

For a woman who had acted onstage with Orson Welles and who had danced with James Dean in Katherine Dunham's studio, this might have felt like slumming. I do remember seeing her perform the two hits on a small stage at The Woods, a gay resort and dance club near California's Russian River. Maybe she was tired of the songs, already. She had sung great standards, and was now reduced to schlock. Maybe it was, as she intimated years later, that she had been seriously underpaid for her vocal work. In any case, she seemed incredibly aloof and bored; she walked off before the final song (which she'd been forced to sing to a prerecorded track) had finished.

I love Eartha, I don't love Eartha. I'm promiscuous in my taste, and she is one of many entertainers I've both enjoyed and winced at. When she missteps, it can be unfortunate. She hasn't chosen as much excruciatingly bad material as Shirley Bassey, but listen some time to her cover of Donovan's "Hurdy Gurdy Man" if you want a challenging earful.

Ten years after the performance at The Woods, I forgave the disdain she had heaped upon her queer '80s audience, and I went to see Eartha performing at Kimball's in Emeryville, California. The man sitting next to me was an überfan; he sighed and clapped and whistled.

She was brilliant, I had to admit: shimmering in an emerald beaded gown, finding every innuendo she could find in Cole Porter's lyrics, suggestively purring her Catwoman purr.

For some complicated reason that I can't quite explain, at one point in the evening Eartha Kitt leaned over the edge of the stage and sang directly to me, in honor of my birthday. It wasn't exactly my birthday, but I didn't know how to correct the situation publicly.

The überfan was impressed. He bought me a drink. Anybody in those days who bought me a drink was a good guy. And, after the concert, he offered to show me how to get backstage, where I could meet the legend herself.

I have since come to learn that, very often, the most ardent admirers of celebrities aren't always the most welcome admirers. Within minutes of arriving backstage, I registered the impatient politeness with which the überfan was being received. He had brought with him an imposing number of albums that he wanted Ms. Kitt to autograph. Though she was clearly feeling taken advantage of—she probably guessed that he would be reselling a number of the discs—she signed each one. She even signed a CD for me, though—again—it was not my birthday. But I couldn't refuse.

Stilted conversation between Eartha and the autograph hound revealed that he had been making many trips backstage. In fact, it seemed he was coming to each show—two performances a night, four or five nights a week. I felt bad for her: having to see this guy so frequently, having to suffer his fawning. And I also felt bad for him: to be so hopelessly star struck and so socially awkward that this small moment was the culmination of his dream.

Finally, Eartha turned her back to us—a sign that it was time for us to leave. I needed to rejoin the friend I had accompanied to the concert, anyway, so I headed back out the side door into the auditorium.

Before I had gone more than a few feet, I felt a tap on my shoulder. It was the enthusiastic young man, Eartha's admirer. He held out his hand to me and said, "Happy Birthday," then pressed a tiny object into my palm. I looked down at my hand, blankly.

"It's a bead. From her dress. I want you to have it."

"Oh . . ." I wanted to seem thankful, but I was also weirded out. "You should keep it for yourself."

"No, no. I have lots of them." He showed me an ounce of glass beads in one hand; a pair of cuticle scissors in the other.

Naturally, when I tell the story, people ask me if I still have the bead. Sad to say, I lost it almost immediately.

There are evenings when I have visitors and I begin to pull out records and compact discs. So many performers that they don't know. Not many seem to know Eartha Kitt's name. But they know her voice. They know that peculiar style she has, that mixture of sultriness and indifference. Sometimes they laugh at her odd phrasing, her worn voice. Sometimes they say, "Where do you find these people?"

They are the faces on the edge of the spotlight. They are the crackling noise of records somebody collected in his lonely adolescence, too many of them, more than one person can hold.

Betty Berzon

Dinners with the Diminutive Diva

Jim Van Buskirk

One afternoon while working as the director of the James C. Hormel Gay and Lesbian Center at the San Francisco Public Library, I received a call: there was someone to see me. Having no appointments, I didn't know what to expect. But soon there stood a lesbian version of Mutt and Jeff. The two women marched toward me confidently and introduced themselves. Betty Berzon was short, with silver hair, clad comfortably in black. Terry De-Crescenzo, also in black, towered above her, as both trophy and protector. I was thrilled to finally meet in person this iconic lesbian couple, familiar from Betty's seminal self-help books: *Positively*

Gay (Berkeley, Calif.: Celestial Arts, 1992), *Permanent Partners* (New York: Dutton, 1988), *Setting Them Straight* (New York: Penguin, 1996), and *The Intimacy Dance* (New York: Dutton, 1996). Betty had often used examples from their own relationship to help readers identify and resolve interpersonal issues.

The two got right to the point: would I sponsor a presentation around the publication of Betty's forthcoming memoir? Betty's "diva-ness" was immediately apparent: instead of the more intimate community meeting room, she wanted the larger, more glamorous auditorium. We planned for a public program in June, at which Betty took to center stage with ease as she read from her powerful memoir, *Surviving Madness: A Therapist's Own Story* (Madison: University of Wisconsin Press, 2001). It was difficult to imagine that this pioneering icon had wrestled with her feelings toward women before coming out at forty. But she had made up for lost time by being the first psychotherapist to publicly declare herself a gay mental health professional, and then by contributing to numerous organizations that continue to support the well-being of the GLBT communities.

After the event Betty and Terry graciously invited my partner, Allen, and me to dinner, where we witnessed their well-documented relationship in action. As Terry instructed the waiter on what "Dr. Berzon" liked, didn't like, and was allergic to, Betty remained silently in charge. While Terry was the "foodie," Betty preferred a simple pasta, green salad, and glass of Chablis. The show they put on was very entertaining, and this evening was the start of our fast friendship. Allen and I were subsequently invited to their annual post-holiday gatherings and birthday parties and arranged for dinners whenever possible despite their living in Los Angeles, a considerable distance from our San Francisco.

When Betty sent me a copy of the revised edition of her classic *Permanent Partners,* I realized that its publication coincided with the first anniversary of the gay and lesbian weddings at San Francisco City Hall. I put together a panel and invited her to participate, but although she enthusiastically accepted, she later called to say she was afraid she had nothing to talk about. I tried to disabuse her, but she was adamant: she couldn't participate without having something significant to offer. Ultimately she acquiesced and, as mother hen–cum–experienced elder, her presentation cut to the heart of the issues and was the highlight of the program. This was typical: Everything she undertook had to be meaningful, to help change the world in some small way. That evening we celebrated at the Equality California Gala at City Hall. It was crowded and noisy, and Betty was so short she had a hard time seeing all the festivities. We must have been a sight: my six-foot-three frame leaning over her, trying to talk against the din.

On October 14, 2005, Betty was scheduled to appear at a symposium celebrating the life and work of her dear friend, the late Paul Monette. I told her we were coming down for the weekend and took for granted we'd all go out to dinner, but Betty e-mailed that she was not feeling well, and then asked if I'd be on the committee for her own memorial. When I realized she wasn't joking, I was stunned. Was she being overly dramatic, or was she really that sick? In any event, I reassured her I would do anything for her—in awe of her unbelievably brave and take-charge approach.

On the day of the event, she arrived late and with obvious effort and discomfort managed to get herself to the dais. As she began to speak, she sounded and looked better. As if being in the spotlight was somehow rejuvenating her. She masterfully presented a poignant portrait of Paul and their relationship. But afterward it was all she could do to get to the car, unable to attend the rest of the day's events and the dinner that evening.

That was to be Betty's last public appearance. Allen and I went over the next day, bringing lunch, and then helped to pull in the patio furniture for the season. On some level, I knew this was the last time we would see her.

I kept in touch as Betty's health failed (though her spirits seldom did). She was as feisty and funny as always. When I called to cheer her up, it was she who made me laugh, remarking how she liked to look at the cute buns of her young male doctor. What I hadn't known was Betty had been diagnosed with breast cancer in 1986 and underwent a mastectomy, that in 2001 it recurred. I'd later learn she had been battling cancer the entire time I knew her. Yet she had never complained, never stopped her important work.

She soon moved into the Beverly Hills Rehabilitation Center, where her room was next to that of Shelley Winters, who was also dying. Terry quipped that she was taking bets as to which diva could hold out longer. When it was apparent nothing more could be done, Betty was brought home to be more comfortable during her last days. On January 24, 2006, six days after her seventy-eighth birthday, Betty died at home (ten days after Shelley), with Terry at her side.

The following April I had the honor of bestowing Betty with the National Center for Lesbian Rights' Founder's Award, which was accepted by Terry.

To the world, Betty was a pioneering gay rights activist, psychotherapist, and bestselling author. To me, she was a dear friend, whose inspiration guides me daily even as her absence deeply affects me.

Jeanne Moreau

Living Dangerously with Jeanne

Collin Kelley

$\mathcal{G}$rowing up gay and poor was a double whammy. Having wanderlust from the age of twelve didn't help either. For the first twenty-four years of my life, I couldn't afford to leave the South, so foreign films became my passport to far-flung locales like Berlin, London, and Paris.

Watching Wim Wenders's angels soar in *Wings of Desire,* Bob Hoskins and Helen Mirren as gangster and moll shooting up the Thames in *The Long Good Friday,* and Jeanne Moreau walk heartbroken through the City of Lights to a jazz riff by Miles Davis in

Elevator to the Gallows transported me to a world I longed to explore. It was Moreau—with her down-turned mouth and dark circles under her eyes—that lit a creative spark in me that has never dimmed. Eventually, I would take my own walk through Paris at night, lamenting over a lover who had spurned me, and like Moreau, I would let the rain soak me in some vain attempt to be washed clean.

Jeanne Moreau is one of the original divas, and she's French, so that makes her allure even stronger. Even now, in her eighties, she remains a beauty so startling that you have to look twice. A lifelong cigarette habit seems to have worked in her favor rather than against. If there is any doubt that French women age differently than other mortals, one only has to look at Moreau to know there must be something in the wine or tobacco. From her unconventional looks, to her high-profile love affairs, to her willingness to take on roles many actresses would run from, Moreau continues to be a vibrant and engaging presence in international cinema.

Moreau has been a muse and a guide to me as a poet. When I crave inspiration, I only need to watch one of her many films to find it in the characters she's created. She refused to let directors and producers lather her up in makeup to hide what they considered flaws. She told them, literally, to go to hell. And to the moralists and critics who decried her "wanton sensuality," she thumbed her nose by choosing even more polarizing and challenging films.

Moreau also famously said in a 1996 interview with film journalist and critic Molly Haskell that she doesn't feel guilt at her choices. "Whatever I wish to do, I do. . . . But if you want to live, and live your life through to the end, you have to live dangerously. And one thing you have to give up is attaching importance to what people see in you" (*Interview Magazine*, September 1, 1996).

This has been my motto as a gay man and writer ever since: no guilt, living the life I want and not one dictated to me by superficial gay men or heterosexuals of any gender, and not worrying what others think of me. I was never a young beauty, or a clotheshorse or interested in clubbing. I was far more interested in using my mind for seduction, exploring the world and my own sexual appetites. I have sought out challenging men, marked them for seduction, just to see where the relationship would go and what I could mine from it for my art. Saying exactly what is on my mind without fear of repercussion has been another hallmark of my life, just as it has been for Moreau. She's been an excellent mentor. Although I've never met her, whenever I walk the streets of Paris, I always feel like she's leading me by the hand.

In 2000 *Salon* magazine declared that "deification of divas" by gay men had become an anachronism. Maybe Judy, Bette, and Joan have become a bit clichéd, but I've always looked for another kind of woman to whom I can build shrines. Sure, divas all have some of the same qualities: larger than life, bucking the system, a string of shitty men. Moreau fits that bill perfectly, but she transcends the stereotype by force of will. Many of the cherished divas died young or created such indelible roles (Judy as Dorothy, Bette as Eve, or Joan as . . . well . . . Joan) that it's hard to separate the icon from the real woman. Moreau has played so many eclectic roles, she's made it impossible to lock her into one "look" or "age."

Certainly she'll be remembered for her breakthrough film, Louis Malle's New Wave noir *Elevator to the Gallows,* but she's just as well known for her turn in *The Lovers,* which shocked even the French with its erotic depiction of sex and infidelity in the 1950s. As the woman who gets in between the homoerotic friendship of *Jules et Jim,* she looks like she's having the gayest of gay old times, even when she's driving them off a bridge to their death.

And while Uma Thurman might be badass in *Kill Bill,* she doesn't touch Moreau in Francois Truffaut's *The Bride Wore Black.* In that film, Moreau's husband is killed on their wedding day and she becomes an assassin, cold-bloodedly dispatching the men involved and looking damn good doing it in Yves Saint Laurent couture.

Many fans of gay cinema will instantly recognize Moreau as whorehouse madam Lysiane in Fassbinder's *Querelle,* which

105

starred hunky homo Brad Davis as a beautiful sailor desired by both men and women.

As mercurial writer Marguerite Duras in *Cet Amour-la,* she takes a twentysomething pretty boy as her lover despite the fact she's old and near the end of her life. The young man is a good trophy at parties and sparks her creativity, but their story should be a primer for any gay man who chases after a youthful beauty hoping to tame him. In *Le Temps Qui Reste* (*Time to Leave*), she is the loving grandmother of a young gay man diagnosed with an inoperable brain tumor. She becomes his confessor, promising to keep his secret, and we learn the family has also shunned her for "inappropriate" behavior after the death of her husband.

My guess is that Jeanne Moreau will die on the set of her latest film. She has refused to retire, still likes to smoke, sleeps in the nude, unapologetic about her many lovers (including being named in Vanessa Redgrave's divorce petition from Tony Richardson) and just for being herself. *Vive la Moreau!*

Jennifer Paterson

Cocktails with Jennifer

Jack Lynch

$\mathcal{A}$ friend who thought I could afford to "put on a few pounds" introduced me to Jennifer Paterson in 1996 when she was starring as that cigarette-smoking, espadrille-wearing, motorcycle-driving matron of the hit British cooking show *Two Fat Ladies*. We never actually met, but for several years she rumbled across the UK—and into my living room—on her Triumph Thunderbird with her younger, fatter costar Clarissa Dickson Wright spilling out of the sidecar. Together they would travel to the most unlikely of places, fighting body-fascism and whipping up delectable dishes for bishops and Boy Scouts alike; and I would go along for the ride. At the end of each episode Jennifer and I would have a cocktail. (Clarissa's a recovering alcoholic and doesn't drink.) Her choice of libation varied depending on the show . . . from the sublime (a caipirinha at the Brazilian embassy in London) to the ridiculous (a pint of breakfast stout at a brewery in North Yorkshire). My choice of cocktail remained pretty consistent: AZT and a protease inhibitor, with a dash of acyclovir (as a chaser).

Although both Jennifer and Clarrisa enjoyed international acclaim, it was Jennifer who was the "true" diva—at least that's what those who knew her were quoted as saying when her obituary appeared in almost every major newspaper across Europe, Australia, and the United States. Just as the world was revving up for the new millennium, Jennifer, and the century that contained her, were coming to a screeching halt.

Born in London in 1928, Jennifer spent the first four years of her life in China, where her father worked for the Asiatic Petroleum Company. When the family returned to England they lived in Rye, East Sussex, across the road from the writer Radclyffe Hall. She attended school at nearby Assumption Convent in Ramsgate, where the food was "exceptionally good" but her behavior wasn't (Andrew Barrow quoting Paterson, in "Obituary: Jennifer Paterson," *The Independent,* August 11, 1999). In fact, the nuns would punish our little diva by making her eat at a table with screens around it. Finally, at age fifteen, she was expelled. "They said if I left, the school might settle down" (Charles Moore quoting Paterson, in "The Fat Lady Sings," *The Spectator,* August 14, 1999). Maybe it did. But Jennifer certainly didn't.

She moved to Berlin to be with her father, who had been posted in the army there. She then went on to live in Portugal, Venice, Sicily, and Libya. After returning to England in 1952, she took various jobs—working behind the scenes for the ITV show *Candid Camera,* cooking for a Ugandan diplomat, being a matron at an all-girls boarding school, to name a few. She gradually found her true calling: being a fixture of the London party scene. "My whole life was one mistake after another, because I was totally unqualified. I took whatever came along" ("A Larger than Life Culinary Star," BBC News Tuesday, August 10, 1999). And a good thing, too, because one of those jobs was cooking a weekly lunch at *The Spectator* magazine, where she met many influential people, princes and TV producers among them. She worked there for more than a decade, cooking and writing articles, but was fired when, after finding her kitchen in a deplorable state, she began tossing dirty coffee mugs and cutlery out the window, shouting, "Those ghastly common people in advertising are cluttering up my kitchen" (Moore quoting Paterson, in "The Fat Lady Sings").

Eventually, a BBC producer hooked her up with Clarissa Dickson Wright and the rest is history.

Two Fat Ladies ran for three seasons, and I saw every episode. I even have the box set! At first I watched the show because I loved the macabre humor and politically incorrect banter. Jennifer and I were kindred spirits. Like her I'd traveled a lot when I was younger and worked a variety of jobs—film and television production, acting, stage managing, banking, cleaning apartments, and interior decorating. But all that was in the past. I hadn't been well enough to work for several years. What I needed was to learn how to cook some good, calorie-rich recipes so I could put some meat on my bones. And thanks to Jennifer, little by little I did.

At the age of forty-one I returned to school. My original plan was to finish my undergraduate degree and perhaps go to culinary school. But plans changed. I'm now finishing my MFA in creative writing, poetry to be exact. I can just hear Jennifer now, doing her best Marlene Dietrich impersonation, shaking her head in mock dismay, lamenting, "Poetry! Poor darhlink, vat could be verse?" Then, lighting one of her fags she'd say (in her very proper British accent), "Off you go then, mustn't keep the headmaster waiting. I'll stay here and cook us up a nice pot of *cog au van,* shall I? It's a lovely dish made with an old cock—not an old hen, an old cock— because they have the flavor. Lot of good in an old cock, but no use keeping one when it's past its prime."

109

Jennifer Paterson died of lung cancer on August 10, 1999. She smoked till the very end, saying, "It's terminal, so why not?"

I'd love to sit and write for hours about my beloved diva; however, I have to get to the gym . . . gotta shed some of this extra weight.

I still have my cocktail about the same time every day, but it's just not the same without her.

Audrey Hepburn

Adoration and the Icon

Joseph Campana

$\mathcal{M}$y poetic adoration of Audrey Hepburn, *The Book of Faces* (St. Paul, Minn.: Graywolf Press, 2005), began as a distraction late one night. One minute beauty distracts, the next it lays waste to us all. Although I was supposed to be reading Plato's *Timaeus* for a seminar, *Charade* was in my DVD player, and I would reward myself with a few scenes for every few pages of Plato, the latter sections of which parse the universe into measurable angles, numbers, and equations. How impressively exact, yet how much less impressive than Audrey Hepburn and Cary Grant in Paris. One minute that film's mysteries titillate and arouse, the next minute someone winds up dead: thrown off a train, drowned in a bathtub, garroted in an elevator, smothered in a plastic bag. Still, Audrey Hepburn can't get enough of Cary Grant, interrupting his elaborate plans to keep her safe with a simple "How do you shave in there?" and a caress of his famously cleft chin. (This line Hepburn added spontaneously during the filming.) And if Hepburn is distracted by Cary Grant (in a towel no less—who wouldn't be?), who wouldn't be distracted by Audrey Hepburn in Givenchy?

Later in *Charade,* in a nightclub, on an early date, Audrey Hepburn and Cary Grant find that they and the other members of the audience will be the entertainment. So they line up to pass an orange to the person next to them without the use of their hands. After some classic Cary Grant shtick with a rather thick and matronly woman, Audrey Hepburn is next. The camera lingers as the game becomes erotic. There's a moment when the camera hovers over the scene and you wonder, as those two iconic bodies move together, would you rather be Audrey Hepburn, Cary Grant, or the orange in between? What poet could ask for a better primal scene? Moments later, Audrey Hepburn has to pass the orange to one of her assailants. When she rushes out afterward to make a call, another one traps her in a telephone booth then lights and drops a series of matches into her lap. How's that for a metaphor?

Petrarch first "saw" Laura on a crowded street. I say "saw" because neither history nor event can address the irrelevance of any actual "Laura" in the *Rime Sparse.* Or was it Dante seeing Beatrice in a crowd in his *Vita Nuova* that Petrarch was thinking of? Of course it was, suspiciously, both. Also, do we believe that Petrarch (no less Dante) actually saw anyone that day? Might it not also be the case that, like Petrarch, we wish to find some reality on which to prop overwhelming desire and rabid fascination because the imagination seems all too slender and unimportant when we consider the things of the actual world? The icon may sit upon a dais or upon an altar; it may be fashioned in stone, as a statue, or carved on a building high above. But the moment of initial contact is that of seeing the icon emerge from a hectic public: a face rising up out of the great crowd of faces in the book of celebrity. The singularity of the icon is always intimately tied to multiplicity: it is an icon drawn from a thronging frenzy to be multiplied endlessly, for adoration requires multiples sites of contact.

My first sighting of Audrey Hepburn I barely remember. I was in high school. It was a snow day, and my parents thought I was at home. How did any of us end up watching *Charade* that afternoon in a house we weren't supposed to be in? The first glance at the icon may or may not be forbidden but it is, certainly, accidental. I can't say I remember anything of that day other than a fascination with Audrey Hepburn (whose face wasn't even immediately memorable then) and with *Charade* (the plot and details of which I had no recollection until later.) At first, devotion to the icon has to it the air of generality, for the icon has obliterated the capacity for immediate relation. I could say "I love Audrey Hepburn" long before I had entered the second phase: the phase of the scholar, of the collector.

Others had famous first sightings of Audrey Hepburn. Collette, for example, saw her on a beach in Nice and cast her immediately for the stage version of *Gigi,* a role that would later be played on screen by Leslie Caron. Audrey Hepburn's screen test for Paramount, the one that landed her first starring role in her first major film (and her first and only Oscar) was a sham. They left the camera running and didn't tell her. The first studio glance is deceitful, for the act of observation deforms the object. Yet when is the icon not observed, even in its infancy?

Her first films are, in fact, about such glances. Take *Sabrina,* whose title character spends her early years spying the delights of the bodies she desires from an unobserved post in a tree. The only one who sees her is the moon above. In those tantalizing early scenes, the camera often shows us Sabrina looking at someone else, which means she seems to be looking at us. Later, Sabrina will appear again, having acquired polish (and some Givenchy) in Paris, but this time she is the indisputable icon. We cannot stop looking at her. The secret truth of the icon is not merely the desire of the devoted. We look at the icon and it looks back at us. The icon creates us with its tender and unmerciful gaze. It will not touch us because it already has.

Everyone knows what it feels like to fall in love. Or, at least, everyone knows what we're supposed to feel like falling in love. It isn't clear to me that everyone knows what it feels like to love or be loved, but that's a different question. You don't have to know anything about a particular icon in order to understand the experience of devotion. Who hasn't had real relationships with imaginary people or imaginary relationships with real people? What else were the arts invented for if not for consummating the deep and necessary loves that can only be lived in the imagination? Is there a way of returning to language an amorous plentitude that is not merely a matter of sex appeal or seduction? The only solution—and it isn't one, really—is to twist oneself into the myriad forms of desire evoked by the beloved icon.

Perhaps Audrey Hepburn's most lucrative film, since she received a hefty share of profits that included massive global sales, was *A Nun's Story*. Audrey Hepburn in the Congo? Perhaps not. But, put Audrey Hepburn with that glorious face in a nun's habit and you can send her anywhere. We'll forgive one of her last appearances in a Spielberg film, since her cameo was as an angel. What else was the close of her career but the elaboration of a perhaps genuine kind of sainthood, with her humanitarian work for the United Nations? In the photographs, holding emaciated children as her own flesh was eaten away from within by cancer, one sees a glimmer of what everyone is looking for when they look up: to ancient gods and goddesses, to saviors and martyrs, to the bright and dark loves of Renaissance sonnets, to the stars and legends of the silver screen and beyond. Either the icon is a beacon that pours out love in exchange for adoration, or it is the cruelest joke of all that we choose to love people and things that cannot love us back because they are nothing if not massive mirrors painted on collapsing screens.

The lover of icons, the lover of divas, hopes for better, because if there is anything that brings together all of us who constitute our very different devotions to mostly incompatible objects, it is some lesson on the nature of love. At the opening of *De Rerum Natura* (*The Nature of Things*), Lucretius invokes the great goddess of love. "Alma Venus," he cries: oh, nourishing Venus. And later, he addresses her as *diva,* which of course means goddess, but this is an archaic form of "god" (*deus, deum*) reserved for instances of supplication. What's more abject than adoration? To be low before the icon, to raise one's gaze up at the barest hem of its garment: that's the desire. Not emulation. Not interaction. Not (generally) conversation. We want the icon to grind us into the dirt under its feet. We love the icon for its disdain, better yet for its disinterested gaze as if it were oblivious to all those supplicating presences done in by their own devotion to a diva glancing elsewhere. Venus appears, later in the epic tradition, in Virgil's *Aeneid* as the elusive mother launching her own scions into imperial glory. Venus appears to Aeneas as a mysterious huntress, but she will not reveal herself to him, not as his mother. Why withhold affection? Because we hunger for it, and the icon knows a little something about power. What lies beyond Audrey Hepburn (or any other star) other than the desire to love something so much that you could imagine, yourself, being loved just that much? The desire for icons is not the desire to become an icon but rather the need to create from nothing a source of nourishing love. *Alma Venus, Diva Venus*: will you not look down?

Ms. Kiki Durane

Her Sound and Fury

Christopher Schmidt

Kiki Durane is the more outgoing half of Kiki and Herb, the drag performance act that has been an underground, and increasingly aboveground, New York institution for the better part of a decade. I mean "better" in the primary sense of the word: Kiki and Herb have brightened my nights and given voice to a whole spectrum of desires and disappointments that I didn't know were in me until given life onstage.

Meet Kiki, a washed-up cabaret singer with an epic backstory who stays afloat with a tumbler of liquor and a talent for the withering comeback. Played by Justin Bond—a dashing, androgynous, let's say late-thirty-something performer—with an inimitable blend of ingenuousness and cynicism, one of Kiki's least heralded virtues is her expansive taste in music. Kiki and Herb bring their lounge-act stylings (Kiki's gravelly baritone is backed by Herb's thundering piano arrangements) to the indie pop canon, covering everything from Joni Mitchell to Kate Bush to Radiohead. Then, just when you think they can't push their sublime ironies any further, they'll unearth the piquancy in some pop trifle like Britney Spears's ". . . Baby One More Time" or Gnarls Barkley's "Crazy"— pure genius.

But the definitive moment in a Kiki and Herb show is when, amid one of many autobiographical vignettes, Kiki sparks to fury, attacking some chimerical or real foe (George W. Bush, for instance). Her anger is cathartic and oddly communal—the only time I've felt the queer fellowship I always anticipated I'd find in New York City. A Kiki and Herb show is more glamorous than a meeting at the LGBT center, less competitive (and generally disappointing) than a night at the bars. Kiki possesses a rare, magical ability to electrify the audience's raw need—that universal need to be rescued from loneliness and obscurity—and transforms that energy into a circuit of queer community and political activism, if only for one dazzling night.

After the show, Kiki's fans will act as if they *own* her, convinced Kiki speaks *only to them*. There are bragging rights. As for me, I'll admit that I did *not* know Justin when he was—as legend has it—a precocious drama student at UC Santa Cruz. Nor did I see Justin/Kiki when s/he began her illustrious career in San Francisco, circa 1993, emerging phoenix-like from the embers of ACT UP.

My own bragging rights are paltry. I once interviewed Bond in his 13th Street tenement apartment for a magazine article. Bond was charming and whip-smart, but confessed to me the toll performing Kiki exacts: "Most people struggle to have a positive outlook in life, and to be productive and to enjoy some sort of . . . pleasantness in their existence. And when I'm doing Kiki five or six days a week, I have to work that much harder—really, fucking hard—to have a positive attitude and be happy. It strains me."

Bond was trying to cut Kiki loose at the time of our interview by adopting alternate personas, like one called the "cool baby-sitter" (short-lived). I've seen Bond perform many times without Kiki's age-makeup and prosthetic birdseed breasts. Bond solo is soigné, smoky-voiced, and dissolute—half Ute Lemper, half Lou Reed. But folks still clamor for Kiki.

Finally, Bond decided that to move on, Kiki had to be killed off. In 2004 Bond and Kenny Mellman (who plays Herb) staged a blowout farewell concert at Carnegie Hall called *Kiki and Herb: We Will Die for You.* I was there, as was half the gay population of the East Village—everyone, it seems, I had ever bedded or wanted to bed. (I attended with my boyfriend.) I had worried that the uptown venue might stifle Kiki, but the performance was better than I could have imagined—in a word, incendiary. For the first of many encores, Kiki lassoed up a gaggle of celebrities, including Rufus Wainwright, Sandra Bernhard, and Debbie Harry, to help her sing "Those Were the Days." Amidst all that star wattage, Kiki still ruled the stage.

After the show, rumors swirled. Were Kiki and Herb really splitting up? Could they be successful doing anything else? Was Bond really off to London to study "scenography"? After a cooling-off period, Kiki and Herb returned to New York in 2006 for a five-week run on Broadway, in a show entitled *Kiki and Herb: Alive on Broadway.* They had been resurrected.

I saw Kiki and Herb perform again last month in a Christmas show at Bowery Ballroom, and they were as angry and brilliant as ever. Bond seems to have reconciled himself to life with Kiki, at least for a little while longer, though his performance of exhausted carelessness was brought very much to the fore. Selfishly, I'd like to see him perform Kiki until performer and persona become one, until Bond no longer needs the painted-on wrinkles to summon his alter ego. Some might call that tragic. But I'd watch.

Elizabeth Taylor

The Über-Diva

Scott F. Stoddart

Ruth Robeline: Now there's a story for you. She is a tortured, twisted soul—her whole life has been an experiment in terror.... I have to tell you, when it comes to sufferin' she's right up there with Elizabeth Taylor!

Truvy Jones (Dolly Parton) to Annelle Dupuy (Daryl Hannah),
"Steel Magnolias" (1989)

It seems as though Elizabeth Taylor is forever suffering. Maybe it was those violet eyes (enhanced with mascara and shadow) that defy belief in most of her sixty-five films—haunting, tragic, yet divine. Maybe it was those marriages—eight in total—each one ending tragically, leaving La Liz turning to her public for sympathy. Or her battles with weight, begun when she gained thirty pounds to play Martha to Oscar-winning glory in *Who's Afraid of Virginia Woolf?* (1966)—becoming a punch line for many late-night comedians. Just as Truvy contends, Taylor has become an icon for suffering in public.

However, let's return to those famous violet eyes; under their gaze, I believe Elizabeth Taylor was the patron saint of my own household in coastal Maine. She was always my mother's favorite actress, and on Sunday afternoons we would sit together through her early movies: watching *National Velvet* (1944), *Jane Eyre* (1944), *Father of the Bride* (1950), we saw the British-born actress mature from a precocious girl to a responsible young woman.

I know that I, as a young gay boy, first recognized her mature power through the pages of a *Look* magazine from 1972: in a photo essay, she romps through the surf with her husband-to-be-redux, flaunting her famed sixty-nine-carat diamond. Reading of her divorces and her desire to find love, I knew that I had found a connection—I was suffering turmoil as a child of divorced parents and fraternal abuse, and Liz's willful spirit reflected in those violet eyes guided me through many a week of high school where I was subject to the usual verbal abuse heaped on gay teens.

The first Taylor film I saw on the big screen was in college: *Suddenly Last Summer* (1959). By then, I was unhappily sleeping with women and happily (though secretly) sleeping with men; wrestling with coming out, I empathized with her story of queer cousin Sebastian's death. While my friends had no understanding of what really happened to Sebastian—I did. Dealing with my own sexuality in a small college town, I knew that the fearful attitudes of these friends prevented me from disclosing my true desires—I felt Catharine/Liz was speaking right to me about the dangers of letting others control you for their own selfish vanity. When Catharine confronts the extraordinary Violet Venable (Katharine

Hepburn) with the truth, she became my own personal diva—confronting falsity at every turn.

In her fifty-two-year career as an actress, Taylor has made an indelible stamp on Hollywood films, and her roles define her progress from playing the ingénue to playing the lead. In George Stevens's *A Place in the Sun* (1951), her first film with friend Montgomery Clift, the nineteen-year-old Liz is accorded the star entrance. Stevens's camera follows the gaze of George (Clift), a poor relation encountering the splendors of his rich relatives. He escapes a well-heeled cocktail party to shoot billiards, and as he ponders (and then makes) a difficult shot, a blur of white frothy chiffon floats by the open door; in walks Angela Vickers (Taylor), soon to be the object of his desire, and in close-up she utters one word, "Wow!" While it is appropriate to give Stevens credit for the progression of the sequence, once Taylor enters the room, the scene is hers, and she becomes more than an object of young lust—she embodies all the possibilities of capitalist success/excess as she gracefully takes control of the conversation, soon falling for the simple desire of George. The dress, designed by Edith Head, was immediately copied on Seventh Avenue, and hundreds of them were sold to adoring fans.

Under further guidance by Tennessee Williams, Liz matured into her role as Maggie "The Cat" Pollitt in *Cat on a Hot Tin Roof* (1957). Williams always said that she was his favorite Maggie, and her sexual energy captures a reading of the character that is now considered iconic. Kneeling on a brass bed in only a slip, her voice quivering to match her restless spirit, Taylor channels her desire for her handsome husband Brick (Paul Newman) by commanding the screen. It was through this role that her talent matured—she holds her own with pretty-boy Newman and cantankerous Burl Ives as the lustful Big Daddy. When Brick and Daddy have a long heart-to-heart over "mendacity," the spectator longs for the return of Maggie.

Taylor achieved more universal diva status with her two Oscar-winning performances. The first was her portrayal of Gloria

121

Wandrous, the "heroine" of John O'Hara's *BUtterfield 8* (1960), a studio vehicle that Liz did not want to make, but did so as her final obligation to MGM. Gloria is a call girl who meanders through the film in an on-again/off-again relationship with a drunken Laurence Harvey. Delbert Mann's direction is hardly the reason for Taylor's Oscar for this over-produced vehicle—Hollywood was simply rewarding her for her subsequent four nominations and her near-death experience some months prior to the awards ceremony—a bout of pneumonia after the death of husband number three (producer Michael Todd) caused her body to shut down, forcing doctors to perform an emergency tracheotomy. She wore a defiantly low-cut Dior gown to the ceremony, proudly showing the scar as she collected her award—an act so very much in line with her on-screen performance, in which she (out of contempt for this watered-down production) boldly makes Gloria's downward spiral less sympathetic: brushing her teeth with a glass of scotch after Harvey leaves her in the morning and then stealing his wife (Dina Merrill)'s mink coat after writing "No Sale" on the living room mirror in ruby lipstick. Diva Liz controls the entire spirit of the film in the face of the Hollywood machine. It made millions.

Her second Oscar was more deserved for her portrayal of the fifty-two-year-old Martha, the embittered wife of a mediocre college professor in the film version of Edward Albee's *Who's Afraid of Virginia Woolf?* Only thirty-four at the time of the film's production, Taylor fought for the role against then-husband Richard Burton and surprised spectators and critics alike. She not only gained weight for the film, but also took on a whole new persona to meet the challenge of Albee's brutal script. The first sight of Taylor and Burton, entering their house after a drunken evening with her father, is a shock—Taylor squinting into the harsh light; her disheveled hair falling onto her bloated face and into those famed eyes physically transformed her to a gorgon. As the film continues, she takes control of the screen with her "bawdy talk," harassing her husband for wasting liquor "on an associate professor's salary," sneering at her silly guest Honey (Sandy Dennis), and coming on to Nick (George Segal), calling him "stud," gyrating her corpulence against him on the dance floor and taking him to the bedroom after Honey passes out—only to learn he is as flaccid as her own husband. The film was the first to successfully challenge the Production Code, leading to the creation of the MPAA ratings system; it is still the pivotal tragicomic performance in Taylor's career.

I have always been drawn to those films of the Taylor canon that did not please the critics—those that elevate her from mere diva status to gay icon. Her vitality in these pictures lifts me out of any sour mood. There is the colossal epic *Cleopatra* (1963), where she earned one million dollars (the first actress to do so) to flaunt the personal trials of her affair with Burton in front of the paparazzi, her carefully designed makeup and jewelry taking on more significance than anything that occurred in the plot of the four-hour epic. There is *The VIPs* (1963), where Taylor, having an affair with Louis Jourdan, wanders through an airport for two hours in a collection of divine Pierre Cardin outfits, chased by her jealous husband, again played by Burton. There is *X, Y, Zee* (1972), a raucous romp where La Liz pulls out all of the stops to prevent her philandering husband (Michael Caine) from leaving her. The vibrant colors of her myriad caftans match the exuberance she displays as she embraces the decadence of 1970s London.

A favorite of mine is *The Sandpiper* (1965), a melodrama my partner and I discovered in a video store bargain bin. Liz plays a female Thoreau, Laura Reynolds, an artist who paints on the beaches of Big Sur. Laura's Bohemian rhapsodies regarding married love and intellectual freedom eventually tempt a minister who heads a boy's school (again played by Burton) away from his conservative wife, Eva Marie Saint. In one scene, the free-spirited Liz poses nude for fellow artist Charles Bronson with her hands covering only her nipples—Burton walks in, and his face is priceless as he tries to carry on a conversation concerning Taylor's son. In another scene, as Liz speaks softly to Burton about her desire for a love of equals, a live sandpiper nests in her unruly hair! The film has become a tradition in our household—our official kick-off to summer.

It is Taylor's audacity reflected in these studio films where one experiences the spark that characterizes the turn her career would take in the 1980s. With the announcement that her long-time friend and co-star Rock Hudson was dying of AIDS, Taylor emerged to take a leading role as celebrity activist. She was the first major Hollywood figure to lend her name to the disease: In 1985 she organized the first AIDS celebrity benefit "A Commitment to Life," and raised 1.3 million dollars. Subsequently, she founded the American Foundation for AIDS Research (AmFAR), an organization that she has personally overseen, raising $83 million in its first ten years of existence. It was through this fight that Taylor turned her public image around—instead of simply suffering in public, she worked to end the suffering of others, particularly the gay men who came to worship her. While she has been accorded many earthly honors for this work—for example, being knighted by Queen Elizabeth II in 1999 and named a 2002 Kennedy Honors recipient—Elizabeth Taylor is known as a patron saint by all members of the gay community for her tireless efforts to find a cure for the pandemic.

Given all of these awards and titles bestowed upon her over the years, I like to think that she would admire my own accolade for her—The "Über-Diva"—the most.

Anna Moffo

Her Funeral

Wayne Koestenbaum

I.

On March 10, 2006, I heard Tchaikovsky's *Mazeppa* at the Metropolitan Opera. In the program I noticed a donor's name: Noffo. Misprint? Someone named Noffo was giving money to the Met? Midnight: I came home to the news (an acquaintance's email) that Anna Moffo, my favorite singer, my nucleus, had died.

2.

Anna Moffo and I never officially met. The two times I approached her for an autograph—after an appearance at Baltimore's Melody Tent, and after a master class at New York's Merkin Concert Hall—don't count.

3.

The day after Anna Moffo died, I bought a fountain pen, red, Waterman, in a blue box, white interior. This sentence is a coffin.

4.

In her performance (live) of *Turandot,* co-starring Franco Corelli and Birgit Nilsson, 1961, at the old Met, Anna Moffo sustains the last note of her first aria, "Signore ascolta," longer than necessary. The glad audience reciprocates.

5.

She has the habit of darkening a note, infusing it with an unrequested, honeyed dram of significance.

6.

At Anna Moffo's wake, I signed the "Relatives and Friends" book, but didn't write down my address. I feared that her stepchild or cousin would send me a chiding letter: "You had no business attending Anna Moffo's wake. Wakes are for intimates."

7.

Anna Moffo's last performance at the Met: March 15, 1976. Exactly thirty years later, her funeral: March 15, 2006. Who else noticed this coincidence?

8.

A *Boston Globe* obituary mentions that she was nominated for a Grammy in 1972 for *Songs of Debussy*: unavailable now. (I found a pirated copy—her tone color resplendently narcotic.)

9.

Anna Moffo's face seems a sugar cookie, a planet, or a pond. Her eyes, in 1972, glow with a glow I can't describe: heightened *élan vital*? Her dark, wide eyes pivot to their corners. Eye-swerve connotes emotional amplitude.

10.

She appeared in Abel Gance's movie *Austerlitz,* impossible to locate. When I read W. G. Sebald's *Austerlitz,* I inwardly saluted Anna Moffo's earlier version.

11.

Her cortège, St. Patrick's Cathedral: the front car transported flowers. The second car, containing the coffin, had a large wayback. I longed to touch the fender but didn't want funeral-home chaps to see me do it.

12.

The heavy coffin sat unsuperintended in St. Patrick's aisle.

13.

The organ pealed loudly at the end of the final processional. I didn't mind being momentarily deafened.

14.

I felt befriended by the closed, compassionate coffin. I paid attention to its quiet bulk.

15.

Anna Moffo debuted at the Chicago Lyric Opera in *La Bohème*: October 15, 1957. Her Rodolfo was Jussi Bjoerling—a duo so divine it seems a mirage. He died three years later.

16.

My favorite screen appearance of Anna Moffo: her German TV performance (early 1970s) of "Depuis le jour," from Charpentier's *Louise*. Her voice is not yet exhausted—its timbre still creamy. She looks like Claudine Longet, Gina Lollobrigida.

17.

In Anna Moffo's duet with Elisabeth Schwarzkopf, "Canzonnetta sull'aria," from *Le Nozze di Figaro,* recorded in 1959, their voices match: Anna's signature tincture of voluptuous innocence, conglobed with Elisabeth's plangent, haughty elevation.

18.

Dream (April 4, 2006): I heard Anna Moffo's end-of-career *Carmen.* She turned out to be in good voice after all. And I (once more) proclaimed her greatness, though no one listened. Her clear, retrained instrument: Anna in 1979 was unbesmirched, her pitch again intact, early. I wish I'd offered timely tribute.

19.

She still appears, a stalwart, in my dreams. March 18, 2008: I dreamt I found Anna Moffo on a train to Philadelphia. Quickly she disappeared, but for a moment she recognized me as her logical traveling companion.

20.

One of my favorite Anna Moffo recordings is Puccini's underrated *La Rondine,* recorded in 1967. Her voice sways, foresees its limits. A beguiling liner-note photo (dimples evident) is captioned, "Miss Moffo explains a point of interpretation."

21.

Outside St. Patrick's, on the sidewalk, a woman with bright lipstick (a retired singer? a garishly dressed fan?) posed for a paparazzo, who was either a hired hand, or an unpaid, self-elected witness.

Nina Simone

I Got It Bad for Bangles and Diamonds

Regie Cabico

$\mathcal{G}$rowing up Filipino American meant piano lessons. It was like an old-school karaoke machine. My mom, a nurse by day and singer by night, gave me piano lessons so I could entertain all the Filipino dinner guests. Belting ballads such as "Memory" from *Cats* was as much a part of the gathering as a plate of pancit noodles and Pepsi. For me, taking classical piano lessons was the bridge to singing show tunes. When I was eleven I wanted to be Andrea McArdle from *Annie,* and when I told the music director of my church, he said that that was "too gay" for the southern Maryland community, but that I could be the lead in *Oliver.* He later died

131

in a crabbing accident, and my dream of being a musical lead ended. I was a frustrated teen slowly becoming a washed-up piano-banging cabaret act and a musical theater freak.

While playing John Robin in the Kennedy Center's Programs for Children & Youth's Production of *Dick Whittington & His Cat,* the premiere of the American cast of *Les Misérables* was performing, and to this day I can play by heart "I Dreamed A Dream," Fantine's musical number, and "On My Own," Eponine's unrequited love ballad—the ultimate closet-case showstopper. So from age sixteen to college, I wanted to do musical theater, but I got tired of playing Chino from *West Side Story.* The list of female vocalists I love is endless: Patti LuPone, Bernadette Peters, Idina Menzel (with whom I accompanied at NYU's Weinstein Hall's coffeehouse show), Betty Buckley, Jennifer Holiday (early), Barbra Streisand, and every incarnation of Judy Garland (I had a *Wizard of Oz* doll set), but the one super vocalist whom I have wedded as an adult gay man is Nina Simone.

While in Chicago for a Poetry Slam master's meeting, I heard Nina Simone sing "Papa, Can You Hear Me?" This velvety voice crooning Barbra Streisand's song: so slow, so full, so processional it could pull a ship of lonely sailors to shore. Nina Simone made the song her own. From then on her songs have crept up and imbedded themselves throughout high and low points of my life.

I agreed to do a reading for *Poets & Writers* where the words "april," "cruelest," and "month" had to be used in a poem. I was completely stuck, and on top of that New York City was then experiencing weeks of gray skies and heavy rains. Then Nina Simone died, which inspired my poem, "i got it bad for nina." Her music seemed to be the perfect accompaniment for urban loneliness, cooking for yourself and doing the dishes.

When I joined the New York Neo-Futurist production of *Too Much Light Makes the Baby Go Blind,* I performed the poem to Nina's recording of "I Got It Bad and That Ain't Good" while holding a glass of red wine and dancing with an audience member in a shaft of light—all this with bubbles being blown from atop a ladder.

I later wrote four short plays with Nina Simone's music. "Little Girl Blue" plays with an audience member being handed three small gifts by the New York Neo-Futurists. "I Think It's Gonna Rain Today" plays as I choreograph losing my virginity in a one-night stand. "Everyone's Gone to the Moon" plays while I put on angel wings, climb a ladder, and watch people say good-bye and eventually drift up toward a cardboard moon as I flap two white poster boards together. "Feeling Good" on the *Six Feet Under* soundtrack inspired me to write a play in which I hire a male dancer to strip and perform a mock wedding.

Nina Simone is ballsy and wise, and just when I think I have heard all there is of her, I'll hear a song—"Consumation" on the radio—and immediately she'll inspire me to write a theater piece with Aileen Cho, my writing partner. Nina Simone is a difficult, hard-to-define artist, sometimes considered jazz when she has always considered herself classical and black. She was a Civil Rights activist, an international star, a musician, a vocalist, and a survivor of abusive marriages, record executive rip-offs, and IRS issues. Her humor and theatricality are the essences of great performance poetry. She takes loss and can wail it off on a long-sustained note. She can take heartbreak and mend it with complex black-and-white chords. Nina Simone is a spoken-word artist, a dramatist who works the piano as a sage. While my poetry-writing Muse of my youth may have been a good-looking, dark-haired, exotic man, my poetry-writing Muse of adulthood is Nina Simone.

Julie Andrews

My First Maria

Mark Wunderlich

One

My father is shaving my head. It is 1975 and I'm seated on a stool in the basement of our Wisconsin farmhouse, and I'm glad he can't hear me crying over the buzz of the Oster clipper. It's the first week of summer vacation, and just as he has done each summer since I was two, my father has given me and my brother matching crew cuts in time for hot weather. My brother and I are both old enough to be traumatized by my father's inexact skills as a barber, and we are old enough to know that in 1975 no one in their right mind has hair as short as ours. We add this to the list of indignities we must suffer: the bread-bag liners of our galoshes, not to mention the galoshes themselves; the venison sandwiches in wax paper packed in our lunch; having to sell sweet corn door to door from our wagon, and worst of all, the lingering smell of cow shit that clings to everything we own and follows us as we get on the school bus. My father palms my head with a huge hand, brushing my blond stubble, and says I'm free to go and take a bath, before he sweeps up and goes in search of my brother.

The television has been left on in the living room, and I turn the knob between our two channels. On one, an overture is beginning with the first notes of a clarinet, then a flute, then strings and more strings. On screen a movie is starting, and we viewers are moving through mist and clouds, over mountains, past a river cutting through a deep valley, a barge far below, past a castle. We move closer and closer and soon we find ourselves in a hay field. We zoom and zoom, and there she is—a tornado of good cheer, soprano authority. She spins in the grass, head thrown back, mouth wide. She's a giant lung in a dirndl, and everything around her is alive with the sound of music because she says it is.

At this point, nothing is going to tear me away from the singular pleasure of Julie Andrews. With my shorn head and bad attitude, I'm left alone by the others, and so I enjoy the movie in solitude, my feet tucked under me on the rug, absentmindedly thumbing the stubble on my head, which is as rough as a cat's tongue.

For some reason, Maria is in trouble with the nuns. This is utterly implausible: what sort of trouble could this woman possibly be? The nuns try to convince us of her rebellious nature by singing in formation, but I'm not fooled. They know they have been outclassed and wish to expel her before anyone cares to make comparisons. Even at a young age I know these movie nuns are laughable. The nuns I know are also sticklers for the rules, but they aren't ambitious enough to actually kick someone out of their ranks. I've seen them in the living room of their small house in back of the rectory, slippered feet up, tilting in their recliners and watching Lawrence Welk. These are not women of action.

Enter the Children. With their Teutonic names and candy-assed uniforms, they are clearly under the thumb of a tyrant. Maria has been sent to them to teach them to sing and play and stage elaborate puppet shows. Gay Uncle Max wants to exploit Maria and the children and make them famous while the Baroness smokes and looks at them as though she'd like to drown them in the mountain lake like a sack of kittens. She decides on boarding school instead, which at the age of seven I understood to be a prison island for the unlikable children of the rich.

I can see that there is a romance or two in the film, but from my vantage point on the rug, I already know the central story: The children are being rescued by Julie Andrews. Because of her, they will move from a world of rigidity and conformity into one of singing and effortless choreography. By pulling down the drapes and turning them into clothes that fit and flatter, Maria makes clear that she is a kind of domestic MacGyver who will stop at nothing to liberate her new subjects.

Maria leads the children in song. Her soprano voice has the power to drive away the rich aristocrat, to melt the dictatorial heart of the Captain. Her voice is more powerful than the willful Nazis who hang swastikas on the entrance of the villa. Her voice is so muscular, so unblemished; it rewrites history, alters geography, vanquishes rivals, wins the hearts of a nation. At the end of the film, in lederhosen and loden capes the Von Trapps slip through the tightening snare of the Nazis and escape into the Alps, but not before putting on a big show and winning the festival competition. Maria's cleverness and the immensity of her voice made it happen.

Two

A Story: I know a man who grew up in one of the many southern California suburbs—we are just the same age, both homosexuals. During the summer of his ninth birthday, his parents took the family on a vacation road trip to the East Coast. When they reached New England, they wound their way north to Vermont, where they had arranged to stay at the Von Trapp Family Lodge. Built by the Baron and Maria Von Trapp and staffed in part by some of the children, the vacationing family enjoyed the mountain setting, and in the evening, Maria—then in her eighties— would visit the tables of those dining in the hotel restaurant. At the end of the family's stay, while his parents loaded up the car, he sat on the bed and began to think that he'd miss them when they left, but that his family would be free to visit him whenever they liked. He had assumed that the only conceivable reason they had driven all that distance was to leave him in Vermont with the Von Trapps, who were more real, more reasonable, than this family that had brought him to Vermont.

Three

In 1987 my high school German club organized a class trip to Europe. We arrived in Berlin and toured the city before boarding a night train through the DDR to Salzburg, where we would take the Sound of Music Tour of the city. The city in June was packed with tourists, and the streets were dusty and smelled of horse manure from the countless tourist carriages that circled the town. After dancing in the famous gazebo and splashing in the fountain in one of Salzburg's many squares, we boarded a bus to take the climb up into the mountains to Maria's meadow. In the parking area, buses were arriving and departing. Leagues of tourists came and went. We disembarked and joined the others there to do one

137

thing: and so we ran, arms spread wide, heads back to spin and spin, until we fell, or just got tired and returned to the bus for the trip back down the mountain. At the end of that summer, I was on my way to college, too old to need rescuing. Soon I would come out and find my own society, Julie Andrews having pointed the way.

Tina Turner

Tina and I

Jim Elledge

Hullabaloo or *Shindig*? I first saw Tina Turner in action on one or the other—in black and white, not color. In those days, it would've been the Ike and Tina Turner Review, not "Tina Turner" or simply "Tina." That would happen years later.

I don't have a clue about which of her songs I saw her perform that first time—a fast number, I'm sure, the type for which she's legendary. I don't remember a single word she sang but won't ever forget the rawness of that performance, her honesty, how she seemed so free—her libido liberated, unencumbered by social concern. Not that, in those days, I knew the word *libido*—although I was acquainted with *hunger, hard-on, urge.* Uninhibited, even public about her body, she kept *who* she was secret, private, in front of millions.

Or so I thought.

I would've been twelve or thirteen at the time. I was a fat sissy-boy, a bookworm. My father cut my hair into a crew cut each summer. I thought I knew exactly who and what I was, and hated both, but I smothered my identity with flab.

At seventeen I left home. I'd saved some money from an after-school job and had earned a scholarship, so I was off to college, paying my own way through a bachelor's program in three years. Because I was so broke, I could only afford to eat one meal a day. I lost fifty pounds of my high school gut my freshman year, grew my hair halfway to my ass, and began fucking anything that was pretty and willing—male or female. It was the '60s. I was learning how to resurrect my identity, blowing life back into the self I had been at twelve or thirteen.

I had discovered Janis Joplin and Jim Morrison in high school, but no one affected me as Tina Turner had, no one presented the body so blatantly, so unapologetically, but kept what made her tick private. I never wanted to be her. I wanted her strength, her self-assuredness, and a body I wasn't ashamed of.

For the next twenty years, I would follow her career, sometimes on FM, mostly on LP.

During my first trip to Chicago, I would join a march to protest the war in Vietnam. Months earlier, the Chicago cops had rioted during the Democratic Convention. The trial of the Chicago Seven was still underway. I noticed flyers all over the Loop and in Old Town announcing a concert by Ike and Tina. I didn't have the money to go.

A few years later, they released "Proud Mary," and clips of her, with Ike in the background, seemed to be on every channel day and night, and I began to realize that her body was as much of who she was as her lyrics, her dancing, her voice. . . . I'd wanted to separate the body from the mind, not integrate them, not recognize then acknowledge that they're interdependent, one relying on the other for existence. I was beginning to understand my fascination with her. It was my own blindness that had kept me from seeing that she was her body as much as anything else, and that her beauty—or was it merely her sexiness? or both combined?—was somehow anchored in the fact of that integration.

In 1984 I was living in Chicago, just off Halsted and Armitage, and had been for fourteen years. Knowing Tina Turner's importance to me, friends took me to her concert at Park West, a slick, hip, rather intimate club. She'd gotten out from under Ike's shadow and had just released *Private Dancer*. She looked different, better, but the moves that I remembered from the early '60s hadn't changed, her body as much to the forefront of her being as her voice, as the songs' lyrics, as the music.

As her band, led by the saxophonist (part Conan the Barbarian, part Mad Max) who, word had it, was a smack freak, began to play "Private Dancer," I got up from my seat and walked up to the stage. All I wanted was to get a different view of her: she was on the opposite side.

I like to believe that she saw me and walked over to give a fan a special thrill, but it was probably just blocking, a move rehearsed for weeks then repeated night after night. It was time, when they began "Private Dancer," for her to move to the other side of the stage. I just happened to be there. That's all.

But there I was, and there she was, coming my way, and then: she was there, right in front of me. And then: she held out her hand.

I can still feel her fingernails digging into the palm of my right hand.

The feeling lasted a few seconds. It lasted a lifetime.

The importance of this moment to me has everything to do with my being gay. That night, I became aware of how wrong our culture was, has always been, in the way it programs us to respond to our bodies—and by extension, to sex. We've been taught to disregard the body's importance to our self-identity because the

141

body's temporary, when we should revere our bodies *because* they're temporary.

These days I understand, at least to some minor degree, the tangle of sexuality with identity and how that knot is power— powerful and liberating—and that's what makes the body so important. It's where sexuality resides with identity, wrapped in one another's arms.

Or so I think now, but then, that night at 10:37 on August 28, 1984, all I was aware of was how beautiful she was and how in charge. In charge—and damned sexy.

Karen Black

Diva of the Deranged

Michael Schiavi

Is Karen Black a diva? Well, she plays one in *Nashville* (1975): B-list country-and-western star Connie White. Buried under miles of blonde wig and a sequined orange organza gown that defies all description, Connie ascends the stage at Opryland to sing—if that's the word—such showstoppers as "Memphis" and "Rolling Stone" (both of which La Black herself composed). Peering at her, political hack Michael Murphy comments, "The last time I saw a dress like that, I was headed to the junior prom. Girl fell out of the car halfway to the dance."

That was my first image of Karen Black, as seen in the basement of American University's Bender Library in March 1988. I was a closeted freshman unearthing as much VHS Altman as I could. Along the way, I accidentally discovered what an underground New York band would later label "The Voluptuous Horror of Karen Black."

Almost beautiful, *almost* brilliant, *almost* human—Black should have been a gay icon to rival Tallulah. I've never quite understood how she missed that distinction. But I'm happy to take up my brothers' slack.

In her forty-year film career, the only time Black has ever played a remotely anchored character was in Francis Ford Coppola's *You're a Big Boy Now* (1966). She's lovesick Amy Partlett, the saccharine goody-two-shoes forever mooning after library assistant Peter Kastner, who has eyes only for evil go-go cage-dancer Elizabeth Hartman. Kastner is completely oblivious to Amy's earnest cross-eyed passes, and who can blame him? Black gives the part a shot but looks uncomfortable in Amy's demure little dresses and teenybopper tops. You keep waiting for her to shove Hartman outta that cage and relieve her of the spangled miniskirts and Julie Christie–esque white eye shadow that caught Kastner's eye in the first place. When will Karen become the '70s sex beast we all know her to be and secretly long to be ourselves?

Luckily, she didn't make us wait long. In *Five Easy Pieces* (1970), Black takes on Rayette Dipesto, Jack Nicholson's neglected dim-bulb girlfriend. When not straining the bodice seams of her orange polyester waitress uniform—whose lower hem misses public indecency by a quarter inch—Rayette favors rabbit-skin coats and chain-bedecked dress creations that one sees only during Sunday brunch at Phyllis Diller's. Rayette also has a Tammy Wynette fetish that allows Black to warble (and damned sweetly at that) "When There's a Fire in Your Heart" to the indifferent Jack. Are you starting to get the Early Black Leitmotif? Straight boys repeatedly overlook KB's freaky charms; discriminating gay boys can't look enough, even when we're not quite sure why we're so compelled to ogle this odd woman with the tonsorial avalanche poised atop her head.

Oscar-hounds will surely know that *Five Easy Pieces* netted Black her only nomination to date, for Best Supporting Actress— but do they also know that, in one of Hollywood's most delicious ironies, KB lost the Oscar to Helen Hayes in *Airport,* the kickoff film to a franchise that Black would soon make her very own?

Airport '75 (1974) tosses together Helen Reddy (as a singing nun), Linda Blair (as a transplant patient), and Gloria Swanson (as herself), seated across the aisle from Nancy Olson, Glo's young rival from *Sunset Boulevard* (1950). This quartet is enough to blowtorch anyone's queer pilot light, but then onto the craft strolls Miss Black as head stewardess Nancy Pryor, consort of skirt-chasing pilot Charlton Heston. Welcome to Gay Paradise; may I offer you a crazed cocktail? It's only a matter of time, of course, before our heroine ends up piloting the plane, a task for which her vision problems would seem to disqualify her, but if she didn't try, you'd never get to see her thrust her tongue eight inches beyond her head while trying to pull a relief pilot (dangling from a passing helicopter, mind you) through the cockpit's shattered window.

A move like that could only send Karen spiraling into the mutant roles that defined her reputation in the 1970s and established her as Diva of the Deranged. Enough ink has already been spilled on TV's *Trilogy of Terror* (1975). The Zuni Warrior Fetish Doll. La Black possessed, sporting long, pointy fangs and a rat's nest 'do, repeatedly slamming a foot-long butcher's knife into the floor as she awaits her harridan mother's arrival. No need to tell you any more about *that,* or about our gal's haute couture turn in Hitchcock's swan song, *Family Plot* (1976)—which belongs entirely to Barbara Harris, anyway. No, we'd do better to focus on *Burnt Offerings* (1976), in which Black struts her paranormal stuff to feature-length effect. She plays Marian Rolf, bland housewife and mother who becomes so creepily obsessed with her rented summerhouse that she manages, no mean feat, to upstage sixty-seven-year-old Bette Davis in a ghastly wig and no makeup. You might squirm some during Karen's love scene with hubby Oliver Reed—they both look seconds away from devouring each other like praying mantises—but stick around through the film's loopy climax, when the noticeably pregnant star morphs into the house's long-dead owner and shoves Reed out an attic window, face-first, *kersplat* through his car windshield.

Don't get me wrong. Karen Black is capable of some wickedly impressive acting: check out *Five Easy Pieces, The Great Gatsby* (1974), *Day of the Locust* (1975), or *Come Back to the Five and Dime, Jimmy Dean, Jimmy Dean* (1982), in which she plays transsexual Joanne without a single note of camp or self-consciousness. But even in her best work, she's always one degree off-center, always hinting at the imminent derangement that cements her diva status. Now: when do we get to see her tackle Baby Jane Hudson? Charles Busch would make a perfect Blanche.

Raquel Welch

As My Mother

Ron Palmer

Raquel Welch is posing in a white space-jumpsuit zippered down to her cleavage; she must be my mother prancing around the movie screen like a panicky cat trapped inside a body (*Fantastic Voyage*, 1966). When your mother is beautiful, there are her breasts snug and big as those on Raquel Welch. It can be confusing when your mother looks like Raquel, because sometimes you substitute her for the woman in the movie, which ultimately recalls Freud's infamous statement on Oedipal desire: "At a very early age the little boy develops an object-cathexis of his mother, which originally related to the mother's breast and is the earliest instance of an object-choice on the anaclitic model" (*The Ego and the Id,* in *The Ego and the Id and Other Works, 1923–1925,* vol. 19 of *The Standard Edition of the Complete Psychological Works of Sigmund Freud,* trans. and ed. James Strachey [London: Hogarth Press, 1961], 31).

Am I the son of Raquel transformed by desire when my mother's breasts so closely resemble hers? I mean to say regret resembles my mouth while feeding on her Raquel-esque breasts as snow falls through the Connecticut moonlight. I mean to say I remember Raquel.

What is a diva anyway? A woman who possesses kindness and beauty without any hint of self-righteousness; surely this is true of our diva pursuits, no? Stunning eyes with the adorable *I DARE YOU* glossing her lips? Raquel challenges the diva genre as she ages and still looks beautiful even after sixty. Have you seen her lately? *Good God,* the woman redefines the relevant dimensions of diva fierceness.

The most likeable diva allows one to pierce her aura and swim around inside her trance for a little while. I experienced this myself as Raquel's room service waiter in 1992. One buzzing midnight of hotel kitchen lights, the phone showed in green block letters: MS. WELCH ROOM 1107. It momentarily blinked out my loneliness, which I have carried like a bag of water inside me my entire life.

A face so stunning I gasped when she opened her hotel room door. I stood dumb with a round tray on my palm balancing a glass of milk and two white porcelain plates: one with a piece of cheesecake, the other with five chocolate chip cookies on a paper doily. Sturdy yet gentle, she was standing with the phone behind her back, wearing a full face of makeup and retying her white terrycloth robe. Smiling, she greeted me:

"You won't tell anyone how naughty I am, will you? I'm on the phone with Japan." She opened the door wider, motioning and backing away, "Oh, let's see . . . [she was immediately motherly] Maybe on the bed . . . Right there, dear, is fine."

So I said, "Here you are, Ma'am," placing the black tray on the white bedspread. I politely leaned toward her as she talked to Japan, sat on the edge of her bed near the lamp-lit pillow, and extended my primal hand with the receipt to be signed. She gave her exquisite neckline shadows while she signed her looping signature lovingly. Everything was completed so sweetly; I was in a trance!

How can you love a diva if she won't let you into her psychological sphere? The diva must be able to rise above social expectations of the cultural heroine and carry herself without negative weights like smugness and evil arrogance, but rather cultivate a graceful air. If she accomplishes this daunting task, then she never needs to save face because she's always impeccably tactful.

My mother wanted to bounce like Raquel and therefore did the doo-wop dancing, hopping left leg to right leg, shifting her weight and be-bopping back and forth; she took Raquel a little too far: inviting all the men to drool into her bathing suit cleavage. This is a preschool memory of my mother dancing at a lake party beside a red cottage. Did I want to be Raquel Welch or my mother?

Something that I respected about my mother is the fact that she never learned shame (especially over the size of her chest, unlike the teenage girls who so often internalize shame of their own development due to constant teasing, girl-group bullying). My mother chose to flaunt her big breasts, which made her a noncelebrated maternal figure among the other wives. This further complicated my diva worship. I wanted to become my mother as Raquel Welch, not in image or beauty but in gratitude. My mother never threw an attitude. And Raquel—so I've heard through the gossipy grapevine—has never been blatantly rude and vicious. I may be wrong to assume this: the idea of Raquel as saintly and unassuming is viscously delicious.

Returning to the diva inspiration for a moment: Raquel could transform an intentionally dumb script and make it more interesting just by looking around the room. (For examples, see *Mother, Jugs & Speed,* and *One Million Years B.C.*) She could be more like Greta Garbo in her brow-contemplative-wrinkle, indicating the complicated cerebral backstory, like when Raquel is thinking about the line right about to be delivered by the other character. True, sometimes her facial expressions read weakly as an emotional shade akin to hollow. But let's not make the mistake of underestimating her supreme talent to awe the customer/consumer of splendor. Even today, Raquel manages to embody what I believe Marilyn Monroe espoused as self-invention, albeit a parody of the American feminine ideal, of the post–World War II sex object, of female power. Raquel always already possesses this female power with dignity and self-styled prowess, so she never has to perpetually reinvent her iconic image from a bifurcated psyche. Instead she pulses out her sublime and substantive glow to show real love for her audience, camera crowd, interviewer, strangers, fans, waiters.

Ms. Welch utilized nonverbal signifiers (posing with a surprised expression) when she "became" Raquel/her public persona. In this sense, like Marilyn Monroe, she could turn the sexual icon on and off. I believe this is true in relationship to her fame, also in regard to her indelible and undeniable impact on how one "produces" oneself, especially on the red carpet, where the production of the twenty-first-century female personality is on display. I would argue that Raquel Welch helped to invent this "production of the self."

In the end, Raquel is not my mother and my mother no longer resembles Raquel. It's a difficult diva image to maintain for sure, and my mother is almost exactly her age. Raquel must have inverted rage and somehow transformed it into glee. Truly mythological is her ability to keep her body together with or without mutation of the skin, the scalpel at the scalp. Regardless, she remains alarmingly radiant and sensitive to the power of that beauty even if it is a performance just like any other addiction.

I think my mother spent tens of thousands of dollars on NutriSlim, SAMI, Weight Watchers, Jenny Craig (I can't even count the diet plans), all to shrivel. In the end we all just slouch down and slack in places we don't even want to see anymore in the scary mirror. As we age, mirrors are horror shows, especially for the true diva. The knife blade in the doctor's office gliding under the big lights can only save so much and then you are (I am, we are . . .) still you knocking around inside yourself like a drunk kitten, all napping and confused.

I don't mean this judgmentally, yet rather in a stab at a grandiose, philosophical summary: eventually every one of us is living out his/her life in a circular spell of our own making—not traveling anywhere beyond the body, beyond the trajectory of the living. But divas somehow let you forget yourself if only for one fleeting moment—like a butterfly landing on your outstretched tongue—you become one with the diva who lets you into her hotel room to sit on her bed while she's talking on the phone with Japan.

Raquel Welch

Julie Christie

The Cocteau Girl

Cyrus Cassells

The super-astute film critic Pauline Kael once described Julie Christie as having "the profile of a Cocteau drawing—tawdry-classical." Bull's-eye! As a Francophile teen in love with Cocteau's sleight-of-hand films and sensuous drawings, Kael's savvy description deepened my fascination with Christie, the androgynous, sunny beauty who seemed to embody the freewheeling, never-be-bored spirit of the '60s.

My first Oscar broadcast was in 1966, and, as an eight-year-old, I was definitely rooting for Julie Andrews and *The Sound of Music,* which I thought was the coolest movie I'd ever seen (singing and cavorting kids, gorgeous Austria, edelweiss, a dimpled Nazi!). My adored musical won Best Picture, but my nun-fresh, puppet-slinging Julie lost, and was supplanted by another more intriguing Julie: Who was that "smashing" girl in the gold miniskirt kissing her Oscar?

In my hometown, we had twin drive-in theaters that opposed each other. My family's bulky blue station wagon featured a plump seat that faced backwards; I recall, on more than one occasion, being hauled off to see innocuous family fare, and sneaking backward glances at the shamelessly grand *Doctor Zhivago,* which was ablaze on the screen behind me: Look! There's that beautiful blonde again—amid the snow and show-stopping daffodils!

The trio of films that garnered Christie fame—*Darling, Billy Liar,* and *Zhivago*—weren't considered kiddie-friendly at all, so it took close to a decade for me to catch up with Christie the actress. I first became enthralled with her as the frizzy-haired, opium-smoking Cockney madam in Robert Altman's innovative Western, *McCabe & Mrs. Miller,* where Christie proved amazingly adept at turning her beauty off and on at will; then as the tuba-blowing "kook" in *Petulia*; as the sometimes coarse, sometimes rueful, dazzlingly sexy Jackie Shawn in the libidinous romp *Shampoo*; as the grieving mother of a drowned child in the splintered, unnerving, coolly erotic gothic thriller *Don't Look Now*; and then finally as the petulant, conniving, upwardly mobile model Diana Scott in her Oscar-winning role in *Darling* (which now feels, in an eerie way, like a jazzy, premonitory variation on the life of Princess Diana!)

If you relish Christie's films, you can't help but notice how often her directors luxuriate in close-ups of Christie's compelling, Cocteau-drawn mask; Tom Courtenay, her stalwart costar in *Zhivago* and *Billy Liar,* remembers being "god-smacked" by that "extraordinary face" the first time Christie came in to audition. It's all too easy to trance out on Julie's legendary good looks and ignore her artist's supple wizardry at conveying moods. Julie Christie has grown into much more than the '60s life-force girl who burst onto the screen, skipping and swinging her purse, as she breezed past city storefronts in *Billy Liar*. She's evolved into a great actress—nuanced, delicately fearless, spontaneous, on the mark. I was surprised at the emotional surge I felt recently as I watched her accept the Screen Actors Guild Award for her performance in *Away from Her*: Christie's kudos from her acting peers, as well her recent lion's share of critical awards, affirmed my longtime faith in her gifts as an actress, not just an iconic It-Girl. Her immensely moving work in *Away from Her,* as a gallant, sophisticated Canadian woman succumbing to Alzheimer's disease—a role comparable to that of Mary Tyrone in O'Neill's masterly *Long Day's Journey into Night*—is the crowning achievement of a fascinating career.

Julie Christie makes for a curious, maverick diva in that the essence of her style is unfettered naturalism and empathy. In the commentary on *Billy Liar,* she's proud that her ebullient, tousled-hair Liz was perhaps the first young woman to appear in mainstream movies without the teased and coiffed, heavily made-up look that made starlets appear immaculate even when "they emerged from the Amazon jungle!" The down-to-earth Christie eschews conventional notions of glamour, but nevertheless remains mysteriously charismatic, stunning.

There's a small moment I've always loved in *Doctor Zhivago,* when Christie as Lara wakes and finds a poem with her name above the title; as she reads, her poet-lover Zhivago starts to interrupt, but she suspends her right hand in the air to hush him as she finishes his verses. It's just that kind of deft physicality and fine-toned expressiveness that makes Julie Christie, as Al Pacino once dubbed her, "the most poetic of actresses." Passionate, intent, the Cocteau girl stays in the poem.

Helen Reddy

Before Anarchy

Richard Jayson

Since I contain multitudes, I will admit the following: before I became addicted to the Sex Pistols and the Clash, I listened to a lot of Helen Reddy. Maybe "listened" is not the best word—more like "idolized" Helen Reddy or "obsessed over" Helen Reddy. It may not sound like an act of subversion as transgressive as blasting "Anarchy in the U.K." or "White Riot," but for a boy on the verge of adolescence to go around singing "I Am Woman" in the quaint white-picket-fence town of Medford, Oregon, was, now that I think about it, pretty daring.

Ever since I'd first heard Carole King's "It's Too Late," I couldn't get enough of female singers. I have a vague recollection of lying on cold concrete in a California basement, just before my family moved to Oregon, and listening over and over to Roberta Flack's "The First Time Ever I Saw Your Face." And then there was the summer day a boy named Troy and I lay out in a grassy field behind Blanche Reynolds Grade School and passed a transistor radio between us as it played Carly Simon's "You're So Vain." But by the time *The Helen Reddy Show* was televised in the summer of '73 Troy was eight hundred miles away, and unfamiliar boys were taking off their shirts across our Oregon town, playing catch and mowing lawns as the sun moved lower across the foreign sky. Against that background Helen Reddy seemed to rise, waiflike, from the ocean-blue spume of my family's TV screen.

It is putting it mildly to say that my parents were concerned about my obsession with Helen Reddy. When they wanted to ground me, they took away my record player and made me go outside, a punishment exactly inverse of other parents who punished their wayward kids by keeping them in their rooms. To stay in my room was exactly what I wanted—no half-naked boys, no questions asked, only the reassuring sound of the phonograph arm clicking into position over a new Helen Reddy album, and the warm, scratching noise as the record began to play. My parents took to withholding my allowance and monitoring the number of records I bought, by any means necessary. I devised various ploys in order to get my music into the house. When *Long Hard Climb* was released I begged my grandmother for money, rode my bike to Sister Ray Records, and convinced the manager to give me a 40 percent discount. Then I rode all the way back and hid my treasure in the hot toolshed behind our house. Diverting my mother's attention by saying that Welcome Wagon had called, I snuck the album in at the sliding glass door of the recreation room, well before it could melt in the uncivilized Oregon heat.

Then came *The Helen Reddy Show*. All during that summer I never missed a broadcast. The only close call came the night my

156

father and brother were watching a baseball game that was clearly going to interfere with my diva hour. So of course I devised a solution and went down the block to the Wilkinson's house. I told Mrs. Wilkinson my sorrowful tale, and she let me in, and all the family sat together, watching Helen croon "I Don't Know How to Love Him" and "Delta Dawn." *This is what I want at my house,* I thought, *everyone talking sheer satins and following the singer's every move!* That was before Mrs. Wilkinson began opining about the differences between sixth and seventh grades, diverting attention from Helen, making me lose focus. She went on about Hoover Grade School versus Hedrick Junior High, and was saying that we'd have to "adapt"—that was the first time I'd heard that word—to a new environment, new teachers, new books, new students, until I couldn't take it and asked her to please be quiet, that Helen was trying to sing. The entire family shut down then, letting me know that I'd obviously crossed an irrevocable line. Though no one said a word for the duration of the show, I felt Mrs. Wilkinson glaring at me. But I wouldn't look at her; I was too busy staring at Helen to care what Mrs. Wilkinson thought, which is probably why I was never invited back to their house.

But that didn't faze me. I loved Helen, not Mrs. Wilkinson in all her dailyness and lack of glamour. She didn't even wear makeup! She didn't stand in front of audiences and sing! She didn't project an unnamable longing, a vulnerability, an androgyny that hooked my attention and held it better than any mother could. Helen's profile and demeanor projected a loneliness, a brittleness. That summer, my last before I entered the unspeakable rigors of adolescence, I felt so fragile that I thought I would break. Helen Reddy looked just like that. Mrs. Wilkinson and all the Oregon mothers were too busy trying to "hold down the fort," as they liked to say, too busy "baking up a storm" to have their photos in *Tiger Beat* and on album covers, for all the world to see.

Ain't No Way to Treat a Lady came out and I began to have the reputation for being obsessed with Helen. John Dancer and Steve Mattos ridiculed me for liking this album, and even though "I

Am Woman" was ancient by now, they called it "Richie's favorite song." Did they know then what I refused to admit: that I was queer, and would spend the next twenty years looking for somebody to love? Did they think this because I didn't play basketball or flirt with girls? Had Heidi Millard told them that I'd refused to kiss her behind the hedge lining Highland Boulevard? It didn't matter to me then; the only thing I wanted to do was write down the American Top 40 every Sunday night, sometimes convincing my parents to leave the radio on while we ate dinner. During the year-end countdown, I felt vindicated when Helen Reddy scored with two singles—"You and Me against the World" at number 57 and "Ruby Red Dress" at 71.

Now—just over thirty-two years after that *American Top 100* broadcast—a well-known writer warned me against idealization. "Idealization makes people smarter than they actually are," he said. "Be careful about any person riding your idealization." Of course I was, from age twelve, trapped by idealization. Helen Reddy was just my *first* drug. I would come to revere other female singers, from Billie Holiday (whom I was obsessed with to the point that my parents refused to answer any of my questions, such as "What was she doing in the bathroom?") to Alanis Morissette, from Stevie Nicks to Suzanne Vega, Diana Ross to Rickie Lee Jones. I would say things like, "Joni Mitchell's *For the Roses* saved my life," and I'd mean it. This was, of course, hyperbolic nonsense. *I* saved my life by writing out my self-loathing, the many varieties of fear, the complex array of deceptions.

Though before writing this essay I hadn't listened to Helen Reddy in years, today I put on the only remaining recording I have of her—a cassette tape of greatest hits—and felt the glory, the verve, the reckless abandon of a kid with his whole life ahead of him, and, yes, the pain. And then the rage against the narrow definition of acceptable behavior in any little white American town. I sit listening to "Peaceful," wondering how much my position in American society has *really* changed, and remember the day I threw out my Helen Reddy records, somewhere around the time of *Love Song for Jeffrey.* I started hanging out with Steve and John, who liked the Sex Pistols and the Pretenders. If you think my parents had a hard time with Helen Reddy, you should have seen their faces when Chrissie Hynde sang "I needed / To find out what the thing was for / Been reading / But man the time came to explore." You got it: they were practically paying me to go back to the safe haven of Helen. But by then, like all things known to passing time, it was far too late.

Wonder Woman

Exploring the Amazon

Jeff Oaks

$\mathcal{I}$ hated Lynda Carter when she became Miss America, so it wasn't her exactly. Standing next to that fawning troll, that singing ham, Bert Parks, she was too gorgeous, too perfect, the living embodiment of buxom, with a perfect smile I had learned by then to distrust.

For one thing, Lynda Carter was a real person. For another, she was the person my father's cousin, Pat, who lived up the street and who liked to wear red, white, and blue clothing, imagined as the perfect American. Pat's children, my cousins, were the All-American dream: large boned, hard working, exuberant, confident. As opposed to me, who was quiet, small, and self-conscious. I distrusted anything that had to do with crowds. I hated being made to stand and put my hand over my heart at parades, to fake patriotism.

But when Lynda Carter became Wonder Woman, she stopped being real. She became a fiction, which was much easier to swallow. Suddenly, I could look at her directly. I became devoted to the show, even taping it, making my parents promise to remain soundless while I taped. Over the course of the next week, I'd listen to it over and over again. I was looking for something.

The essence of a diva is her ability to be apart from humanity, to be larger than life, to be beyond it, like a goddess. Divas do not do dishes or wash underwear or drive cars or hook worms or fish for anything, even compliments. They are driven, possessed by greater powers. Often they seem demonically controlled, which explains their frequent mood swings, their tantrums. And yet, Wonder Woman was calm, unflappable. She was not invulnerable but pretty much so. Able to toss a car around. Outrun a train. She could break your arm. She hated bullies but was not a bully herself.

I had already rejected the Judeo-Christian model of the heart, never mind the universe. I knew I was not fallen. I knew it was unfair to blame us for the sins of our fathers. It was clear no one else around me was really a Christian anyway, despite their protestations. No kids I knew loved others before themselves. I always heard someone clipping fingernails in the back pews during the services, as if he or she were waiting for a bus rather than waiting on the Word.

When I asked one day why we needed to give our change to UNICEF, why God couldn't simply make things better for the children around the world, no one answered. I asked how it could be that Father and the Son were different beings, when it seemed

161

only logical that if the Son were separate, then God was not everything, and God had to be infinite in order to be God. People looked away.

Greek mythology gave a truer description of my complicated insides.

The Christian God was tyrannical, cruel, and ridiculously passive-aggressive. There was no Eros in Him. On the other hand, the Greek gods visited, blessed, and handed out gifts. They transformed and chased and embraced and fought and drank and flashed their eyes.

So when I said to my mother I didn't want to go to church anymore, her answer was to sigh and say okay. My father, I remember, looked relieved. The pews were hard. Besides, no one did anything after but go home and get drunk watching football.

When I was nine or ten, in Phelps, New York—a village where you knew everyone's business in 1975, and they knew yours—I cut the bottoms off of two Dixie cups and slipped them over my wrists. Rode around town that way on my bicycle, which had a banana seat and a sissy bar. Rode around until someone asked me why I had those things on my wrists.

At nine years old I read the tragic story of Apollo and Hyacinth, a story that has haunted me ever since. I still remember where I was in that TV room when I first imagined the two men in love, hunting together, playing together, sharing their lives, so in love that Apollo forgot what he was and tossed his discus at Hyacinth, his dear love. It killed him. There is no calling mistakes back, said Greek mythology. There is tragedy and it is often our own fault. Even the gods make mistakes. In his grief and guilt, Apollo turned his lover into the purple flower I grow now in my little patio garden.

Still, the story meant that it was possible for the powerful to be swept away by the beautiful.

Hadn't my mother fallen in love with my father despite the prediction in her yearbook that she'd go to medical school and that he'd end up working in a bean factory because of his propensity for farting and fart jokes?

Hadn't I fallen in love with a younger, blond-haired, blue-eyed, baseball-playing boy whose initials were R. C.? When he stayed the night we kissed each other passionately. We told no one. I wrote in blue pen "Me and my RC" on the rubber rim of the heels of my sneakers. I thought if anyone asked about it, I'd just say I loved RC Cola. But the first time my friend Randy read it, he asked me outright if I loved the boy. I felt myself blush but said no. And yet I wanted someone to know that I did love him.

At home, I practiced, with an old length of clothesline, lassoing fence posts as my father sweated in the garden behind the house. Not once did he ask for my help. In the woods, I lassoed branches, climbed up them. When Wonder Woman lassoed bad guys, they froze in place. When I lassoed any of my friends, they usually ran toward me, trying to tackle me, despite my saying, STOP, STOP, STOP. They were not compelled.

Here was a woman imbued with gifts from the Greek gods themselves. Wonder Woman was the verge where things overlapped, where male and female touched, embraced, conjoined without catastrophe. Her symbols were open enough to interpretation, mutual penetration by men and women.

Her bracelets were not girlie bangles of plastic or silver. They were gladiatorial, forged, heavy. The lasso was a cowboy's, a breaker of horses as well as wills. The only way she might lose her powers were for those bracelets to be welded together into handcuffs.

Wonder Woman had an invisible plane she controlled telepathically. Where did she hide it, I wondered? How did she find it again? Did it just float above her, waiting?

Her tiara might become a boomerang in a pinch.

Still, Major Trevor was a problem—he was so obviously inferior to her. Why did she, how could she have fallen in love with him?

Like my mother, Wonder Woman had a secret identity. It showed up at night when our "Major Trevor" came home drunk from the American Legion, having gone to escape the sense he had missed out on life by having accepted his father's sand and gravel business when he came home from the Korean War. During that war, he'd spent his time directing air traffic on that magical faraway island called England. There he was a hero simply for being an American and handsome. Here he was an ordinary man with taxes, mortgages, anxieties, both his parents dead by the time he was thirty-two, the only boy in a large family of women, the only one who could pass on his father's last name. When he came home late at night, he slammed the door, threatened to kill himself if we didn't say we loved him, cried right there in front of us.

How to protect myself was a real question for me. Not from my father, who only spanked me three times as a kid: once for running away for about a half an hour; once for threatening to kill myself with a butter knife if I didn't get my way about something; and once for, in a pique of frustration, taking a rock from the driveway and dragging it along the side of the green Pontiac of some people whose house we were staying too long at (and then trying to pin the blame on their son). I understood why all of those happened.

What I didn't understand was the way I saw boys suddenly punch each other or challenge each other to fight. I stayed quiet enough generally to avoid all those awful challenges the bullies in school made to the stranger kids around me, but I knew that I was at least as strange as the ones who were routinely humiliated on our playgrounds. I knew I had secrets that would make me vulnerable.

When my friends saw me with my wristbands and my looped length of clothesline, I said I was Wonder Man. I knew I shouldn't pretend I was Woman; simply implying that I'd taken my model of power from a woman could have gotten me in trouble, made me suspect. But I got away with it somehow. It made me nearly tremble to get away with it. It was subtler, if only by a little. As if I were telling them something about myself and yet not saying it directly. I'm not sure any of my friends got it. Maybe they were just not that interested in playing superheroes. They liked more real things like cops and cowboys and robbers and Indians.

They thought that Elvis's death was a tragedy. One of my mother's friends didn't stop crying over him for a year.

So why not Superman, who had greater powers in the end, who would have been far more socially acceptable? Why not Batman or the Flash or Green Lantern? Because I fundamentally didn't trust masculinity enough to inhabit one of those characters for long. Men were dangerous and unstable. They fought with one another. As a boy I knew I had no real power to fight. I couldn't stand the idea of fighting, partly because I hated the idea that my inadequacies would at last be revealed. I had already been beaten up in second or third grade by Judy Erdle for calling her Erdle the Turtle at recess. When she tackled me and sat on top of me, I pretended to fall asleep, the embarrassment was so fierce. She knew it and didn't even make me apologize before she got up.

For me I could not imagine power through the bodies of men, which always seemed distant, closed off, untouchable. Once my interest in their bodies started to manifest itself, I knew I had a problem. If I wanted to live, men had to be untouchable in that small town where everyone knew your business. Still, I had hopes they might be deflected, lassoed, compelled to speak the truth occasionally.

I wanted people to tell the truth. I was always trying to find out the truth.

I didn't know why Major Trevor had crashed on Paradise Island. To me, every man I knew seemed to have just crawled out of some war-related wreckage. (I stood there many nights, waiting for the man to speak coherently.) And it isn't, I think, a coincidence that on Paradise Island was the Amazonian's Purple Healing Ray, that great female invention that rewrote the tragedy of Apollo and Hyacinth, so that the doomed mortal lover gets to live, the two lovers get to enjoy their lives together.

And if worse came to worst, no one knew where I had set down my invisible plane, its engines always running, ready for escape. I had only to imagine it floating above my house at night, its invisible ladder tapping on my bedroom window for it to be so.

Diana Ross

How to Reign Supreme

Jericho Brown

#1

I am not an objective source. I am a poet.

#1

When company comes, they play cards and dominoes. My parents put on the *diana* album because disco is one life, and some nights, we live it.

I climb from lap to lap, begging for sips of beer, whiskey, and wine until cigarette smoke is thick enough to blind me, and I run to my room.

But my father won't have it. Everybody here is here to party. This is his house. "Tenderness" is playing, and he's as drunk as he will be. He calls me from my room and tells me to dance.

I do whatever he tells me. I'm that kind of kid. Our company encircles me with yelps and claps while I stomp and slide all over the den. I do as Daddy tells me. I dance to Diana Ross.

#1

I was getting all kinds of messages to get off the stage . . . and I had an electric mic in my hand. . . . but I knew that if I would have left the stage, the lights would go out and there would have been some form of panic, and I knew people would have been hurt.

Diana Ross

I want cartoons—superheroes who fly. The skinny black woman with the widest smile in America wears a beaded orange bodysuit. She raises her arms, and the winds blow. She squints—her eyes delicious and round—the bright blue sky goes black. She tilts her head back and opens her mouth, and her orange cape and mane of black hair rise in the wind. Isn't she flying?

Then comes the voice. A soprano at once clear and breathy calls to the multitudes screaming her name. She makes it rain.

#1

I prefer lyric sopranos to dramatic ones. I prefer worship to praise.

And so I love poems. They are, each of them, part woman, part lioness, all angel, on stage at Central Park in New York City. Poems are the jeopardy involved with making lightning strike, with singing in and against a downpour that might drown us all, a rain the singer herself summons.

Who wouldn't want all that artifice—the hair, the smile, the costume, the dancers, and dear Jesus, those eyes—just to hear the voice, just to see the way the bones jut as if to escape the body of the thin woman singing? Just to watch her, with her arms wide in triumph, accept and command the ovation that mortals call thunder?

The poem is a woman in danger, who loves danger. Throngs of women and children stand in the rain to see her. So many men miss work to hear her. Diana Ross is a superhero, and so many of the men want to be saved. It's 1983: so many of the men are dying.

When I began my life as a writer, I only had in mind to get onto paper some version of that iconic image: a black woman dripping in sequins holding the final note of a song with both her hands raised in praise of astounding applause. She is, somehow, as ferocious as she is elegant. I wanted to signify the isolation of the lead singer, even when she travels and shares her fame with the background harmonies made popular by the two Supremes singing next to her.

I thought what I knew of that image would be enough for a statement about art and the artist . . . about the poet, who is expected to be a member of her community and at the same time, as a being possessed by music, separate from that community.

Diana Ross

169

Soon, though, given the time period of Diana Ross and the Supremes' popularity, I saw in each of my poems an opportunity to make use of history and culture. For my muse, I turned specifically to Ross, the queen of crossover, as a performer who might have something of interest to say about black art and black existence in the United States of the turbulent late '60s. I attempt to make lyric revelations about the self, about race, and even about the often contradictory life of the minority artist and her relationship to a paying establishment—an audience that may know nothing firsthand of the background that inspires that artist's material.

#1

I seek to be moved. I move to manipulate.

#1

When I was ten years old, three brothers attending a college near our home rented the house next door. Yes, they were all three beautiful boys. And yes, I knew it.

They were all three beautiful boys, but only one of them mowed the lawn shirtless, trained his dog shirtless. He was, of course, my favorite. He would read holding a book above his head to block the sun with his bare back on the grass of the back yard, and I had only an iron fence—one million diamond-shaped holes—separating me from touching him.

If he was outside, I was outside. And I didn't need a book or a lawn mower or a dog. I stared in the way we let rude ten-year-olds stare. He waved, or he smiled.

As the months passed, he became inventive. He'd come outside wearing a shirt just so I could watch him unbutton it or pull it over his head, and no matter the season, as soon as his chest was bare before me, he'd say something about how hot it was.

Only once did he ball a fist and threaten me for swallowing his torso with my eyes:

"Say, little man. For real. Why you come out here being nosy and staring every time I come out the house?"

"Huh? Oh, I'm not staring. I'm practicing."

"Practicing? Practicing what?"

"My song."

"I never hear you singing."

"Because I'm singing to myself. I'm not singing all out loud. I'm just practicing, so I ain't ready for singing it all out loud yet."

"You been practicing that song a long time. You're probably ready to sing it by now. It's a song for church?"

"No. I don't know no church songs. It's an old song."

"You like old songs?"

"Yeah."

"And where you gon' sing it?"

"Why you so nosy?"

"Well if you got a song you been singing, I wanna hear it."

And he sat down on the other side of the fence my father had put up when I was born. I was afraid *not* to sing. The watcher became the watched. I knew all the words to only one song, so I sang it:

> *Do you know where you're going to?*
> *Do you like the things that life is showing you?*
> *Where are you going to?*
> *Do you know?*

From that day on, when he wanted to do some staring of his own, he'd unbutton two, maybe three buttons, motion for me to come over to the fence, and tell me to sing it to him. By the end of the song, every button was undone, and the shirt lie crumpled on the grass that grew on the other side of an iron fence.

Rocío Dúrcal

The Day She Died

Rigoberto González

𝒯he day Rocío Dúrcal died I received a text message from a friend with the news. I sat by myself at the movies, and the announcement was devastating enough to send me out of the theater and into the bustling streets of Manhattan to drown out the screaming in my head. To this day I cannot recall the name of the movie, but I do remember the day of the week—a Saturday, March 25 to be exact. It was late afternoon, and I didn't want to be alone with this knowledge. Immediately, I called or e-mailed every friend who knew who she was and repeated the pronouncement, as if the repetition of it would lessen the sharp sting of the phrase: *Rocío Dúrcal is dead.*

With her passing, I truly felt bereaved. Since 1982, the year of my mother's death, Rocío Dúrcal and I had had a personal relationship, since that moment I stood frozen in front of my aunt's television in Mexico, where movies of the '50s and '60s (usually sentimental dramas or flicks with singing actors) were the standard fare at the network's family hour. I was mesmerized by this young girl who danced and sang her way into the hearts of her leading men, and into mine that day. I wanted to *be* this vivacious beauty queen, not the twelve-year-old orphan whose immediate future was uncertain. We both knew what awaited *her* at the conclusion of the movie: a happy ending.

"She's old now," my cousin informed me after I inquired about her name. "But she still sings."

I began to collect her music on tape, to my father's chagrin. (Already he was having a hard time understanding why I was so enthralled with this old lady on *Murder, She Wrote.*) Rocío Dúrcal's name leapt out at me on the glossy covers of the celebrity magazines on the U.S.-Mexico border. Her face, slightly worn ivory, still showed traces of her younger self. Still, I made it my mission to memorize all of her songs, so that I could move my lips with hers, and picture myself inside her body, and inside the glamour of her dress. I wanted to *be* Rocío Dúrcal and swim inside the admiration of others.

Each year my collection grew. La Dúrcal was prolific and popular with the best songwriters of Latin America—Juan Gabriel, Marco Antonio Solis, Roberto Livi, Rafael Pérez Botija, Bebu Silvetti—they composed the best poetry for her voice, and how she could sing it, quivering the final notes to prolong the life of the dying syllable at the end of a line.

At night, when I could not escape inside books, I could escape into the sound of her, picturing myself on a stage, glittery and glowing like angelic light, the object of all the affection I wasn't getting from my family. Why listen to people fight over money when I could listen to Rocío, the *c* of her name a lisp, like the Spaniards say it, like the effeminate boy in me says it? Why remind myself that I was as miserable as the second-hand clothing coming out of the washer for the fiftieth time, when I could pretend I was wrapped in the newness of evening gowns?

I celebrated my adolescence with her, and when I left home I insisted on taking my Rocío Dúrcal tapes to college, where I moved through the strange campus inside the safety and familiarity of her song.

"Why do you listen to that Spanish woman?" a friend asked with disdain. I had become a politicized Chicano, raza-centered and nationalistic. "Haven't you heard of Los Lobos?"

I liked Los Lobos surely, but Rocío Dúrcal was my diva, my drag queen identity, the woman who could transport me into fantasy painlessness. I kept my adoration for her quiet, but belted out the songs in the shower, where even in my nudity I didn't feel so vulnerable or exposed.

The 1990s passed by and my Rocío collection grew, though now I was trading in my tapes for this new invention, the CD. My musical taste had expanded to include everything from rap to industrial house, but the place of honor was still held by my diva, who once kept me company in the backseat of my father's broken-down car—the only resort for privacy. But as a graduate student, I didn't have to apologize for my love for Rocío Dúrcal, because I met other gay Latinos who also admired and praised her, who also collected her music as anthems for Latino queerness. That Rocío, she knew about loss and heartbreak and longing and revenge, all the relationship dramas we were living, all in the same language we were using against our Spanish-speaking significant others.

I finally had a chance to see Rocío Dúrcal in 2000, in a Madison Square Garden concert. I had traveled with Rocío's voice through my three college degrees, and we were now going to breathe the same air in the same city at the same time. The experience did not

174

disappoint. Rocío gave her performance every bone and muscle and artery, and I could feel her songs go through me like electricity. Tears threatened to pour down my face. Rocío Dúrcal was real, alive and *real*. And if she existed, so did all those moments of my past in which I needed her. I walked out at the end of the concert feeling somehow validated and complete.

But something else changed that evening of the concert. I realized I didn't need Rocío Dúrcal anymore—not for the same reasons anyway. She was now simply an echo from my past life. I was now a professional, living well and removed from my days of hunger and want. I was a relatively happy gay man in a committed relationship with another professional. We had spats, sure, but we also had our glorious nights out in the city. We could afford it. I didn't need to escape my present anymore because I was enjoying it. If I continued to buy her music and to listen to her voice, it was because of my loyalty to her, perhaps even my gratitude. I had moved on. The truth was that at the concert, I forced myself to go through some kind of spiritual experience because one didn't come to me naturally, the way I always thought it would should I ever come face to face with my diva. I didn't fault her for that. Instead, I thanked her for getting me through.

So when she died, having lost a battle to cervical cancer, I mourned her passing like any other of her fans, knowing that each of us had made some personal connection with her and claimed her above anyone else. That's the way it always is with celebrities. That's why we love them and then become discombobulated when we can live without them after we have convinced ourselves that we can't. But, we move on.

However, when I bought my new gadget, the iPod, Rocío Dúrcal went into the playlist first. She continues to be my only fixed variable in a life of changes. Even in death she is always there, faithful as oxygen.

Bette Midler

First Loves

Steven Cordova

$\mathcal{P}$eople tend not to believe me when I tell them this, but I haven't always associated Bette Midler with gay men, gay liberation, or even gay men who happen to have been show-tune queens living in New York City during the 1960s and '70s. I did, however, discover Bette in a gay community—a young, emerging community of two.

It was summer 1979. I was fifteen years old, and one of my best friends was Rick Dunlap. I was still too young to work, so I went to Rick's everyday, boarding the bus on the west side of San Antonio, Texas (not the best part of town to be from, meaning it

176

was black and Latino), and getting off on the north (wealthier and whiter) side. Rick and I spent hours there, listening to music, and smoking pot while his father holed up in his large, air-conditioned bedroom at the back of the sprawling Dunlap house.

What must have happened in the marijuana haze to bring Bette Midler into our lives was that one day Rick and I got tired of listening to San Antonio fare—AC/DC, Cheap Trick, Heart, Rush, and Yes—so we unearthed his sister's LP collection. Not much grabbed us, but there was one album entitled *The Divine Miss M.* We put it on, and it sounded all the better for being scratched, for clicking and snapping as it played. We tapped our feet and shook our hips to the World War II–vintage tune "Boogie Woogie Bugle Boy." Filled with adolescent ideas of romance, we kept time to "Going to the Chapel." And we were probably unwittingly shocked by how sweet girly songs, like "Do You Want to Dance," "Superstar," and "Leader of the Pack," could be transformed into sultry displays of lust.

"Leader of the Pack" sounded as though it had been recorded live in a high school gymnasium. I've always imagined that Midler and company recorded the song on a hot summer day. Bette stripped down to a cheap full slip and ran around the gym, occasionally collapsing, belly up on the gym floor, in fits of passion. Twenty years later, I still walk down the streets of New York—where I've lived since I was twenty-two—bellowing "Hello in There," the version Bette performs on *The Divine Miss M.* It's a spare arrangement, just Bette, singing slow and sad to the equally adagio Barry Manilow on piano.

> *We had an apartment in the city,*
> *me and my husband liked living there.*
> *It's been years since the kids have grown,*
> *a life of their own, left us alone.*

Well, it wasn't long before Rick and I lit up with our straight Speech and Drama Team friends—Becky, Kathy, Jason, and

Elisa—and turned them on to Bette, too. In fact, drama, as much as love, must be what I first associated Bette with. The six of us spent a lot of time together, traveling the state with the team, competing with other high school students in categories like dramatic interpretation, humorous interpretation, and prose and poetry reading. We rehearsed late into most school nights, and we brought home trophies to show for our work. So it must be the moments on *The Divine Miss M*—when Bette practically speaks the lyrics, or when she throws in an aside for levity—that perked up the ears of an adolescent group of thespians, a little troupe of comedians that took itself very seriously.

Rick and I were, of course, gay. We weren't open about it to each other yet, but soon we would be. Our friends, our drama coach, everyone except our parents would soon know it too. At one tournament in Corpus Christi, I even steamed up the back seat of a car with a boy from another team, a competitor whose name I've forgotten. I remember he was cute, and very forward. My teammates and friends had gay experiences, too. (Well, some of them did.) Theirs usually happened on nights they drank too much or the first time they dropped a Quaalude. There were theater-scene cities like New York and San Francisco, where the Divine Miss M enjoyed largely gay audiences. In San Antonio, my friends and I provided the theater.

The summer of 1979 became the fall semester; 1979 became 1980. I turned sixteen during my sophomore year and, inevitably, fell in love. It was lunchtime. I was standing in line. I looked to my right, and there he was, leaning on one leg, looking shy and worried—the angelic John Límon. He was about my size but had blond hair. I thought he was a white boy at first. But no, it turned out he was a highly acculturated Mexican American, like me. And he was interested in theater.

We became friends quickly. In fact, we'd steal time alone together from our teammates, who, like any clique, could be possessive. We drove around in his car in those stolen hours—drinking, sometimes; talking about deep, meaningful things, always. And it was John who introduced me to the rest of Bette's discography: the self-titled *Bette Midler, Songs for the New Depression, Broken Blossom, Live at Last,* and *Thighs and Whispers.* After John graduated (he was a grade ahead of me), I played hooky with him twice to see *The Rose,* Midler's first screen-acting stint and the only one to date that approaches excellence. She played a character based on Janis Joplin—more theater, more drama!

I finally told John how I felt about him. And he loved me, too—but as a pal. His affections were focused on a jock who, I recall, made a dramatic foray into our school's production of *Bye Bye Birdie.* He was straight and inaccessible. But, no matter, the jock was taller and less acne-riddled than I was. John was fixated on him and later on other more accessible men. We stuck it out though, remaining difficult but close friends. I wanted magic to happen, for his feelings to somehow change. They didn't change, and I would periodically try to break away. He, in turn, would periodically try to let me go. He knew I was hurting. But I was the only gay friend he had. The sad truth is that John Límon just didn't love me that way.

The happier conclusion is that I still love Bette Midler. I still listen to the early albums, and I buy newer recordings if they're passable. I can listen to my collection, to boot, without wallowing in bittersweet memories of John. Bette's fiery feelings on *The Divine Miss M* were, thank the gay gods, my own. Those silly torch songs that she reinterpreted for my generation were cathartic for a boy growing up gay in San Antonio. They had all the art I needed to move on and, eventually, continue my search for love.

Jessye Norman

Als Ob Ich Säuseln Hörte

Dante Micheaux

*T*he pull was instant—as if a tether that had always been there, convinced of independence, suddenly conceded to the demands of its source. I was in the eighth grade and had just returned from my first trip to Boston. Mom was waiting, late that Sunday night, with the rest of the parents at school for our charter bus to pull in. Enthused by this latest adventure, masking fatigue, I hopped into our Plymouth Horizon ready for the forty-five-minute debriefing—the highlight of which was either the view from John Hancock Tower or chocolate-covered strawberries in Quincy Market.

When I arrived home, I dumped my bag, took off my shoes, and began (what was at age fourteen) my only devotion—television. I was becoming quite the fencer at that time, and my hand-eye coordination was stellar. Having all the buttons on the Magnavox remote memorized, I let the channels whiz by, knowing that if something caught my attention, I could recall the station and get back to it in a blink. And catch my attention she did. There, on PBS of all places (not appreciated for its late-night programming before I was savvy enough to watch the interviews given by Charlie Rose), was a black woman . . . at Avery Fisher Hall . . . singing! Though she had a snowy orchestra as backdrop and an even snowier audience, she appeared to be all by herself. Draped in what must have been a stolen Pollock canvas, it was her voice—all three Sirens rolled into a voluptuous brown goddess—that called to me. Recruited by the American Boychoir at age nine, veteran of the Trenton Children's Chorus at age thirteen, and in the midst of an internal struggle between surging levels of testosterone and a platinum soprano voice, I knew a little about singing. I also knew that I was under the sound of a voice that would change me forever.

I have always been lucky. I could have gone immediately to bed and, considering I had school the next morning, was not sure why Mom hadn't forced me to do so. Readying for school meant Mom and I would be up at 5:30 a.m., so she would have enough time to unload me the aforementioned forty-five minutes away and get to her security post by 7 a.m. at the Justice Complex. I have never thought of my mother as a Super Friend (long replaced by '80s ringers like *Transformers, Gem and the Holograms,* and, the cartoon to end all cartoons, *ThunderCats*) but she did actually have employment in a hall of justice and wore a uniform. And in this instance, because of her allowing me to stay up, I had stumbled upon an episode of *Great Performances,* when the PBS executives weren't afraid of the effects opera had on ratings and scheduled back-to-back broadcasts. If I had been home at eight, I would surely have watched something else and would have been

181

heading to bed at ten. Scratch luck; I was destined to hear this voice.

I recognized the German from a Bavarian children's song I knew. The tone was velvet, the most plush, most comfortable thing in which I had ever been enveloped. I was surrounded, held-up and stolen from myself. To quote Toni Morrison, "how can I say what that was like? The taste, the taste unlid my eyes." I was certain of two things: she was not Marian Anderson and I was not who I had been just a moment ago. At the end of her breathy lieder, she had made slaves of the audience—with me as its most intimate member, clapping so hard I thought my hands would shatter when Mom ran into the living room, wanting to know what the matter was.

The matter was, and has been since, Jessye Norman.

Liza Minnelli

Everybody Loves a Winner

Jason Schneiderman

The summer I was fourteen, I stayed in and watched *Cabaret* on video loan from the local library. Over and over again, I watched. It was my summer of close reading. On the first viewing, I fell in love. On the second viewing, I realized that I needed to study this. On the third viewing, I noticed that the film gradually *conceals* the character of Sally Bowles through song, instead of revealing it as you might expect from a movie musical. On the sixth or seventh viewing, I realized how the songs were related to the action—thematically replicating on the lyric level inside the Kit Kat Club whatever was going on at the narrative level outside in the streets and apartment houses of Berlin. It took me until the tenth or eleventh viewing to realize that Michael York and Helmut Griem were having an affair with each other, in addition to both having affairs with Liza. Michael York's Brian states it explicitly, but I was rather dense—at fourteen I just didn't think such a thing was possible. In time, I learned to apply the skills the film taught me. I learned that I wanted to wear blue cashmere sweaters against my bare chest. I learned that I wanted to travel abroad and have adventures in which I mingled indiscriminately with fellow expatriates and native citizens (in whose tongue I would invariably be fluent). In other words, I was ruining myself, and in time, I realized that I had to unlearn most of the lessons if I wanted my life to go on beyond the last frame.

1. Act as though whatever flatters you is the height of fashion

Sally's haircut flatters one person in this world, and it's her. Those costumes flatter one body: hers. She doesn't live by trends, or make trends, or care about trends—she has a calling and a vision. She is the vision.

2. Present myself as a problem to be solved

The first thing that Sally does to endear herself to Brian is to offer him a wretched concoction called "prairie oysters" (a raw egg with Worcester sauce). Brian responds, "Peppermint," to which Liza responds, "Oh, that's the toothbrush glass!" Brian's options are to respond with amusement or with anger. He chooses, of course, to be amused. Years later, I would realize that the proper response to this kind of overture is to run. In other words, I learned to remove from my life the Brians who liked the Liza I had become.

3. Present myself as unavailable and tragic

Wounded is the key to Liza-Sally. It's a wonderful aphrodisiac. *Wounded* is *always* a component of wisdom. In some ways, it's the same as Lesson 2—any man who wants to salve your wounds is good for at least a few movies and dinners. Of course, *wounded* is also *exhausting*. You have to keep playing the same script over and over—and the same break up can get really tiring. My husband broke me of this cycle by breaking up with me. You have to stop being so wounded, he said as he dumped me. We got back together. We got married (Lady Peaceful, Lady Happy).

4. Express enough interest for the man to make the first move

I found this *very* handy in college. I used the sorority girls' mating call ("I'm so drunk") to great efficacy more than once. Hold up a half empty bottle of Zima, pretend it's your third, and you'll have your pick of at least three rides home. The kind of man I wanted took pride in having picked me. Loved that one. If I'm ever single again, this lesson will definitely come back off the shelf.

5. Enjoy it while it lasts

The end of *Cabaret* is not happy. Sally has an abortion, Brian goes back to England, and you know what's about to happen? *The HOLOCAUST.* The young Jews find love, but we never find out if they escape the gas chambers or not. And Sally handles it perfectly. Leaving Brian at the train station, she waves without turning as she walks away. I love movies with unhappy endings. Annie Hall refusing to go back to New York with Alvie Singer. Faye

185

Dunaway realizing that she should have joined Steve McQueen in his life of aristocratic crime. Dustin Hoffman dying at the back of the bus while John Voigt gazes out the window. Michael York/Brian wants long term, but he can't have it—there is no long term with Nazism on the rise. Politics is bigger than we are. Careers are bigger than we are. Liza/Sally isn't fooled by a dream of domestic motherhood—she knows what she is, and she burns the candle at both ends. Perhaps the biggest surprise to me was that I don't burn the candle at both ends. I'm not a club kid; I'm not an actor; I don't have a larger-than-life talent whose expression cruelly dominates my life. I'm bourgeois. I'm happy—with a husband and a house and a graduate degree. I want it to last.

Postscript

My love of Liza was limited to *Cabaret*. My adoration of Liza didn't spread. I didn't track down copies of *Liza with a Z,* or *Tell Me You Love Me, Junie Moon*. I didn't read Liza biographies, and when I watched the Queen Tribute concert, I didn't even recognize Liza Minnelli—I was watching it for Cyndi Lauper anyway. At some point I saw *Arthur 2: On the Rocks,* and realized that I'd better stick to *Cabaret*. Liza was teaching me to protect myself—to keep myself self-contained, and not to rely on anyone. Liza was the key to my closet—like her mother was for gay men of my father's generation.

But at some point, we have to *unlock* the door and throw away the key. When I came back to Liza as an adult, I realized how much I needed that film version of her then, and how different my life became. Now, I have a curious attraction/repulsion, shame/pride relationship that's not entirely separate from my relationship to my younger self, sitting on the couch, watching *Cabaret* again and again and again. Now, I listen to *Results* (her collaboration with the Pet Shop Boys) and go see her in concert when I can. I love the grandiosity and excess of her talent—but also the way it seems incompatible with a real life. Now that I love my real life, she's less of an escape, and more . . . well . . . decorative. In a very literal way, she helped me survive—I built this life by implementing the lessons of *Cabaret,* but I survived it by unlearning those lessons. When I see her on Larry King or *Arrested Development,* I don't want to protect her, or keep her safe or anything like that. I want her to keep on sparkling—to keep on being the cold, hard gem whose gleam held me captive that long, hot summer.

Liza Minnelli

Cher

History (1987–2000)

Aaron Smith

The First Time (1998)

Cher has written a book, and she's doing a signing at Tower Records on Newbury Street in Boston. Drag queens, gay men, kids, teenagers, fans from the sixties. The line is zigzagging down the sidewalk. *Cher will sign two items.* I have the book and the *Believe* CD; the line inches forward and two hours later, it's my turn. I approach the table and something inside me rises up, something I couldn't have guessed was there: a ridiculous, consuming, awestruck panic. (It never occurred to me to plan what to say!) I say: "You're so glamorous and beautiful." Then I think: Did I really just say that? I want to die. I want to hide. I want to get back in line and try again. I don't think I've ever said that sentence in my life, and yet of all the sentences possible, the universe sends this one, right now, today. Every Cher-moment in my life has led me to this, and I just screwed it up. I should have just said, *Once, I accidentally peed on someone's shoe in the bathroom.* It would have been just as ridiculous. She kind of just nods and it's over.

"I Found Someone" (1987)

Don't you know. Those three words float from my sister's boom box, and suddenly I am beautiful. I am thirteen years old—roller skates strapped to my sneakers—making up dance routines in the garage. I'm a terrible dancer (and skater), but it doesn't matter: I'm inventing a world I can live in from my loneliness. I pretend turning a smooth corner on the concrete floor with my arms stretched wide is a feat only an expert can accomplish, and because I can do it perfectly, people like me, applaud me. I know the guys at school who call me *faggot* are incapable of moving with such grace. I fill that cinder-block room with the possibility that I, too, can find a way *to take away the heartache.* Though I'm too afraid to imagine what that might look like.

Moonstruck (1987)

Because my parents don't go to movies, I don't get to see *Moonstruck* until it comes out on video. I'm happy it's rated PG because I'm not allowed to watch R-rated movies. (I sneak occasionally: I smuggled a copy of *Working Girl* home from school that a friend recorded off HBO and watched it when my parents were sleeping. Melanie Griffith topless and shocking as she ran the sweeper!)

Maybe it's Cher's transformation that draws me to the movie (the gray removed from her hair before the opera, her eyebrows plucked, the perfect shade of lipstick)? Maybe it's the delicious secrets all the characters in the movie are keeping? Maybe it's being picked up by a hairy man with a wooden hand and hauled off to his bed and enjoying it (though I know I'm not supposed to)? Whatever it is, I rent that movie from Kimberly's Video and Tanning so many times that my mother finally asks: *Are you sure you want to spend your allowance on* Moonstruck *again?*

Will & Grace (2000)

His name was Mark, and he had me over for dinner at his house when I lived in Pittsburgh. I almost didn't accept the date because that was the night Cher was to make her first of two guest appearances on *Will & Grace,* but he promised we could watch TV. He wanted to fool around. I managed to hold him off until after Cher slapped Jack (who had mistaken her for a drag queen) and told him to snap out of it. Mark came all over my black Gap sweater.

The *Believe* Tour (1999)

JFK Jr. is missing, and we are afraid Cher is going to cancel the concert (she doesn't). "I think they're friends," Brian says. She's playing the Tweeter Center in Mansfield, Massachusetts, and we've looked forward to it for months. Brian has a red convertible, and it's perfect for driving while wearing the Cher wig (of course we have a Cher wig). We push to the front of the outdoor pavilion. Cyndi Lauper opens. She comes out into the audience and Brian touches her hand. When Cher rises from the floor singing "I Still Haven't Found What I'm Looking For," Brian cries. I clap, sing along, but I'm worried because I'm afraid I have testicular cancer.

I will find out the next week that I don't. In those days, I always worried I was dying of something. I worried about everything. On the ride home, Brian stands in the back seat—wind whipping the long black hair—and sings "All or Nothing" while we speed down the interstate toward Boston.

The *Believe* Tour
(For a Second Time with My Friend Fran)

Fran comes out of the bathroom at the concert and says, "I've never seen so many leather cigarette cases and cans of aerosol hairspray." When Cher rises from the floor singing "I Still Haven't Found What I'm Looking For," Fran and I stand up and sing along. The audience is full of old people, mean people. Someone asks security to make us sit down. When we sit down, our section applauds. Cher was great, but that ruined our evening. That's the last time I see her in concert.

"If I Could Turn Back Time" (2000)

I have just swallowed a tab of ecstasy. Josh and I are boarding a boat for an all-night cruise in Boston Harbor to kick off gay pride weekend. I have never tried anything other than pot, and I'm nervous: If something goes wrong, I'm stuck in the middle of the harbor until dawn. We find our friends—Marc, Greg, Amiko—and make small talk until the boat pulls away from the dock. The music starts: *If I could turn back time . . .* What better song for a boat full of boys? It's cold, but not too cold. The boat moves fast, but not too fast. I don't know if it's the pill or Cher or the fact that I have friends and am living in Boston—so far away from where I started—but I feel light and calm, like I'm floating above the boat in the perfect black (black as Cher's revealing outfit). Cher throws out big notes that crack and crash with what feels like a strange

191

hope in my throat. We dance in a circle. The city blinks and fades in the distance beside us.

Cher

Laura Nyro

All She Asked of Living

Michael Klein

In 1968 there was a record store on 85th Street and Broadway in New York where my twin brother Kevin and I would go every other Saturday to search through the new releases. For us, this was a rite of passage—one of those intimacies in which we could feel something about the world (in this case, what there was in music that we wanted) without any parental influence. In this phase of our pull toward music, one of our great bonds was an almost obsessive interest in the singer-songwriter—that rare artist (troubadour, really) who, unlike everyone in the music business today, signed off on a creation *before* signing the recording contract.

My brother and I came across an album one Saturday called *Eli and the 13th Confession* by someone named Laura Nyro—an excitingly odd-titled new release that came wrapped in a lavender lyric sheet that had unbelievably been sprayed with a fragrance (hyacinth?). "Who's Laura Nyro?" my brother asked the shopkeeper. "Never heard of her," he replied. But Kevin and I liked the package and the title and the smell and brought that Saturday's singer-songwriter home with us. We then spent the next week, month (the entire winter?), devouring *Eli and the 13th Confession,* which entailed, because all devotion requires imitation, memorizing the lyrics and immediately sounding out the songs on the funky upright piano my mother gave us for Christmas.

"Well, there's an avenue of Devil who believe in stone. / You can meet the captain at the dead-end zone" (a line almost private in meaning), Laura Nyro joyfully tells us in the first track, "Luckie." And for twelve songs afterwards, Nyro rapturously chronicles a woman's sexual and spiritual awakening ("Luckie inside of me, / inside of my mind," which in the end track "The Confession" becomes "Love my love thing / love is surely gospel") in a way that is so moving that only Billie Holiday comes to mind as a sister artist of similar intent, as someone whose singing voice was intended to lean against her own consciousness. Nyro's voice, of course, was amazing—earthy *and* ethereal, paint-stripped, and vibratory. Along with the vocals, this was the most compelling and complex, dissonant yet soulful music Kevin and I had ever heard: Copland meets Stravinsky meets Motown.

Aside from falling in love with her music, we also immediately identified with her on so many levels—a sexually ambiguous New Yorker who went to the high school we had just been accepted into (Music and Art), and she couldn't read a note of music! All things true for Kevin and me. We also discovered that we were able to find her melody lines on the keyboard because somewhere under the complexity, her chord progressions were actually pretty accessible.

Her vocal lines, too, miraculously could be located in the throats of two fourteen-year-old twins, and so we sang "Poverty Train," "Timer," and even the rarified, hard to sing "December's Boudoir" all through our fourteenth year. And while *Eli and the 13th Confession* put Laura Nyro on the map—a small map, but a prodigious one—her next album, *New York Tendaberry,* put her in the same company with the most influential songwriters of her time, particularly Joni Mitchell, who, like Nyro, was a woman who wrote confessional music (unheard of outside of contemporary poetry).

On the cover of *New York Tendaberry*—that rare album that elevated popular song to art—she is posing for the picture sitting on a rooftop in New York; it's her rooftop, I'm sure, because in everything I had ever read about Laura Nyro (and I read everything I could get my hands on and saw her perform at least a dozen times), she came across as completely raw and unaffected. Her rooftop, her city.

More raw and unaffected pictures: She opened for Miles Davis at Fillmore East, and if I remember right (I was drugged and in love with everything), they played together. She ate tuna fish sandwiches every day (like someone going to school) and called her music publishing company Tuna Fish Music, which she started with her manager, a young David Geffen. Her first audition for Clive Davis was in a room the size of a closet whose only light came out of a portable black-and-white television.

Back to the *New York Tendaberry* picture: You can tell by the way the fire escape climbs behind her head that this is probably a walk-up, and something about the light (gray, indirect) makes it look like a scene after rain. Because her eyes are closed, you know she is somewhere else. It's a photograph that *shows* us everything about what we're going to hear when the music starts playing: moody, distinct, and unbridled—music after (or is it before?) a storm.

The album's essence is New York City—complex, iconic—and yet, it is delivered spare—mostly Nyro alone at the piano: jazzy, dissonant, and primal—and it's about the street that never closes, the bad neighborhood, the struggling artist, the woman with the man who doesn't understand the woman, and—like every Nyro album—God and the Devil. I never thought of Laura Nyro as a particularly religious artist, but she was most definitely a songwriter who embraced opposites: temptation *and* redemption, the funky *and* the traditional. Here, at this nexus, is where the soul aspect of this album and all of Nyro's music really lives—radically positioned between jazz and art song, between the lyric that rhymes and the lyric that won't.

I think her music meant so much to me because it was so brazenly unlike anything else that was out there at the time and you really had to listen to it, and in that way, like all great artists, she gave others of us, who were just beginning a musical life, permission to let the pain be a guide, as well as the ecstasy.

Her music was a surprise to the ear and to the body. And, like Joni Mitchell, Rickie Lee Jones, Tom Waits, and Stephen Sondheim, most apparently, I don't think I ever fully comprehended the music until the second or third hearing. (What phenomenon *is* that?) I couldn't even get some of the words: "Two mainstream die / You don't love me when I cry." Well, I get the latter part of the statement, but what exactly is *two mainstream die*? It didn't matter. By the end of the song, I knew what it meant as a whole, and my joy may have come from the fact that this was music that didn't feel engineered for an audience. She was anti-famous, a woman on a New York rooftop after the rain and her music was going to get written with or without us.

The day she died in 1997 (at forty-nine, of ovarian cancer—by the same cause and in the same year of life as her mother) I wrote a short homage to her and her music, which I gave to my agent Henry Dunow to try and get placed somewhere. He sent it over to a young editor at the *New Yorker* (where only the young can thrive), and after circulating it around the magazine for comments to, I imagine, the cadre of other young editors, someone came back to Henry a few days later and said, "I'm sorry, no one here ever heard of Laura Nyro."

Stevie Nicks

"And Wouldn't You Love to Love Her?"

Michael Montlack

"Hold Me"

Picture it: 1982. Long Island. Just another one of the aluminum-sided split-levels in the town's sprawling line of them. A twelve-year-old boy sits on the family room sofa. Faintly aware of the MTV playing (that still-new phenomenon that seems to be always on in any kid's home). Until he is awakened from his after-school stupor by imagery he will never forget.

Picture *this*: A vast desert. In an undetermined time and place. Populated by the five members of Fleetwood Mac, each one engaged in his or her own peculiar behavior (or *Mirage,* as was the name of their current album). The drummer (Mick) and bassist (John) crawling through a junkyard of guitars and keyboards, dusting off the sands in a desperate attempt to see what can be salvaged. The floppy-haired and sleepy-eyed keyboardist (Christine) staring through a telescope before taking her green-polka-dotted stallion for a stroll under the blazing sun. And then the handsome guitarist (Lindsey) standing tall, in his safari hat and khaki trousers, before an easel, obviously struggling to capture what could never be captured fully on canvas (or for that matter in words.)

But let me try:

The petite vocalist (Stevie), in slinky red gown, reclining demurely on a lush olive-green velvet divan, sultry but not sweating in the dry winds, occasionally brushing away strands of her wavy gold hair from those heavily glossed lips. She sits patiently, waiting to be portrayed. Until in frustration, or distraction, the handsome man, without a word or even a wave good-bye, walks away, leaving her.

So *what* does she do? What any true diva would do.

She gets up, trudges the distance in her platform boots to that easel, picks up the brush and palette, and starts to paint herself into the scene, craning her neck to peer around the canvas's edge at her other self: still posing there casually, still stunning in the sun, undisturbed (at least on the surface) by the abandonment. She will finish the job herself. She will create her *own* image, painstakingly and independently, before lifting the considerably large painting to lug it across the dunes: a slow graceful march in those chunky heels to an unclear destination that you *just know* will be as surreal and beautiful as this one she is leaving.

And you—or at least I—will want to go with her . . .

"Sisters of the Moon"

That "Hold Me" video may have been my visual introduction to Stevie Nicks. But the seduction started years earlier, with her faceless rasp that bellowed through the halls of my household in between the Led Zeppelin and Eagles and other '70s fare.

Yes, my older sister, Pam, had a lot to do with it all: stomping around the house in platform clogs, constantly re-feathering her hair and blasting Fleetwood Mac's *Rumours* every time my parents pulled out of the drive, leaving her to babysit me. That was 1977, when I was seven but already well aware that I was different, especially when Pam's biker boyfriends came by to smoke pot with her, and I couldn't keep my eyes off their tight Levis and the newly sprouted chest hair they showcased through unbuttoned flannel shirts. Before I had even heard the name *Stevie Nicks,* her husky growl had been the soundtrack to my childhood: "And wouldn't you love to love her?" "Thunder only happens when it's raining." "Till the landslide brought me down."

And my own sister, the pretty portrait of tough, was aiming in her own way to be the next, sexier Stevie. Pam may have been a lousy babysitter, leaving me to float in the pool by myself for hours while she tripped on mescaline or acid, but the moment any boy on the block said anything even remotely hinting at my being *faggy,* she was on him like a watchdog, chasing him down the street (nearly stumbling in those clogs) or actually pushing his face into the lawn: "Just try it again, ya little fucker. And see what happens." So is there any wonder I'd develop an affinity for wispy but hard-edged blondes?

"Leather and Lace"

A few years later, when I was eleven, Pam, then in her own struggling rock band, took me to a record shop so I could spend my first allowance on a 45, one of Stevie's first solo singles: "Leather and Lace." Already I was admiring those contrasts: the raw, gutsy howls that erupted from the frail chiffon-strewn femme. The ultrasoft against the hardened. Was this a gender blur of sorts? Perhaps that duality was part of the attraction for a seemingly masculine (first to shave in his grade) but sensitive boy.

But there were other dualities: The troubled, drug-addicted rock star versus the humble singer-songwriter introduced on stage by her proud "Daddy." The spinning, black-caped vamp accused of witchcraft versus the doe-eyed angel about to take flight in those layers of white gauze and lace. When once asked during a radio interview how she could explain this multiplicity, she simply answered, "I'm a Gemini." It wasn't long before I was at the local bookstore, poring through the astrology books, trying to better understand this woman. And it wasn't hard at all to identify with her "twin" existence because I too felt split: the public Michael (regular soccer-playing wholesome boy) versus the real Michael (who was hiding a "dark" side—even masturbating with one of his teammates after practice).

But clearer to me was the unclear. Her lyrics, like her wardrobe and sex appeal, relied on mystery or veils: what was not seen, what could not be fully discerned. On stage and in videos, her emotions were always on the surface—in her streaming tears and furrowed brow—but her meaning was not. Stevie was the goddess of codes, symbols, secrets. She told her own personal stories through sometimes muddled Welsh mythology ("Rhiannon"), natural phenomena ("Storms," "Landslide"), and fairy tales ("Alice," "The Highwayman"). And fans were left to decipher or just guess what her real story was.

Yet even through that fog, and from a distance, she would teach me how to survive the closet: for example, how to feel and communicate without being caught. This was when I started to write (lyrics, poems, and stories: my own codes) not to mention read more seriously—first mythology and fairy tales to keep up with Stevie's references and then classic literature. For the remaining part of my adolescence, I would be wrapped safely in Stevie's sheer shawls and capes, a perfect hiding place for the already invisible.

"Edge of Seventeen"

And I did hide, especially in high school, when she would become another kind of buffer. Perhaps Michael didn't date because he was waiting for a Stevie type to twirl into his life and enchant him? Maybe no girl was sexy or romantic enough for him at East Meadow High? And, after all, it did seem that I liked girls considering that barrage of seductive Stevies staring at me from my heavily postered bedroom walls. She appeared, to my friends and family, to be a surrogate lover but was actually an adopted fairy godmother, who like all good godmothers (and big sisters) provided protection, acceptance, and guidance, perhaps offering even more to kids like me who needed more but couldn't ask for it.

"Has Anyone Ever Written Anything for You?"

A couple of years ago, I wrote a line in a poem about Stevie that no doubt started me on the path to the self-examination and community study that became this book:

Childless fairy godmother, mother the fairy child.

In recent years, Stevie makes it clear that she has made the hard but right decision to not have a family of her own, in order to do successfully what she feels she "came here to do": create music, fulfill her destiny as an artist, and hopefully make an impact. When asked by one interviewer if she considered herself a teacher, she, without hesitation, said, "Yes." But I can't help but wonder if she knows to what extent she has taken her mission.

Stevie Nicks was an outlet—and an out—for all those unexpressed emotions, like love, confusion, and loneliness, and everything else that comes with growing up and being different. It could have been Barbra, Janis Joplin, or Beyoncé that hooked me.

But in the end, whom we choose as our divas may be less important than what they come to do for us, generation after generation, and often without even knowing it.

"Has anyone ever written anything for you?" Stevie sings in a song by that title.

"Well, I have. I have given that to you. If it's all I ever do, this is your song."

Jessica Lange

Isn't It a Laugh?

Allen Smith

The laugh. Unmistakable. Natural no matter what god-awful shade her hair had been dyed or how poorly she lip-synced when she played Patsy Cline in *Sweet Dreams*. Though drawn through the years to drama, and with an acting style praised by Pauline Kael for its physicality more than Meryl Streep's prowess at accents, Jessica Lange's laugh, for me, defined her appeal. And, yes, it was her own solo, her own aria.

It came at odd times, as when she was mildly annoyed at Cline's mother in the hardscrabble upbringing that Lange portrayed in *Sweet Dreams*.

"Oh, Mama," she'd chide, sandwiched between that laugh, needling Ann Wedgeworth (as Cline's mother) to fib on the *Ed Sullivan Show* and act like her agent. Of course, Lange and Wedgeworth were busy with their own fibs, portraying people they weren't. How easy that's been for me to attempt through the years.

To pretend with steely conviction as I had in high school that I did not have a hopeless crush on an English teacher with silver streaks passing cometlike through his beard. To act as though I wrote that love letter to a hall counselor in college my freshman year not because I really loved him (as I had written) but because I was troubled by abusive parents, as I quickly followed up in subsequent notes, thick as the *Oxford English Dictionary* to ensure absolute burial of the authentic sentiment.

So small wonder then that I was interested in an actress, particularly one who found humor when things were bleak, as my love life was when Lange won an Oscar for best supporting actress in *Tootsie* and was nominated for best actress in *Frances.* The comedy turned out to be an uncharacteristic setting for Lange, but the gender-bending theme of *Tootsie,* though campy and embarrassing in retrospect, had some daring to it for its time. Still, I much preferred *Frances,* yet another Lange role about a performer, this time actress Frances Farmer. Something of a maverick during the Depression, Farmer apparently tried to abandon the old, rigid Hollywood studio system (which for me perhaps symbolized the conventional hetero marriage factory) for meatier roles on Broadway. Farmer ultimately found herself performing for a psychiatrist at a mental ward where she'd been hospitalized after a breakdown, trying to persuade him she was normal, a common, ironic theme in Lange's work, as in the HBO gender-bending film *Normal.*

Normalcy, so easy for most, was out of Farmer's reach, as Lange portrayed her. It was far too much fun taunting the doctor, making him nervous, getting on his nerves and having a laugh, or at least a smile or smirk, at his smug expense. I really think the psychiatrist, so wrongheadedly judgmental, in a way symbolized society at large for me and its scorn for my sexuality.

Yet, if this was the picture's morality tale for me, it took a while to absorb. I watched and rewatched it an insane number of times while in college. I was, at the time, perhaps wondering if I was going crazy, newly aware of and frustrated by my unfulfilled sexuality, which seemed in that early era of AIDS frighteningly far from the norm.

How was I to act in a straight world that considered my romantic instincts sinful or backwards? My answer advanced little beyond watching *Frances* during college. Once, to my friends' bewildered amusement, the answer was shearing my head of hair, then unfathomably thick, short as Frances Farmer's had been clipped in the scene when she was institutionalized. As I grew bald as an Oscar, I found more of the courage to turn—as did so many characters Lange had played—and blurt out the truth (however abnormal or unsettling it might at first seem to others) about who I was. Increasingly, I was turning away from "acting."

Still, I enjoyed Lange's more infrequent roles. A friend brought me an autographed poster from her performance as Blanche DuBois in *A Streetcar Named Desire,* which I eventually got to see televised. I was particularly struck by how offhand some of her most shocking revelations were, like when she couldn't muzzle her attraction to a young man, in fact a boy as she calls him, who happened by—yet another sign of an abnormal love threatening to undermine her sanity, if not a mental deterioration already in progress.

When I was in high school, the one unquestionably open gay hangout that I knew of in my hometown, apart from a few out-of-the-way bathrooms and the occasional modern dance performance, was the old movie palace, the Carolina Theatre, built originally in 1927 for vaudeville and then in a gloriously kitschy, unrestored state of disrepair. It was there that I'd seen gay characters or couples take center focus in movies, as in *Colonel Redl, My Beautiful Laundrette,* and *I've Heard the Mermaids Singing.*

Other than that scene in *Sweet Dreams* when Patsy Cline zooms into North Carolina to see her sweetheart at Fort Bragg,

Lange hadn't set foot in my home state, at least not to my knowledge. But gradually I heard from other guys I met that she'd visited at least once in the flesh—to shoot *Crimes of the Heart* in Wilmington, back when its movie industry far outstripped more recent upstarts like Toronto.

These informants were pals I met when I started going to the gay bars that gradually sprang up. I recall chatting with one guy about how he'd once seen her in the area—the spotting gave some momentary fizz to a relationship that quickly fizzled out.

Another barfly, as irreverent as Bob Fosse in one of Lange's earliest films (*All That Jazz*), invited me back to his place, where, among his many portraits of friends, I found his one drawing of a celebrity: Lange. He recounted meeting her when he was in graduate school in Charlottesville, recalling some way in which she coolly snubbed him, as her longtime boyfriend Sam Shepard joined her at her table.

For years, Lange and Shepard lived together, like a married couple, though they remained unmarried. This unconventional arrangement was further evidence to me, however slight, that she was a kindred spirit. So too was her Oscar-winning reproach in *Blue Sky* to fellow performers on an army base who were talking about her behind her back as, Lange's character defiantly declares, others had done all her life. The sting of others' sport with innuendo—that was another thing we shared. And then, more recently, her turn as someone attracted to someone else who happened to be the same sex in *Broken Flowers*.

But by the early 1990s, Lange had moved past some of her more soul-searching roles (*Country* or *Music Box* or *Far North*), as I had many of mine. Maybe she too felt more comfortable and less anguished with who she was. I, for one, did: coming out to my parents, forgoing a career in the practice of law (which seemed impossibly closeted in North Carolina even as recently as 1991), and pursuing one in writing—one in which I could find my own songs and music, if not actual arias.

On a road trip in 1994 with my partner (to his family reunion in Kentucky), we were forced to take refuge from torrential rains in a dilapidated motel in Covington, Virginia. In the morning, on my way back from a quick visit to the motel office, I saw a woman with a baseball cap accompanying three dogs, one of which was large and white as a child in some cheesy ghost costume.

"What kind of dog is that?" I asked.

"A komondor," she said. "Most people think it's a poodle!" She laughed.

That laugh. Unmistakable. Only then did I recognize her.

Patti LuPone

Patti's Turn, In the Key of Diva

Jonathan Howle

It is March 27, 2008: opening night for the newest Broadway revival of *Gypsy,* arguably the greatest musical ever. Here I sit, dead center, front row/front mezzanine of the St. James Theater. Lauren Bacall is sitting directly below me in the orchestra! The atmosphere is electrifying. The show was to start at 6:45, but it's almost 7:10. However, the delay is nothing when you consider that this night was never supposed to happen. Even Patti LuPone's most loyal fans had once resigned themselves to that fact. (Back in the '80s, a major fall-out with the show's book writer, Arthur Laurents, prompted him to publicly decry that she would never play Mama Rose.) But that was then; fortunately, they kissed and made up. And she will be marching down the aisle any minute now.

Only . . . everyone around me is talking about the wrong things: *American Idol,* Bernadette Peters, Mayor Bloomberg, leg room, and get this, Whole Foods! While in my mind serious questions are swirling: How will Patti not be paralyzed by all the money at stake, all the longings of those who want her to succeed, and all the inevitable secret desires of those who want to see her fail miserably? (After all, just nine months earlier, the chief theater critic for the *New York Times,* Ben Brantley, was not impressed by LuPone's Mama Rose in a concert version of the show.) So what if these reviews don't glow too? And the musical closes next week? What if this is such a flop, Patti publicly vows never to sing in New York again?

Beads of sweat trickle down my face. My friend asks if I am all right, to which I reply, "My mother might as well be opening on Broadway tonight."

Suddenly, the lights dim. I've never really believed in out-of-body experiences. Until now—this night. I am about to discover that when a gay man finds himself in the same room with his first (and ultimate) diva, strange, marvelous, frightening, and most of all, enlightening, things can happen.

Opening Bars

They're a call to action. Sit down, shut up, and take notice. You are in the presence of greatness. Suddenly, on stage I see myself at age seventeen. Listening, really listening, to Patti for the first time. I'd heard her vocal prowess on the recordings of *Evita* and *Anything Goes* before, but it was her live recording of "Being Alive" at Carnegie Hall that did it. I wish I could articulate exactly what it is about her voice. It's not just the typical "Broadway diva" voice. All I know is that once I heard this song I never listened to music the same way again.

"Everything's Coming Up Roses"

More applause. Perhaps the most widely recognized song from the show. Brassy and rapturous—it ends act 1. The opening scene disappears, and now I see myself in October 1996: the first time I ever saw Patti live, in Terrence McNally's play *Master Class*. It was a Saturday afternoon, and there were hurricane-sized rains and winds in New York. No other meteorological scenario would have been more appropriate.

It was my sophomore year of college, a rather confusing time. I was not out; in fact, I was doing everything I could think of to turn straight, including rushing a fraternity. I figured if I could get in, that meant I was heterosexual. That I would live out the All-American-Preacher's-Kid dream my parents had planned for me. Although I can laugh now about it quite heartily, getting rejected was quite painful for me then.

However, as I walked from the Howard Johnson's restaurant (which I miss terribly) to the John Golden Theater that afternoon, for the first time in weeks, I did not think about that frat and the rejection. Instead I was nauseated, giddy, and just overwhelmed that this woman, previously only real to me on tape and CD, was about to appear. In the flesh.

When the doors to the set opened, and she walked through them, again, it was a defining moment that renewed my confidence. When I returned home to North Carolina, that frat experience was fully behind me. The only pledge I could make was to Patti.

"You'll Never Get Away from Me"

A major change in mood to the romantic (yet sad) duet between Rose and Herbie. Here's one of those "Why in the hell am I thinking about this?" moments.

210

In December 2000, I saw Patti in her concert *Matters of the Heart* at Lincoln Center. She was singing "Where Love Resides," a selection I'd heard on her CD a few times but had never fully appreciated. But again, you have to see Patti live . . .

In the song, there is a cello solo, one that lasts for only thirteen seconds. On this particular night, however, Patti actually stopped and listened to this solo, and when she resumed singing, she was clearly overcome by emotion. I've always wondered what she experienced in that moment. The ushers said it had never happened before. She did not give way to tears; instead, she struggled with the well of emotion, which is far more interesting. When she finished the song, there was not a dry eye around me.

"Small World"

A gorgeous moment in *Gypsy*. The most popular romantic ballad in the show. Tender. A moment of real connection between two people who have been disappointed by love. Suddenly, there is Patti in 2004 in a concert performance of the musical *Can Can,* which showcases some of Cole Porter's best-known ballads, including one that Patti sang called "I Love Paris." This piece too had never particularly resonated with me until I heard it live. She had inspired a thrilling orchestration of the song, and all of the theatrical elements magically coalesced. Hence, the familiar became completely original. The audience was so enraptured and surprised that their applause lasted a few minutes. She then went back and sang the entire song again. I'd only heard about this happening a few times in theater history. (Had Ben Brantley been around for *that*?)

"Rose's Turn"

Oh, hell. Musical Theater Fireworks. The greatest song in American Musical Theater. The song you can only sing if you're a survivor of a certain age. Has Patti earned the right to sing it? You bet your ass she has. The words "survivor" and "resilience" are as synonymous with Patti as "diva" is. She's been knocked down quite a few times. Unfairly fired from *Sunset Boulevard* by Andrew Lloyd Weber and replaced by Glenn Close—knocked down, to be sure, but knocked out? Not on your life. She returned in a blaze of glory to New York in show after show and concert after concert. When Arthur Laurents said she'd never play Mama Rose on Broadway, did she give up entirely on her dream to play in the musical? Not on your life. Instead, she went to Illinois to the Ravinia Musical Festival and played the role to such critical acclaim that Laurents was forced to reconsider his vendetta. He then said she'd play the role as long as he could direct her. Did she say, "Not on your life, Mister"? Not on your life. Here she is. About to arrive on stage in just a few minutes. Which just goes to show that the words "diva" and "unmitigated ego" are not always synonymous.

"Mr. Goldstone"

A quick march, blaring trumpets . . . leading up to the lyrics "I had a dream." The overture's almost over. I'm more panicked than ever. And here I go . . . Why am I seeing this? I don't want to see this, but there it is. There I am: October 1997. Frightened for my life. One year ago, I was rushing a fraternity, dating girls, and walking through a hurricane to see Patti on stage for the first time. Now, I'm driving my red Buick LeSabre home to come out to my parents, who are in their sixties. I am afraid I might back down. What do I do? Play one CD, and one track only. Over and over. "Being Alive." Carnegie Hall. Live. Patti LuPone. I make it home. I speak my truth. And it feels like being alive.

Last Three Punches of the Orchestra

The overture finishes. The show begins. All of a sudden: her first line. "Sing out, Louise." The audience goes nuts before she can even speak the word "out." And there she is. On Broadway, in *Gypsy.* As promised, marching down the aisle. All my questions now seem irrelevant, even senseless. This survivor has put all her fears aside and is simply investing everything she has into text and song.

I have never heard such lengthy entrance applause. It does not seem as though it will ever stop. Finally, I can't control myself. I've never done anything like this before. But I have to do it. I don't care if I get kicked out or hushed. I've come this far, and I just have to: As she walks on stage, I say aloud, "Thank you, Patti!" Even if I'd screamed the words, no one would have heard me.

(And tomorrow, Ben Brantley will change his mind and write Patti a rapturous love letter of a review.)

Wendy Waldman

Seeds and Orphans

Paul Lisicky

$\mathcal{I}$f I played Wendy Waldman for you for the first time, I wouldn't be wounded if you didn't get her right away. I wouldn't pick a fight if you made a crack about "'70s California Singer-Songwriters" and heard only the indulgences of the genre: the earnestness, the sunny harmonies. You might say, "Where's the irony?" and I might say back, "What irony?" And I'd be just as likely to point out that she's not a consistently assured singer, or say she's written too many songs that don't bear the stamp of personal signature, as if they've been intended for other voices. As for the whole earth-mother spirituality thing—well, where's the *edge*?

214

The truth is that her contribution to songwriting is hard to articulate, and I'm wondering if that's part of the reason she's worked, for the better part of the last thirty-five years, on the margins. As far as I know, she's never dressed in feathers at the Oscars. She's never cast aspersions, at least publicly, on another female performer, or been voted "Old Lady of the Year" in *Rolling Stone*. When I look past the heap of frizzed-out hair, the gypsy skirts and bracelets on her early album photos, two things come to mind: *sweet, quick to laugh.* She's the earthy, smart Jewish girl who might have been your high school best friend; she'd sit across from you in the cafeteria and do her best to cheer you up when some clown called you a fag. But she'd be careful not to take up too much space about it, and she'd certainly leave you alone if you wanted to mope. Someday she'd even ask you to play in her band. Maybe the most noteworthy extracurricular fact about her is that she was Linda Ronstadt's opening act at the height of her stadium-era fame. Also, she's the daughter of Fred Steiner, the film and TV composer best known for writing the theme to the old *Perry Mason Show,* with its kitschy associations of both testosterone and striptease.

But none of that's exactly fodder for the journalist. And it probably hasn't helped that her music is difficult to categorize. There's been a country Wendy Waldman, a hard rock Wendy Waldman, a symphonic Wendy Waldman. Early in her career she was known as the "West Coast Laura Nyro," which makes a kind of half-sense: both share a knowledge of American songwriting tradition—whether it be blues or Broadway—and its metaphors. But other than that, Wendy's her own animal—or many animals. In a song on her first album she's the daughter of a vaudeville performer who's learning the tricks of pleasing the crowd from her old ham of a father. In "The Walkacross" on her most recent, she's the matriarch of a family running ahead of a flood. Where is the self behind these gestures? Who is Wendy Waldman? But that's part of what's engaging about this work: the disappearance into character, into the mask it's trying on. It would probably be pushing it to say that Waldman knows her queer theory, but I'm sure one of the reasons she matters to me has something to do with her fluidity, her refusal to be any one thing. Why wear one costume when you could be a blues guitarist one minute and a tarted-up girl on the town in the next? How else to keep yourself awake before the mirror?

Of course, the modesty of this strategy has come at some cost. Unlike Joni Mitchell, she doesn't have her "Help Me," which hammers down the persona: the hunger for attachment alongside the need for sexual freedom. She doesn't have PJ Harvey's "Big Exit" with its exuberant pistol waved at anyone in her way. She's finally more character actor than leading lady, and since her interest in inhabiting multiple voices isn't the explicit subject of her work (as it is in, say, Dylan—or at least in Todd Haynes's queering of Dylan), I suspect that her achievement has been hard to see and hear.

What Wendy Waldman excels at is writing wised-up, tender songs. They're not especially concerned with extremity. They're not interested in revenge or outcry. Some are bold enough to engage old-school sentiments like hope and joy. In that way they're closer in spirit to the best songs of the '40s, by which I mean a musical landscape that assumes its listener is living in hardship and doesn't need to be reminded of that every two seconds. (Imagine the old World War II–era standard "I'll Be Seeing You" in gauzy pants with little bells around the hems.) Not that they offer cheap consolation, but they put a high value on intimacy and contact, as if they believe those things are sustaining. I'm thinking about my favorites from *Seeds and Orphans,* which have the eerie sense of being addressed to a lover who never was, who might—or might not—be dead. But the moves are subtle, easy to miss if you don't give them your complete attention. You can pay taxes or scrub vegetables to them and trick yourself into believing they sound like a dozen other songs, but then you'd be missing their little gifts: the leap of melodic line, the unexpected harmonic shift.

Maybe years from now Waldman's music will get the recognition it deserves. I'm talking about that distinct category of praise we reserve for the neglected or the underdog. I'd like to think that she'll be held up regularly alongside Joni and Laura, and younger counterparts like Feist and Joan Wasser, but Wendy Waldman proceeds as if reputation and fame are distraction. Occasionally you hear the tug of missed possibility inside her voice, the shock of something huge left behind, but it's never a whine, or laced with entitlement or self-pity. She might have a better sense of these matters than I do, anyway. In "My Last Thought" on *My Time in the Desert,* she sings: "Nothing much around here's going to stand the test of time. / The things we fought and died for will all be left behind." That insistence on ongoingness, without futurity, without descendents, yet open to experience—doesn't that sound familiar to what many of us might know about ourselves? She soldiers on. She writes beautiful songs in an era that doesn't care about beautiful songs.

Cyndi Lauper

The Sadness in Her Rasp

Steven Riel

$\mathscr{I}$ found out about Cyndi Lauper because my aerobics instructor included a few of Lauper's hits ("Girls Just Wanna Have Fun," "She Bop") on our workout tapes in the mid-1980s. At that point my husband and I had been together for about five years, and I was no longer clubbing nor keeping up with popular music, so I enjoyed feeling a little bit in-the-know about some then-current music.

When I bought Lauper's first album, *She's So Unusual,* I studied her image on its cover, which was packed with primary colors. There she twirled, dancing in a red sundress, with her red pumps kicked to one side. She twisted within a circle of blue sand. Behind her stood a dilapidated, blue brick building called "The Wax Musée." The museum's doors were painted a bold yellow. I was intrigued by the unique persona Lauper projected with what seemed to be extreme deliberateness.

A major reason for my attraction to certain female celebrities and characters is that I am drawn to the strength and originality of the personas that these women project. No one else could be Lauren Bacall, for instance: she was unforgettable, unmistakable, and irreducibly herself. As for fictional characters, no one else could be Cruella De Vil.

Unlike the male stars at the time, female celebrities were given rein to express themselves more distinctively, through a greater range of modes (clothing, hairstyle, voice, mannerisms, etc.). Male stars did not have as many options—for instance, the colors of men's clothing were generally limited to a much narrower palette. Likewise, men generally were allowed a narrower range for the expression of emotions in their acting and singing styles. I was drawn to women because they could express the range of strong emotions I was feeling.

I was also fascinated by women stars with clearly defined personas because, as a boy who felt he could never be who he actually was, I was conscious of needing to create an exterior "self." Even if the ordinary, school-day "drag" and mannerisms I self-consciously put on were all about toning down my flamboyant personality (in middle school, I practiced *walking* like a boy), what they added up to remained an act, just one played in a costume of gray and brown instead of canary and magenta.

What most attracted me to Lauper, however, was not her hair dyed in loud colors, nor the brassy, sassy whirling dervish with the heavy New York accent. Cyndi became my virtual soul mate through those songs in which she expressed sadness, desperation, and hesitancy. Sometimes the sadness was framed by driving anger, as in "Change of Heart," which became my private anthem while I was estranged from a sister who would not accept my gayness.

Lauper could run her voice along heartbreak, whether with baby talk ("Time after Time") or a full-out wail ("My First Night without You"). By contrast, the sterile sweetness of Julie Andrews's voice had never fastened itself in my imagination. Lauper's rasp, like a burr, took hold and grew.

When in 2003 she released *At Last,* a collection of covers of classic songs she had heard growing up, it seemed like a culmination of what I liked best about her work. Free of rock-and-roll arrangements, her voice takes center stage, and in songs like "If You Go Away," she lingers achingly over anguish. Like this CD's music, the graphics on its container are simpler and emphasize the classic. Leaving behind the zany hues and self-referential imagery of her earlier album covers, in a nighttime scene of blue, black, and white, Lauper emerges from what seems to be a manhole while wearing a strapless black dress and arm-length black gloves. On the back of the CD's container, she is depicted facing the Statue of Liberty, her arms raised in either a dance or a gesture. If this is an ecstatic swaying in the moonlight, it appears restrained, slow moving, meditative—far from the frenetic movements of the Cyndi of my younger years.

During the summer of 2007, my husband and I were able to catch Lauper's outdoor concert beside the harbor in South Boston. This was a stop on her "True Colors" tour, which benefits the Human Rights Campaign. Naturally my passionately political side was very pleased to witness the results of her leadership and hard work for our human rights. The lonely and frightened gay little boy I once was still marvels at the courage and strength he can find when joining in with hundreds, if not thousands, of gays, lesbians, and our friends, and in this particular instance singing "Girls Just Wanna Have Fun" at the top of our lungs. Curiously, however, it wasn't Lauper's progressive politics that impressed me most that evening, but how restive she is as a creative soul. Another singer would simply keep relying on his or her greatest hits, realizing that that was what audiences mostly want anyway. Instead Cyndi introduced several new songs and presented very different acoustic arrangements of some of her most famous tunes, as if she is constantly exploring what more she can discover in them.

On the red carpet before the 2008 Grammy Awards show, Lauper defended nominee Amy Winehouse from criticism of her wild behavior, saying, "This is rock and roll. We should not be conservative and we should not be safe." I admire Cyndi Lauper's willingness to take her material and her voice where risk enlightens us.

Rickie Lee Jones

The Duchess of Coolsville

Timothy Liu

$\mathcal{B}$efore I'd ever read a book of poems, before I'd ever listened to an opera all the way through, I'd already come to understand what a "diva" meant even though I knew no Italian. Born in the United States, I was a child of immigrant parents from mainland China and grew up in the somewhat affluent suburbs of South San Jose. Maybe it was after the fact of my parents' divorce when my mother ran off with her Gestalt therapist (only to get dumped after she'd spent all of her $60,000 community-property settlement on him and later wound up in an institution), or maybe it was just typical adolescent angst on the one hand and joining the

Mormon church against my father's wishes on the other (while blowing cock at the local mall every chance I could get), but whatever the case, I felt in need of being *rescued,* as if life had become some sort of psychic emergency that cruising and shoplifting couldn't answer. So you could say I was predisposed to certain frequencies. For Rilke, it was an archaic torso. For my lonesome, it was the album *Pirates* by Rickie Lee Jones, a record I'd first encountered by way of a review in the September 3, 1981, issue of *Rolling Stone* with a photo of Stevie Nicks (+ cockatoo) gracing the cover. Not yet sixteen years old, I'd subscribed to nothing else but. The title of Stephen Holden's five-star encomium was simply "A real treasure. Rickie Lee Jones: exile on pain street." He was astonished by "the bravura way it weaves autobiography and personal myth into a flexible musical setting that conjures a lifetime's worth of character and incident." Was this not my initiation into the land of divadom?

Seven months later, with California driver's license fresh in hand, I lied to my mother on the night of April 11, 1982. The whole afternoon after having been pelted by rain with no sign of letting up, I was in need. A particular need: her '79 Dodge Dart, which she rarely drove. Said I was heading out to a church social that evening and would she mind? Her only condition: that I bring the car back by eleven. This was in the days before Google, before Mapquest. I'd never driven outside of Santa Clara County before, hardly even knew where Berkeley exactly was by way of roads and highways (had only taken BART there from the Fremont station once before), but I still have the ticket stub:

BERKELEY COMMUNITY THEATER
Allston Way and Grove
BILL GRAHAM PRESENTS
RICKIE LEE JONES
Sunday, April 11, 1982 8:00 PM $10

The stage set was a bunch of rooftops with a single grand piano nestled among them. And a big full moon behind it all. You can get some sense of what I heard by listening to her mini-LP *Girl at Her Volcano,* portions of which were recorded live less than a week later in L.A. (just give "My Funny Valentine" or "Something Cool" a spin, both remastered on her *Duchess of Coolsville* CD). With a bottle of bourbon propped up next to the damper pedal, she tore the roof off that theater. "She lost her baby that night!" her ex-lover and coconspirator Sal Bernardi would tell me almost a decade later backstage in Atlanta after I had driven all night from Houston just to catch her *Flying Cowboys* tour there, since that was the closest it would get to where I'd shacked up for grad school. But back to Berkeley. I couldn't stay for the encore because I had to get the car back. I drove through flashing rain in the dark at 80 m.p.h. all the way home.

The divine can make a diva only insomuch as the fanatic can make a fan. You have to change your life as Rilke did and leave Rodin and follow after Lou Andreas Salome on a train to Siberia. I could tell you about all of Rickie Lee Jones's subsequent tours, her reputation for walking offstage without coming back for an encore, her love-hate relationship with the audience. My partner's favorite diva would have to be Nina Simone, another feisty lioness full of kinetic temperament. And when Rickie Lee goes from teenage runaway to paramour of Tom Waits to a miscarrying sot all the way to her current incarnation as a nondenominational born again, you just have to go with her, for better *and* for worse. And now, after the thousands of poetry books that I have read and after the hundreds of live vocal performances that I have attended, some of which have made me see God Almighty himself (Victoria de los Angeles, Jessye Norman, Kathleen Battle, Renee Fleming, Anna Netrebko, and Juan Diego Flórez among them), I have to pause and remember where it all started, where the poetry in my life began.

Annie Lennox

Desire, Despair, Desire

RJ Gibson

$\mathcal{M}$aybe it's a sort of fogeyism, but I find so much contemporary pop music boring. Lyrically, radio-oriented pop has always been a little lacking in heft, so it's not that. I know it's supposed to be disposable: I'm not looking for truth or universality, really. Part of my distaste is the over-reliance of wailing melismas and show-offy vocals passing as soul or something engaging. It leaves me thinking, "Great, you went to church, and you've got range. What else ya got?" And don't get me started on the other end of things: the digitally treated, the overproduced, the lip-sync reliant. What galls me most, perhaps, is that these new chanteuses just aren't that visually interesting. Sure, they're groomed and styled within an inch of their lives; they have nice bodies and good hair, but there's a superficiality to it that just doesn't charm. Calling some of them mannequins is insulting to mannequins—their sole purpose is to highlight an ensemble. It's the difference between pretty and beautiful. Pretty is easy. Beauty isn't. Their mass-market, *FHM*, *Maxim*, men's magazine quality leaves me cold. I want something a little more complicated, a little less easily digested. I want old-school Annie Lennox.

She's been a fact of my life since I was eleven or twelve years old. I knew of Eurythmics from the radio and catching a video here or there, but I wasn't too caught up in them. I remember her cover photo on one of my sister's *Rolling Stones*: cropped orange hair, black leather jacket, New Romantics' mask of eye makeup. There was something unusual about her; she definitely caught my eye, but I didn't really latch onto her then. I didn't feel any strong interest in or connection to her until I saw her in full-on rockabilly-drag at the 1984 Grammy Awards: that black suit and pompadour wig with sideburns hooked me. This little voice inside my head went, "Oooooooh, so that's it." It took me a couple of years to figure out what "it" was, but from that moment I was a devotee. I remember my mother noticing her and asking, "Is that a man?" It was my first chance to be knowing and (I imagined) a little sophisticated when I said, "No, it's a woman."

The tension she created that evening attracted me—appearing in full drag, singing in her lower register, passing as a man. (What's surprising to me now is that people still ask if she's a man in that clip. Go to YouTube. Look up the clip and read the comments; more people are fooled than you'd think.) It's why I love her videos. There's a fascinating combination of visuals at work. Her video for "Money Can't Buy It" has her cast as a chic Vermeer socialite rapping about her wealth. "No More 'I Love You's'" reminds me of Nora Desmond in a Lautrec painting. She appeared on David Letterman once in a PVC and cotton Minnie Mouse outfit, looking like a collaboration between Disney and Gaultier. High art and

Annie Lennox

pop art, cartoon and sex club, this theatricality counterpoints her restrained delivery. The multiplicity of visual references is amped up when she plays multiple characters, switching from male to female to neuter with amazing ease. The "Love Is a Stranger" video (originally banned from MTV for gay content, when one of the "men" in question was actually Lennox in drag) is a perfect example. Toward the end of the video, through a series of close-up shots, her face shifts between the sexes and the sexless simply by tricks of light and angle. My personal favorite is the "Little Bird" video. It takes her filmic past and turns it on its ear as psychodrama. Costumed like the love child of Sally Bowles and the Emcee, she fights for stage space against her past video and concert personae, an array of Annies played by men and women, shot in a way that you're never *quite* sure until later in the video who's who. These ideas—of playing with identity, defying easy definition, unsettling people—appealed to me when I was younger. There was a sense of possibility there. It was a means of defiance and strength while feeling outside the norm.

The tension she creates in videos and performances carries over musically to the way she sells a song. She sings around the lyric, never really trying to emote her way through. Her obsession as a lyricist is relationships, the failings and the limits of people to love one another, to fulfill each other—bleak stuff, really. Yet what might be bleak comes across instead as radiantly stark. Where another singer might take songs like "You Have Placed a Chill in My Heart," "Savage," or "Why" and go all out, filling the spaces between the words with vocal gymnastics, she sings just enough. The songs come across as matter-of-fact, as more truthful to me for their lack of out-front ornamentation. This isn't to say that she doesn't play with descants and melismas—she does. They're usually relegated further back in the mix, treated as another instrument in the bridge or break.

But her sangfroid serves another purpose—she doesn't read as the typical pop vocalist doing a "woman done wrong" number. She may be desperate, she may be unfulfilled, she may be demanding, but none of it consumes her. That remove, that restraint, gives her a power missing in a lot of pop music. Where some might try to play up the vulnerability of a piece, she lets it stand. Her shifting vocal attack in "Who's That Girl?"—the dry delivery of the verse versus the more passionate take on the chorus—elevates a song that could be only the despair of thwarted passion. Instead, she purrs out indictments and accusations that make them as much a caress as a slap. Although I love those songs, she appeals to me most when she's more aggressive: "I Need a Man," "Missionary Man," "Would I Lie to You?" and "Wide Eyed Girl" are cock-rock songs, delivered by a woman. That assertiveness, that sexual baiting without stooping to crassness, appeals to me. Her restraint, her command, her use of tensions attract me as a man and a writer— they are essentially what I aspire to in my own life and work.

And this is where it becomes tough to pinpoint just exactly how she's mattered to me—the tricky split between me as a gay man and me as a poet. I don't necessarily make the distinction myself. Art's been what fed my life, my own development as a man, and at the same time my life informs my poetry. It's where I found beauty and strength and a way to act upon the world. I see her as a model, a mentor, a goddess. Perhaps it's the tension she creates that draws me: her ability to be everything and nothing and be frank about it, to confront her audience with it and still be alluring. She isn't glamorous in the way of other icons and divas; she doesn't have a single sort of performance persona the audience can hang onto and cherish, but she has a commanding presence. Hers is a voice worth listening to. Ultimately, as both gay man and poet, that is what I want.

Siouxsie Sioux

Black Eyeliner and Dark Dreams

Benjamin Harper

As I was standing impatiently among the crowd of malcontents at Irving Plaza in New York City waiting for Siouxsie Sioux to appear, I realized that I had been doing the exact same thing twenty years ago, almost to the date, in St. Petersburg, Florida, at Jannus Landing.

Not much in my life has changed.

Hers, on the other hand, has been upheaved several times. First the Banshees, her band since the mid-'70s, disintegrated, which left her with the Creatures (her side project with husband Budgie). Then she and Budgie divorced, which she revealed to the world in 2007—and she's on her own musically and emotionally for the first time in three decades.

I wondered what she would be like now.

The Banshees carried me through most of my adolescence and young adult life. I remember very vividly the moment my friend Carolyn handed me the albums (yes, LPs) *Tinderbox* and *Hyaena* in the tenth grade. Carolyn had been horrified by my mainstream sensibilities, and, trying to usher me past the world of Top 40, had taken it upon herself to be my musical tutor.

What Carolyn didn't realize was that she was introducing me to the one who would come closest to being a "diva" in my life. Some have Madonna, some have Judy, and some even have one of those talentless "divas" littering the airways these days.

I have Siouxsie.

I doubt Siouxsie would embrace the term "diva." I am quite sure she would have a vulgar slur ready to hurl at anyone who would dare to say such a thing—and that is one of the things that made her such an important figure for me as a teenager. She had no need to adhere to the rules and regulations set forth by society. She broke through them and became a true individual.

As a chubby, alienated gay teen, I was searching for someone—anyone—who could tell me being different was okay. When I saw Siouxsie in her signature thick eyeliner and hair teased as if she had just stuck her finger in an electrical outlet, something clicked. This woman was a weirdo—and completely unrepentant about it. I knew she was the one for me.

Soon my room was littered with posters and images clipped from alternative music magazines. I would lie on the floor and fan out my ever-growing collection of albums and singles, inspecting each and every one over and over until even the most minute detail in the cover's artwork was memorized. When I saw her on the "Song from the Edge of the World" tour in 1987, I was filled with angst-ridden awe that I was about to witness live, in the flesh, the bleak matron of sinister music who had enriched my nights with visions of a happy apocalypse. As a disenfranchised kid, I envisioned an end to conformity and superficiality, and in my mind's eye, she was the avenging angel who would swoop down and rid me of the vacuous throngs that littered my school's classrooms.

I was shocked that she was actually gracing St. Petersburg—home of shuffleboard courts and mah-jongg tournaments—with her presence.

As I warbled along to giddy lyrics about cities being engulfed in lava and women suffering from multiple personality disorders, I felt as if Siouxsie were speaking to me—she was feeding an as-yet untapped need in my brain for the morbid, macabre, and mysterious.

Following her lead, I eschewed the once-important ritual of being dressed head to toe in brand-name clothing—realizing that labels prove only one thing: you spent a ton of money to give some designer free advertising—and took to wearing black, and plenty of it. I put eye shadow under—yes, under—my eyelids so I would have the pallid visage of someone who had spent decades living in a cave. Fishnets, rosaries, John Fluevog Swordfish shoes, black velvet leggings, and the final goth male accessory—the black floor-length skirt—all made their way into my wardrobe. I was given wide berth when traversing the high school (and later college) hallways, and I couldn't complain—I didn't want to talk to those people anyway.

Twenty-two years have passed since Carolyn introduced me, but Siouxsie continues to alter my perception of the world. In 2007 she released her first solo album, *Mantaray*, and I was ecstatic. As most chanteuses grow older, they seem to fade into bland routine. I was hopeful that she hadn't settled for something less than perfect. The first single, "Into a Swan," had me hooked instantly, detailing a personal transformation, the nature of which was left to the listener's imagination. The lyrics, when taken at surface level, speak to the possibility for change at any time in a person's life, regardless of age or situation. Make of your existence what you will—after all, it is yours, and no one else's. I could have used this song when struggling with being gay in the less-than-friendly '80s.

She proved through this release that, Banshees or not, she kicks just as much ass by herself—perhaps even more. Siouxsie has managed to retain the disdain she held for pretty much everything when the Banshees formed in 1976, molding it to suit her as her life changes, without falling into a "comfort zone." As one of the few originators of the punk genre who survived its disintegration from cutting edge to mainstream, Siouxsie ignored musical trends first through the Banshees, and later through the Creatures, her spin-off band that relied on tribal beats and native instruments. She never compromised her sound or vision in order to sell singles.

After waiting at Irving Plaza for nearly five hours for Ms. Sioux to grace the stage, I was getting impatient. I'm not one to stay up past ten o'clock these days, having become prematurely geriatric, and she was crossing the line. I wanted to get to bed, needed my routine. My back was hurting; I hadn't gotten to do my daily yoga sequences. Yet all of that peevishness faded the moment she slinked onstage.

Anyone who happened upon recent photos of Siouxsie, who turned fifty in 2007, immediately said the same thing: "Oh, that took some major Photoshopping," because she looks flawless. But there was no Photoshop work done. From the front row, I could see she looks better now than when I saw her in 1987.

She danced hypnotically throughout the entire show, spinning, kicking, undulating, performing slightly suggestive pelvic thrusts. At one point she fixed her gaze on a google-eyed goth standing near to me and grabbed her left foot in her hand, singing all the while. Not breaking eye contact or concentration on the song, she lifted her left leg into a standing split, bringing her foot over her head.

Her unmoving glare was telling that goth and everyone else, *That's right. I am a badass.*

A badass who is just as important to me today as she was when I was sixteen. As she and I both age, I make use of her words and actions differently. I no longer wear floor-length black skirts. I no longer linger in the dark shadows of nightclubs chain-smoking clove cigarettes. But I still at least attempt as much as humanly possible to exist separate from mainstream culture—just in a more mature way.

She ended her set with "Into a Swan," sending the entire audience into a foaming frenzy that lasted long after the band walked offstage. Her first concert in the United States as a solo performer had been a smashing success, and she had proven that she did not need to rely on anyone.

When the show was over, the friend I had attended the performance with turned to me and said, "She really did turn into a swan."

And he was right.

Auntie Mame

"I'm Going to Open Doors for You, Doors You Never Even Dreamed Existed"

Lewis DeSimone

Mame Dennis made me long to be an orphan. I was already in my twenties when I discovered her—dark hair in a bouffant, bracelets jangling on dramatically gesturing wrists as she floated in an orange dress across my TV screen—and immediately I envied her young nephew, Patrick, who had been entrusted to her after the death of his father. Laughing wildly at her antics, I nevertheless felt a perverse pang of self-pity. Why couldn't I have been raised by such a flamboyant and adventurous woman? Why couldn't I have attended glamorous, decadent parties and been introduced to all that culture and style when I was young enough not to be intimidated by it? Of course, I didn't seriously wish my parents away, but if it meant spending my formative years with my own Auntie Mame, I was willing to consider it.

Mame is the kind of aunt every little gay boy needs, and the role model so few of us ever get. I had had my share of divas before—mostly the usual suspects: Cher, Bette Midler, even (in a brief, delirious moment) Liza. But Mame was altogether different, and not just because she was fictional. All the women in my imaginary Valhalla of Divas share a take-no-prisoners attitude, a sense of absolute certainty about who they are and a cry of defiance to anyone who disapproves. But with Mame, there's also a maternal quality. If I long to party with the rest of them, Mame is the one I imagine tucking me in at night, or mixing me a sidecar in the morning to relieve the hangover I got from an evening of carousing with Bette and the girls.

I never had an Auntie Mame in my life when I was growing up—nowhere near. Sure, my mother introduced me to soap operas and took me to see *Cabaret* when I was all of ten (hence, the brief flirtation with Liza), but hers was a passive approach, not an encouraging one. When it came to discovering the world and imagining a place for myself in it, I was on my own.

One of my favorite moments in the film occurs when Mame first meets Patrick, in the middle of one of her bootleg parties. Distracted by her hostess duties, she gives the boy a pad of paper and a pencil, and sends him off into the party to eavesdrop and write down all the words he doesn't understand. When they reconnect a little later, she smiles proudly as he reads off the words: *free love, Cubism, libido, Karl Marx*. Only when he gets to the word *heterosexual* does she take on a bug-eyed look and toss the paper away. Ever the nonconformist, Mame is thrilled to see Patrick learning about the unconventional; it's the so-called normal that she feels obliged to protect him from.

I could have used some of that brand of protection when my father shamed me into throwing away my Barbies, when the kids in the schoolyard judged my value as a human being by my ability to catch a ball, when I began to question my self-worth because I had more crushes on boys than girls. Auntie Mame would have understood all that.

Maybe that's why I couldn't get enough of her once I'd found her. Seeing *Auntie Mame* for the first time was a bit like discovering a long-lost relative. I rented the movie at first, then bought my own VHS copy, and years later, when the technology changed, the DVD. I watched it obsessively at first, several times a year. Even now, all these years later, settling down with Mame's motley crew is at least an annual event.

I even tried the book once, hoping to find a more in-depth portrait of this woman I'd fallen in love with, but it was completely dull by comparison. Mame Dennis did not come to life until the great Rosalind Russell stepped into her high heels. (One of my boyfriends kept trying to convince me that the Lucille Ball version was better. We're no longer together.)

Few actresses have ever inhabited a character as convincingly as Russell did Mame—certainly in comedy. If Russell is over the top in this role, it's because Mame herself is over the top. Her wild gestures and vocal calisthenics are as right for the part as Meryl Streep's brooding looks and Polish accent are for *Sophie's Choice.* But she does it all—the madcap gestures, the vaudevillian pratfalls—with a depth of feeling that makes the character completely believable. Mame's genuine love for Patrick undergirds every aspect of her performance. It is Russell's ability to embody unconditional love without compromising Mame's unconventional and authentic self that lifts her performance and inspires.

Mame is the perfect parent in large part because she is so woefully unprepared. She has no training in the traditional methods of relating to children—either ignore or infantilize them—so she treats Patrick like a small adult instead. Spared the dangers and inconveniences of his infancy (oh, the comic opportunities missed by not showing Mame changing a diaper!), she feels little need to shelter Patrick from the world; instead, she welcomes him into it.

The film is virtually bracketed by one resonant line—among many memorable ones—that Mame speaks to Patrick when they meet and that she utters again years later, to his son, Michael, as she takes him, too, under her wing. As she and Michael climb her majestic staircase at the end of the film, she practically sings the line, the words that epitomize her essence: "I'm going to open doors for you," she croons, "doors you never even dreamed existed."

That's not something my own mother would have said. My mother didn't know much about what lay on the other side of our own front door. The great world that energizes Mame terrified her. Products of the Great Depression, she and my father had more sensible advice: pointing out the dangers inherent in dreams, they always wanted me to have "something to fall back on." But, as Mame clearly knew, when you get too used to the net and too invested in maintaining it, you stop taking risks altogether, and you never move beyond where you started.

When I need courage to speak my truth or to go off in a new direction, it is Mame's voice that I hear. Around the time I discovered her, I was taking my first tentative steps out of the closet, so her words rang especially true. The doors that Mame Dennis opens are closet doors. As I began to tell the world who I really was, I could see Mame's hand on the knob, feel the draft of wind as she yanked the door open and pulled me out into the light of day.

But there are all sorts of closets in the world. Any kind of conformity is a closet. The high-strung trustee, Mr. Babcock, is in a closet of money and rules; Patrick's lockjawed fiancée, Gloria, is in a closet of nouveau riche social climbing—both unable to fathom a world outside their own circumscribed lives. (How fitting that in Gloria's signature speech, the climax of her absurdly uninteresting story is a confrontation with a locked closet door.) These are the type of people Mame's talking about in her most famous line, "Life is a banquet, and most poor suckers are starving to death!" There's a feast laid just outside the closet door, and the vast majority of people are too afraid to step out of their comfort zone to partake.

Real or fictional, we all need an Auntie Mame in our lives—or perhaps an Uncle Mame. My ambitions are set: Let my brother be the disciplinarian for his kids and the cheering section at Little League games; I'll gladly be the one to introduce them to Picasso and Proust, caviar and curry—everything impractical that they don't need to survive but sorely need to truly live.

Kate Bush

The Invisible Diva

Reginald Shepherd

𝒥 first (and last) saw Kate Bush perform on *Saturday Night Live* in late 1978; I was fifteen. My mother had died that spring, and I had been removed from New York City, where I grew up, to an aunt's house in Macon, Georgia, where my mother's family lived. I could barely stay awake for Bush's appearance (it was far past my usual bedtime), but I also couldn't bear to miss it. She sang "Wuthering Heights" and "Them Heavy People," from her first album, *The Kick Inside.* Once I heard that music, I wanted to hear it again, to reenter a world far from that stifling southern town and that house crowded with ignorant, hostile relatives in which I

239

lived as an unwanted or at best barely tolerated guest. I got that sense of Bush as an emissary from another realm not just because she was British (though that helped separate her from everything I knew and hated around me) but also because she created her own worlds in her songs. I think that *Saturday Night Live* appearance was Kate Bush's only trip to America.

I had read about Kate Bush in magazines in bookstores at the Macon Mall, but like so much of the music I read about, before that night I had never heard her. (Sometimes that gave me the opportunity to imagine music much more interesting and profound than any actual act could produce, though Bush's music fully lived up to my imaginings.) They certainly didn't play her on the radio in Macon. But the things that reviewers said about her, even the negative things, struck a chord in me: that her music was dreamy and introverted, based in a world of fantasy, self-consciously literate and literary ("Wuthering Heights," one of her most famous songs, is in the voice of Cathy's ghost from Emily Brontë's novel), and highly eccentric. Several of her songs were about the power and pleasures of music (the dangers, too, in at least one song, "Experiment IV"), including what I'm certain is the only pop song about the British composer Frederick Delius (I had no idea what she was singing about when I first heard it).

Kate Bush was a little odd, undoubtedly a misfit, and I, with my lack of fit anywhere and my ambitions to be an artist, could identify with her as a more successful imago of myself. Something *could* be made of being an outsider. She was a version of the singer-songwriters I had loved for years, from Neil Young to Patti Smith, weirdos and misfits every one. And that early in my relationship with poetry, the lyrics of those singers were among my models of what poetry could be, along with T. S. Eliot and Wallace Stevens and W. B. Yeats. I wanted to write poems that created the kind of mental landscapes those songs produced for me, poems that had the visceral effect that songs like Bush's "The Man with the Child in His Eyes," Young's "Winterlong," or Smith's "Easter" had on me.

Like so many gay men that it's a cliché, I've always identified with female voices, whether in pop, jazz, or opera, perhaps because however idolized they are also marginalized, as women speaking out of turn, speaking too much and too loudly, making their presence too known. Divas tend to be both revered and marginalized, adored by some, reviled by others. (No real diva is loved by all. Without detractors, one can't be a diva.) I already had both the marginalization and the sense of being or making myself too conspicuous. I hoped to turn that outspoken marginalization into a source of strength, maybe even into the basis of the social recognition otherwise denied me.

For me, Kate Bush is a kind of anti-diva. I know little about her except that her family is Irish (and her father and brother have appeared on her records), she has a fear of flying, and she has a private recording studio near her home. She seems to be an astute businesswoman, as she owns her own recordings, which is quite unusual. (David Bowie owns his, as do the Pet Shop Boys.) Nor have I ever sought to find out much about her. My sole relationship to her has been through her music, and the eccentric personae the music presents. While I presume that the topics of her songs reflect her interests and preoccupations (which are clearly quite diverse), Bush's songs don't engage in personal revelation or direct self-expression. Instead, many if not most of her songs create personae, adopting other voices either explicitly (Cathy from *Wuthering Heights,* a Viet Cong guerrilla, Harry Houdini's wife, a scientist working to produce a sound that kills from a distance) or implicitly (*The Ninth Wave* from *Hounds of Love* is a song cycle with a definite if not fully defined narrative arc, going from loss to trials and tests to spiritual rebirth), and creating worlds (musical and material) for those alternative selves to inhabit. One would be hard pressed to pick out one persona that was "hers."

As far as I can tell, Kate Bush is a very private person who doesn't impose herself on the public, preferring to let her music speak for her. She gives few interviews, rarely performs live (perhaps because she is a perfectionist who wants total control over her music), and puts out new material when and as she's moved to do so. She has only done one full-scale tour, in support of *The Kick Inside* in 1979. (I presume that her earlier appearance on *Saturday Night Live* was part of that promotional effort.) Four years elapsed between her albums *Hounds of Love* (my personal favorite, along with 1982's *The Dreaming*), which appeared in 1985, and *The Sensual World* (1989). Another twelve years passed between 1993's *The Red Shoes* (her weakest album, though there are some lovely songs on it) and 2005's double album *Aerial.* I don't know why she went so long without producing music for public consumption, and I'm not terribly curious. From some of the songs on *Aerial,* it seems she spent quite a bit of that time doing laundry, and contemplating the square root of pi.

One can be a great singer and not be a diva. All it takes is a certain degree of modesty or even shyness, an unwillingness to make a spectacle of oneself, a lack of desire to put oneself on display. No matter how "personal" or distinctive one's songs or one's mode of performing them, one needs a public image to be a diva. Conversely, one can be a singer of limited technical means and be a great diva: Billie Holiday (whose voice at first grated on me terribly) and, more recently, Diana Ross would both fall into this latter category. Divadom is not about ability, innate or acquired, or even about what one does with that ability, but about the public projection of personality. It isn't about the "real" self, whatever that might be, but it is very much about self-presentation, the production and performance of a public self. It is this projection to which fans, to which fanatics, attach themselves. Their fantasies, their hopes, their dreams, and their disappointments are transfigured, transubstantiated, into the diva's triumphs and tragedies.

In this sense, for me Kate Bush is not a diva at all. All I know of her triumphs and tragedies is what is in the music, transubstantiated indeed, from personal anecdote to aesthetic archetype. That is one definition of art, and one reason why I love Kate Bush.

Jamie Lee Curtis

When the Artist Met His Muse

Vince A. Liaguno

$\mathcal{B}$e forewarned: I am a Jamie Lee Curtis fan. A big one. The biggest. And while I stake claim to being a fan like no other, please don't rush to assumptions. My lifelong obsession with the preeminent scream queen of '80s horror films is not of the creepy Kathy-Bates-stalking-James-Caan-in-*Misery* variety; it's more of the I'd-love-to-ask-her-to-tea-and-pick-her-brain variety. Stalking is so unbecoming of a gay man, after all. No, my love of Jamie Lee Curtis is culled from an early fascination that somehow never ebbed, instead strengthening and threading through the fabric of my life and personality over nearly thirty years and counting.

Just like many people identify the important events of their lives by particular songs or other compass points on the pop culture landscape, Jamie Lee's films and accomplishments serve as mile markers on the highway of my memories.

As early as my love of slasher films developed, so did my adoration for Jamie Lee. I can still remember the first time I ever laid eyes on her celluloid image as a terrorized babysitter in John Carpenter's classic *Halloween*. I'm not quite sure if it was her vaguely androgynous looks, or slightly crooked smile, or eyes that looked out from behind the windows of an old soul, but Curtis's portrayal of Laurie Strode (in her feature film debut) captured my heart—and hasn't let go since. Now I admit that my relationship with Jamie Lee is terribly one-sided; I've only met her once, yet my admiration of the offspring of Tony Curtis and the late Janet Leigh goes deep.

Since 1978 I have followed her career highs and lows and personal milestones. I've amassed what can only be described as the future Jamie Lee Curtis museum . . . clipping articles and blurbs that mention her name from countless newspapers and magazines; collecting posters, lobby stand-ups, and other memorabilia from most of her forty-plus feature films and TV movies; and tracking down every professional and candid photo ever taken of her from infancy to the fabulous woman she's become at fifty. I've snatched up any autograph I could find, acquired multiple signed copies of all of her illustrated children's books, taped her talk show appearances, and have even come to be the proud owner of a Jamie Lee Curtis bobble head. (Yes, bobble head—you *were* forewarned.) I also wear T-shirts emblazoned with such cheesy slogans as "Property of Jamie Lee Curtis" and have a license plate holder proclaiming my status as #1 fan.

It's important to note that my devotion to this amazing actress, author, and activist goes far beyond the contributions she made to the horror genre with her early appearances in *Halloween, The Fog, Prom Night,* and *Terror Train.* These were but the catalysts that launched, and then cemented, my fandom. I have been equally

smitten by her work as a deft comedian in films like *Trading Places,*
A Fish Called Wanda, Drowning Mona, and her ABC sitcom *Any-*
thing but Love. Have been thrilled by her roles as an action film
star in *Blue Steel, True Lies,* and *Virus.* Have marveled at her subtle,
thoughtful performances in supporting roles in smaller art-house
films like *Amazing Grace and Chuck, Dominick & Eugene, A Man*
in Love, and *Queens Logic.* Been bowled over by tour-de-force
dramatic turns in *Love Letters, Nicholas' Gift,* and *The Heidi Chron-*
icles. Even warmed by her motherly roles in sweet coming-of-age
films like *My Girl, Forever Young,* and *House Arrest.*

I remember being moved to tears when noted *New York Times*
movie critic A. O. Schwartz singled out Curtis's virtuoso performance in Disney's *Freaky Friday* remake as being Oscar worthy,
committing his words of praise to memory: "Ms. Curtis's performance is a marvel . . . there is a verve and conviction here that is
downright breathtaking . . . it is likely that Ms. Curtis will be overlooked when Oscar season rolls around. This is a shame, since it is
unlikely that any other actress this year will match the loose, ener-
getic wit she brings to this delightful movie." I shouted with glee
that year when Golden Globe nominations were announced and
threatened a boycott of the Academy Awards when she was passed
over by the Academy as Schwartz had predicted. I also remember
proudly exclaiming, "That's my girl!" when female friends of a
certain age were impressed by Jamie Lee's now-infamous *More*
magazine spread, which was done sans makeup or touch-ups to
dispel Hollywood glamour myths. And I squealed with delight
when one of her publications hit the *New York Times* bestseller list
for children's books.

Why the strong kinship? Perhaps it started with her publicly
stated feelings of being an outcast as a teen . . . similar to my own
feelings growing up gay, scared, and alone in suburban New Jersey. Perhaps it is our shared status as being the products of divorce. Perhaps it is the fact that she later embraced the gift of
adoption in forming her own family—similar to the gift my own
biological mother gave me when she put me up for adoption at

birth. Perhaps it is the conviction of her opinions, the fierceness for the causes she believes in. Or her ability to successfully reinvent herself, to keep from being pigeonholed as a single commodity.

Yes, it will be difficult to boil her legacy down to one specific film or life event: Scream queen . . . comedian . . . sexy starlet . . . sitcom star . . . children's book author . . . adoption advocate . . . champion of women's aging . . . because these are all titles she's earned and can wear proudly into her golden years. I derive inspiration from her tenacity at surviving in the fickle world of Hollywood, her courage in often eschewing career safety nets and following her heart in new creative directions, and in her struggle to accept herself for who she is—flaws intact. But more likely, my affinity for Jamie Lee comes down to an amalgamation of all these things, she being the female counterpart, the kindred spirit, to my own.

At the height of a successful career as an award-winning healthcare executive, I ripped a page from the Jamie Lee Curtis playbook and reinvented myself as a writer. Now she has become my writing muse. I believe that it's no small coincidence that my very first magazine cover was a feature article I wrote on her for a small national magazine; on the contrary, I think it's nothing short of divine intervention . . . a sign. My first novel, *The Literary Six,* sprang from my fondness for those early Jamie Lee slasher films, and the book is co-dedicated to her. The penultimate moment in my fandom came when I presented a copy of the book to Curtis in the fall of 2006, in person, with the precisely worded dedication and my handwritten inscription that conveyed her profound impact on my life spread out naked in print before her as she stared down at the page, incredulous and genuinely moved.

There are no words to adequately describe the sight of Jamie Lee Curtis rising up from her chair and leaning across the table toward me with beautiful, intimately familiar facial features etched with delicate lines that bespoke an experiential wisdom framed by gloriously defiant salt-and-pepper hair. Nor are there words to describe the appreciative kiss she planted on my cheek.

Mere words also fail to capture the sensation of having a woman I have so adored for so long wrapping her arms around my neck and looking toward a camera strategically placed to record the long-awaited moment when artist met his muse, the zenith of nearly three decades of deifying one extraordinary woman.

Sade

The *Other* Material Girl

Christopher Lee Nutter

Diamond life.

Nothing sums up Sade like the first line from the single that made her a star, 1985's "Smooth Operator."

I was fifteen when I saw the international pop chanteuse in the video for the first time. There she was on the screen in a sleek white backless evening gown with a silky jet-black ponytail draped over skin the color of clay, performing in an impossibly glamorous nightclub lounge in some exotic place (Istanbul? Marrakech? Monte Carlo?) beneath a glimmering disco ball. She barely moved, and yet she radiated sexuality. And she sang like a desert goddess romancing the moon: throaty, sultry, deep. I had never seen nor heard anything like her. I was positively *mesmerized*. If I didn't know what a diamond life was before, I knew what it was then.

As a clueless closeted teenager growing up in the southern country club world of suburban Birmingham, Alabama, little did I know that something monumental had happened: I had discovered my diva.

At the time countless young gay boys like me all over the world were discovering Madonna. And they had the same reaction—that they were watching someone on the screen who spoke to them in a way the people around them did not. From watching their diva they were learning that there was a world somewhere that suited them better than the world they'd been born into. And they saw that in Madonna.

But I did not. I saw it in Sade.

There were many reasons why. Unlike Madonna, who stunned us with overstatement, Sade was a masterpiece of understatement. There were no backbreaking dance routines. She exposed nothing, and yet you couldn't keep your eyes off of her. Her life off-stage was a total mystery. She released albums seemingly at her own whim (or as graffiti on a Sade concert poster I read years later put it, "this bitch sings when she wants to"). She sailed above trend. And while Madonna's Material Girl was sheer, unadulterated artifice, Sade's materialness was genuine—her Diamond Life was *real*. In short, Sade did not have to work for your attention. She simply *was*.

The difference between Madonna and Sade was the difference between performance and presence; between a celebrity and a star. From Sade I learned that being a diva is not about being at the head of the crowd, as Madonna demonstrated on her death-defying climb to the top, but about not being one of the crowd at all.

This was a very important lesson, for I myself am a diva. I always have been. Being a diva isn't a choice. It's like being an alpha dog or a silverback—you're born that way. But it is not an easy destiny. Unlike alpha dogs and silverbacks, divas are not meant to lead. Nor are they led. Outside of the herd altogether, they have only themselves to seek direction from. And if you do not learn how, you're as good as dead.

From Sade, I learned how.

And this wisdom saved me. From my adolescent vantage point, there were two paths that I could follow: I could stay in the closet and become a married southern lawyer like all the other boys I grew up with, or I could come out and be a gay cliché. Both seemed like death to me.

From taking Sade's cue, I learned I could follow my own path.

My exit out of the closet was a perfect exercise in this. When I was twenty-four I wrote an essay for *Details* magazine about life inside the closet, thereby coming out to the entire world without having to "come out" to a single person, thus avoiding the whole "I'm gay" cliché altogether. Even my mom had to read about it. In doing it on my terms in my own way, I didn't just come out as gay. I came out as a diva.

Given that this was 1994, when coming out was starting to become common, finding a way to do so that set me apart from the crowd was critical to my coming out at all. And it proved just as critical to my finding a way to be openly gay but on my own terms.

I entered New York's gay scene in full force in 1995 in the heyday of the "Chelsea Boy." Defined by their herd mentality, Chelsea Boys had the same bodies and hair cuts, went to the same parties, held the same opinions, said the same things in the same ways, traveled in packs . . . *and they all worshiped Madonna.*

Following the Sade diva model, I knew I could be in the gay scene without being a member of the herd. So at the pinnacle of the "gay clone," I was an individual: I had a trademark look (which, like Sade, has hardly changed over the years), made a name for myself in the scene as a nightlife columnist, and became a classic disco aficionado at the apex of the "pots and pans" symphony. I even physically set myself apart from the crowds by working as a bartender and a doorman. While Chelsea Boys overstated their sexuality, I always played it cool. I *never* traveled in a pack. And while everybody was "acting" like a diva, I was—as a friend complimented me at the time—the real deal.

Even in my thirties when I became a spirituality author, I continued to embrace my diva qualities despite the prevailing idea that somehow being a diva is *un*spiritual because I knew instinctively that being a diva is *very* spiritual. After all, the ultimate realization of life is that no matter how it seems, you only ever answer to yourself. For divas this is not a philosophy—it's something they know viscerally.

I finally got to see Sade in person at Madison Square Garden while she was on tour for *Lover's Rock* in 2001. Marching in slowly to the concert hall with thousands of people, it felt more like a pilgrimage than a concert. There was a tangible sense that we were all coming home somehow, and I marveled at the thought that we all had a diva in common.

And it was, ironically, the only time I didn't mind being one of the crowd.

Taylor Dayne

"Tell It to My Heart"

Peter Covino

Okay, why would Taylor Dayne be standing outside Penn Station?

And (no offense) why would she need bodyguards anymore?

Taylor of the famous Barry White cover song and the soul-inflected, freestyle groove—pop diva of, what was it, the late '80s, early '90s? Bona fide crossover star, first white girl to appropriate black musical phrasing: "saying goodbye is never an easy thing" becomes an "essay thang," a warning and extended sassy dare at once.

For two weeks now, the same love songs in my head, forecasting a breakup—a move to another state and only Taylor understands—straight out of Freeport, Long Island, via years of the demanding Brighton Beach Russian nightclub scene, as the liner notes remind us. . . .

She was standing *this* close to me and thanked me for recognizing her, right in front of Penn Station with two bodyguards on a Tuesday, 2:45 in the afternoon.

Well, at least I think it was her: four-foot-nine bundle of joy in heels and hand-stitched jeans. Maybe it was spring fever, and nostalgia, or the way that girl standing next to us with the barky Shih Tzu made me crazy by droning on, on her cell phone, about bungee jumping and needing another cup of coffee. Could have been an honest case of mistaken identity like my friend Richard who looks uncannily like Kevin Spacey.

Maybe she decided not to burst my bubble, to go along with the happy coincidence, me her number one fan, after all, who's belted out many a version of "Tell It to My Heart" . . . *tell me I'm the only one* . . . after a couple of martinis at the local karaoke.

If it's true that God paints some people, and with others he forgets the paintbrush altogether—well, I'll tell you, Taylor's his masterpiece! Pronounced features and all: a natural beauty. And who cares if she plays second-rate clubs now like the Mohegan Sun and the Suncoast Casino in Vegas? I admit it, I thought she was black too when I first heard her, just like all the kids did back in the '80s. And to think now you can catch her on the MTV Jewish Suburban Legends Special or vote for her latest video on her Web site. For only $9.95 you can download three of her most famous songs and even get a voiced-over complimentary dedication! If you're lucky, provided you've got decent credit, "you can all feel your body rock . . . when she calls your name . . ."

In conclusion, I thought I'd share part of this open letter I wrote to Britney Spears (though it could be for any of those young singers aiming for diva status):

Okay, so maybe you're a little taller and we feel bad about your recent marital/rehab problems, but your voice can't touch Taylor's, and your clothes: way too sleazy. Taylor would never get her belly button pierced. She only started wearing risqué outfits in the '90s after folks like you made clothes passé. Check out those bedroom eyes and the pouty lips on her *Greatest Hits* album. Taylor's in a knit top and a leather skirt plenty long enough. You were barely in grammar school, Brit! Not even a Mickey Mouse clubber yet in 1989 when Taylor's mega-hit ballad "Love Will Lead You Back" . . . "to my arms, I know my love will lead you back" . . . topped the charts for a steady six weeks, just in time for the summer wedding rush.

Can't you just hear it now? That misty, languid electric piano, the wispy drumbeats, the rhythmic cymbal . . . quintessential lounge music; is there any doubt Taylor's "love" could set anyone "free"?

Who can say, after all that spandex and dreadful news of the 1980s, just how many slow, jubilant dances I danced at Italian weddings in places such as Leonard's of Great Neck or Terrace on the Park?

Oh, Taylor, you were the sing-along at many an engagement party, you slowed a lot of us down, you made a lot of mascara run, and tonight as your voice careens through the air, there's not a box of Kleenex anywhere that's safe.

Endora

Afternoons as Endora

Richard Blanco

$\mathcal{I}$ was a boy who hated being a boy. I couldn't catch a football or throw a baseball. I didn't learn to ride a bike until I was nine years old and never played outside with those boorish boys next door— Randy and Ricky. Instead, I made Pillsbury Dough cookies and latch-hook rugs, drew flowers in my notebooks, and proudly displayed my paint-by-number scenes of Paris. I hated dogs but loved my cats—Miso, Ferbi, Butter—combing and dabbing them every day with baby cologne. I preferred my mother's Tupperware parties to Clint Eastwood movies and fancied her gossip magazines over all the butch toys—the Erector set, Hot Wheels cars, and cap guns that were approved "for boys" by my grandmother.

According to her, I was a no-good sissy—*un mariconcito*—the queer shame of the family. And she let me know it all the time: *Why don't we just sign you up for ballet lessons? Everyone thinks you are a girl on the phone—can't you talk like a man? I'd rather have a granddaughter who's a whore than a grandson who is a faggot like you.* And other such offenses whenever I struck out at bat, put my hand on my hip, or whined a little too loudly. She was a witch, and I was terrified of her; but ironically it was also a witch who helped me get through some of the verbal and psychological abuse during the years my sweet, dear *abuelita* lived with us.

Every afternoon around 3:30, while my grandmother was busy checking her lottery tickets or gossiping with her sisters on the phone, I'd quietly lock the door to my room and turn to channel 6 to watch my diva—Endora—on reruns of *Bewitched*. I'd pull the bedspread off and tie it around my chest into a full-length dress, drape the bedsheets over my shoulders, wrap a towel around my head like her bouffant, and paint my fingernails with carmine and cornflower-blue crayons. All dressed up, I'd wait for Endora to magically appear out of thin air sitting on top of a lamp shade or the banister. For half an hour every afternoon, I was a witch too—imitating the flair and drama of her every gesture, floating around in *our* chiffon muumuu, flaunting *our* mauve cape, and waving *our* billowy sleeves. We'd give Darrin cat-eye scowls, scoff at Samantha for being such a fool for love, and cast secret spells in *our* raspy voice. Together we'd turn Mrs. Kravitz into a chihuahua, *Derwood* into a donkey, or Uncle Arthur into a chair. We were unstoppable—as long as my grandmother didn't pick the lock.

I never told anyone about those afternoons as Endora until I was well into my thirties. In part because of the fear and shame still buried in my psyche, still scared of my grandmother's ghost. It also took me years to forgive her—not until she was on her deathbed—and come to view and accept her abuse as almost a gift. Her constant attacks made me an extremely self-conscious and quiet child, but it also made me a keen observer focused on the world around me, because my interior world was far too painful. This inadvertently led me to become a writer, a recorder of images and details. But mostly, I hadn't "confessed" because even I had trouble making sense out of those eight-year-old afternoons in drag. I mean, there's nothing drag-queenish about me now; I've no desire to slip on a pair of pumps or smudge on a little lipstick every now and then, even if just for fun during Halloween. For years I couldn't reconcile those years of my childhood with my life as an adult. In retrospect, however, it now seems obvious why I loved and wanted to be Endora—why she is, and remains, my diva of divas.

I was a helpless and scared child, powerless against my grandmother, while Endora was a mighty witch with limitless powers. Unlike Samantha, her foolish daughter, she was a witch who wasn't afraid of being a witch, and used her magic to get her way or enact revenge every time she had the chance. I wanted to be as powerful as her, and for a little while every afternoon I could pretend I was. I could conjure up thunderstorms so I wouldn't have to go to baseball practice, and cast spells to turn the boys who shoved me at recess into toads. I could concoct love potions that would make me like girls instead of boys and make my grandmother love me. With a wave of my hand I could make her a mute, put her in shackles until she apologized, or simply make her disappear forever. Imagination was my only escape—a coping mechanism, as I would learn in therapy years later. From 3:30 until 4:30 every weekday afternoon, life was wonderful and livable: me and Endora sitting on clouds, sipping bubbly brews from cognac glasses, and laughing at the world under our control. Then she and my powers would vanish in a poof of smoke, leaving me—the boy afraid of being a boy, dressed like a witch, alone in his room, wanting to vanish into another place and time away from the pain of his world.

Björk

With Regards to Ms. Guðmundsdóttir

John Dimes

Björk was at a London airport. She was isolated within a thick circle of paparazzi and news crew cameras. Rigidly she stood, with her head slightly bowed. Her expression? Pensive. I mean, for all intents and purposes, she was the proverbial cornered animal.

Now, most of those assembled were savvy enough to give Ms. Guðmundsdóttir a wide berth. Not so for the intrepid lady reporter who was foolish enough to enter into the ring and badger Björk with a seemingly endless succession of questions and comments. About what, I can't recall.

Well, the only things that truly registered any of Björk's rage were her hands, which were fanned and apoplectically twitching at her sides. But the lady reporter kept at Björk, hounding her relentlessly with questions. And before you could say "When Animals Attack," Björk suddenly turned on the reporter and swatted (or "pimp-slapped") the hapless woman to the ground with her open palms!

It . . . was . . . *MAGNIFICENT!*

For propriety's sake, I wouldn't normally condone violence. But, hasn't Björk established herself as a person of somewhat unbridled energy and passion? I've been to her concerts. On stage, she can appear surprisingly subdued, as if she were some frail British Dame holding court. After every song there was a rather curt "Thank you very much," said in that cute Icelandic accent of hers, which reminded me of Latka Gravas, that character from the TV show *Taxi*. Then she was off to her next song, where her shyness would acquiesce to her more primal instincts, and she'd kick into a maddening overdrive that dazzled and pleasurably exhausted the brain. At these moments, in my opinion—mind you, I'm a weirdo—she became less of a human being and something of an avatar for all things primal and mystical.

Björk's incident at Heathrow airport only served to cement my already strong appreciation for her and her music. I mean I always loved her, way back when she was in the group the Sugarcubes, Iceland's answer to the B-52's. Her puckishly youthful, and sometimes stunningly choirlike, vocals always stood out, even on the dullest of songs. It was only during Björk's solo career that I truly took notice of her unique vocal phrasing, which I found to be reminiscent of Bulgarian folk singing. Yes, yes, I know about Bulgarian folk singers! Sadly, however, most people don't normally have the same access to Bulgarian folk singers as myself, so Björk would naturally come across as some shrill, unfortunate harpy to most.

And as for her clothing sense (swan dress) and her mercurial ways. What can I say? She's the last of a breed of true actor/singer/

songwriter/performance art rockers who enjoy flouting convention. David Bowie did it with his various costume/personae changes over the years. Grace Jones did it with her bizarre runway fashions and her severe female/masculine gender bending. The same can be said for Annie Lennox during her '80s tenure with the Eurythmics. One never knew whether she was going to be in a ballerina's tutu or a pinstripe suit à la Marlene Dietrich. It was, and is, all about being unconventional, while being original and innovative. It seems to me Björk is all about being an artist, in the exact sense as an artist paints or illustrates. She's dabbled in all the mediums of music, from jazz to classical. Yet her uniquely ethereal vocal stylings, I feel, somehow manage to complement these forms with a surprising amount of "naturalness."

Also surprising is how popular Björk is, even though she is clearly on the fringe of things. It's a testament to her talent and creativity, otherworldly though she may be. There have been skits about her on *Mad TV*. And one definitely knows one has made it when Britain's French and Saunders imitate you, right? They parodied Björk's video "Big Time Sensuality." Dawn French was a riot as Björk. She had the corkscrew hairdo, all the quirkily impish expressions, and the childlike jubilation just right. All the moments that I enjoy the most about Björk were captured right there, save, of course, for the off lyrics, the "singing," and the ampleness of Dawn French.

Impishness and childlike jubilation—the very qualities I'm drawn to also in her lyrics. Her playful innocence, mixed with maturity. I wonder how a person can navigate these extremes, where she can craft songs about cutlery hurled over a cliff side, while imagining herself as the objects thrown ("Hyper Ballad"), to songs of inflexible men taking advantage of her flexible or mutable nature ("Where Is the Line") without missing a beat. Or without ringing falsely and jarring the listener during the experience. Again, it's a testament to her talent and uncanny ability to comfortably affect people with her "Serendipitous Unexpectedness."

Björk's dichotomous balance as an adult successfully harnessing and channeling childlike forces resonates with me as a queer gent because I recognize that "balance" within myself. When I came out, physically there was no denying I was an adult. Yet my spiritual/sexual identity hadn't yet caught up, due in part to outmoded social mores and their resultant impact on my core beliefs. My self-esteem. A body was allowed to mature and flourish in every other aspect of daily life . . . *save for one.* So, there's little wonder that sometimes one explodes upon the queer scene with such alarming intensity! Björk—by her very nature, by her artistry—puts all those pent-up frustrations, all those festering uncertainties (Am I acting too *quirky*—too "gay"—for a guy my size?) into much healthier perspectives.

Björk

Kristin Hersh

"Is Sticky Ever Blue?"

Mark Bibbins

That's the kind of question Kristin Hersh is always asking: provocative, evocative, unanswerable and answering itself, delivered in a half snarl, half coo. I've learned as much about the possibilities of language from her lyrics as from almost any poem; she's been coming up with such sophisticated and bizarre questions, and no shortage of answers, since she was a teenager. Her logic is internal but not inscrutable. She talks about having started writing songs without realizing she was doing it, experiencing synesthesia—describing chords as pink or turquoise, for instance—and of being a conduit for music that she hears in her head, and "writes" itself. I know I'm not the only poet to have had similar experiences.

My problem, one of them anyway, is that I can't pick a diva. I'm not the diva type. Etymologically, *divinity* is right up front, but my tastes are, shall we say, more secular. And I can't muster the kind of devotion (not gods this time, but vows) that most divas require. This is going to be about Kristin, because she's actually what I'd call an anti-diva, but it pains me to leave out a dozen other figures—Lisa Gerrard (Dead Can Dance), Beth Gibbons (Portishead), and Alison Goldfrapp—so there they are, at least a few, not left out. But in the end, it has to be Kristin, even though I know I can't fix this enough to do her justice.

A little background noise: Top 40 radio was a different place during my '70s boyhood than it is now (if a "Top 40" even exists anymore—no idea, no interest, what's a boyhood, etc.). I heard Patti Smith, Chrissie Hynde, Donna Summer, Dolly Parton, and Janis Joplin all on the same AM radio station in my parents' sky blue Volkswagen Bug. It seems impossible now. Was it? At home, Edith Piaf and Joni Mitchell albums spent more time on the shelf than on the record player, but I heard enough to get me going.

Patti and Chrissie were punk—not a scene an eight-year-old kid in the upstate New York section of the middle of nowhere would have had much exposure to, at least not without an older sibling moping around the house and blasting music behind a locked bedroom door. (This would later be my role.) Blondie's "Heart of Glass" was the first single I bought, at a Faye's drugstore, and I didn't care that I couldn't understand the words. My first live show was Missing Persons, 1982: Dale Bozzio squeaking and vamping and strutting around a stage covered in white fabric, sporting a clear plastic bra and pink-and-blue-streaked platinum hair, the black-clad guys in the band as pretty and painted as she was—watch the "Words" video online, and you'll see. The distant planet they had come from is called Los Angeles.

Things got darker after '84, when I was turned on to Cocteau Twins, Kate Bush, Siouxsie and the Banshees—you better believe the gay guys still turn out for Siouxsie—and a couple of years later, Throwing Muses. Kristin Hersh, their lead singer, guitarist, and songwriter, wrote in the liner notes to *In a Doghouse,* "I swear to God, we thought we were a party band. As Throwing Muses, at age oh, sixteen or seventeen, we were gleefully impressed with ourselves and our ability to bring joy to people through sound. We were then stunned and horrified to see audiences react with something like stunned horror."

September, 1986: My friend Sean and I had dropped some speedy blotter and were merrily riding it out at his house, when his father arrived home unexpectedly. Shit. We dashed upstairs to hide out in Sean's room, where the only distraction was a clock radio, which would have to amuse us for the next several hours. Some time after midnight, one of the college stations was playing an album by a band we'd never heard before; we missed the beginning and had no idea what it was. What *was* this? Bizarre time-signature changes, lyrics about blowjobs and pigeons on tires and smack freaks and deep holes. And that *voice.* I kept thinking Marianne Faithful—raw, keening, brittle, destructive, and/or destroyed. Then came "Delicate Cutters," which sounded for about five seconds like it would be a pretty acoustic respite from the spiked smear of electric guitars and drums. Nope. It was about the bleakest, most visceral thing we'd ever heard—not necessarily something you want clawing through your little suburban bedroom while you're tripping your face off. But it was exactly what we wanted. Stunned horror indeed, in the best possible way. It was Throwing Muses' first self-titled album, and we had to have it.

More than twenty years later, Kristin is still making incredible music, still very much on her terms, despite "alternative" rock getting mainstreamed and homogenized long ago. Throwing Muses have been on hiatus for the last ten of those years, although they reconvene to play live occasionally, even releasing a new record in 2003. Kristin makes albums and tours, on her own and with her other band, 50 Foot Wave, who, rather ironically, opened for the Pixies a few times on their big reunion tour. (Ironic because Pixies used to open for the Muses in the '80s—I adore them both, so I'm not going to bitch about injustice, but still.) She is also active online, blogging and posting free downloads of demos and new songs at Throwingmusic.com.

Though she's earned the right to one, Kristin doesn't have a diva persona in the least. In interviews and onstage she's funny, down to earth, and self-deprecating; you would never guess the darkness she's been through and is capable of conveying. In concert, though, she lets it out, gazing over the heads of the crowd, seemingly transfixed by some mesmerizing thing at the back of the venue or beyond, her head slowly wavering back and forth, the rest of her body barely moving as she makes her Rickenbacker roar. Throwing Muses' live shows were also exciting because you never knew which Kristin would show up. Blonde or brunette? Little anecdotes and asides, or silence between songs? Or would there even be betweens? When the band toured their album *University*, they charged through the set, thrillingly running many of the songs together. Eventually some guy in the audience yelled, "Please slow down," to which she cheerfully responded, "I can't. I'm speedy."

As a gay person and as a poet, it's doubly inspiring to know that someone like Kristin has figured out how to exist outside "the system" and can live the art she needs, creating a kind of community in the process. She thumbs her nose at an industry that turned its back on her and cynically coopted a genre of music she helped to invent—an industry, thankfully, that becomes less relevant every day: "I don't care and you don't move," she sings in "Devil's Roof" (the same song that wonders about the sticky and the blue).

Kristin has no interest in dumbing her work down, as she puts it, in pursuit of fame or huge record sales; she makes her own space and fills it with glorious noise, and the fans who want to share it know how to seek her out and show their dedication and support; she gives unreservedly back to them in return. She wrote recently on her blog, "It's a nice little 'yay!' and 'f*ck you!' when music shouldn't work but does anyway." I feel pretty much the same way, without the asterisk, about the poetry I choose to read and write. Hers is not some quaint indie-rock fairy tale: she has spoken openly about her struggles, not merely with the music industry, but with her own illness, notably bipolarity that was misdiagnosed and treated incorrectly for years. While she doesn't romanticize it, she has the ability to stare down madness and make something pungent but glorious, without being sensational or sentimental. Yes, it can be damn scary down there; I'm grateful not to have to go too often myself, but even more grateful for what Kristin drags back up.

Céline Dion

Cirque du Céline

Jim Nason

So, Céline Dion walks into a bar and the bartender says, 'Céline, why the long face?'"

Well, Céline's response could be: "Because I drove all night," or, "I'm all by myself," or, simply, "Heh, I was born that way." Céline Dion has a Quebec face. A small-town-girl-turned-great face with no big breasts, big attitude, or big drug habit. And, as the joke suggests, she isn't the most beautiful pop star either. Céline just can't win. I dare anyone to bring her name up over lunch in the office cafeteria. The response will go something like this: *She's so tacky, mannish, ugly, sappy.* . . . So, what makes her a diva?

After many false starts, I finally came to realize that my musings about Céline Dion had to go beyond those gaminelike characteristics that offended some sensibilities. I had to focus on the epic event that signified her rise to "divadom."

First, we need a little background. Long before she sang it big in *Titanic*, Céline, in overteased hair and bushy eyebrows, paid her dues in tacky suburban malls around Quebec. She tried to be Michael Jackson with a bad accent and absolutely no ability to dance.

One night, shortly after I came out, I was in Montreal at le Stud. At two in the morning, a bizarre, intense song came on: "Je danse dans ma tête" (I Dance in My Head). The girl's voice was as big as Whitney's, and as theatrical as Cher's or Barbra's. "Who is this goddess?" I asked the DJ. It was Céline all grown up. That song became an enormous dance hit in Quebec and to this day it is my poet's anthem.

Like all writers, I dance in my head. I create. Think. Play. I compose in my head. The day after my encounter with Céline at le Stud, I bought her *Live at the Paris Olympia* CD. It was Céline's coming out as well. She sang in French but was making her way into the Anglo world. She was in love with the audience and they were in love with her. You could tell by their reaction: they thought Edith Piaf, the other French diva, had come home. The *Olympia* CD has the feeling of Judy or Barbra live at Carnegie Hall. And yes, "Je danse . . ." is on the album, but there is also a gorgeous ballad called "Ziggy: Un garçon pas comme les autres." In this song, Céline sings about her friend with whom she is in love, *a boy not like the others*. And as the lyrics unfold you realize that Ziggy is gay, "*il aime les garçons*." It's a beautiful tribute to the love a diva can have with a gay man. And we all know that divas love their gay boys. So of course, I felt that it was my personal duty to tell the world about Céline—particularly my American friends who hadn't yet heard of her.

It turned out I didn't have to do a blessed thing. Like Tina, Barbra, or Cher, Céline came from a young life of adversity that made her perfectly capable of fighting her way up from a blue-collar, small-town Quebec family of fourteen children to become the largest-selling female recording artist of all time.

I, too, come from a large, poor, but Anglophone Quebec family and know how it feels to be different from others. A "tappette" is what I was called (the French word for queer). But finally, in my late twenties, I found someone who knew me. Someone with astonishing passion. I understood Céline, the awkward ugly duckling determined to become a swan, and knew if only we could meet somehow, she would understand the same about me.

In France many resent Céline's mainstream success. They call her *Dairy Queen*—the implication being that she has sold out, become monotone, homogenized, packaged like a '60s eight-track. Like any star, a lot of packaging has occurred. But Céline's transformation has astonished and inspired us. And like most divas, her transformation has become a public legend and belongs to everyone. Céline went from speaking absolutely no English to becoming a number one English pop star in less than a year. Vegas has not made her more beautiful or less contrived, but Céline has found a forum that mirrors the "dancing in her head." Cirque du Soleil, the inspiration for her show, has its roots in Quebec. The sublime gets blended with the surreal.

Céline's ability to manifest what's below the surface is phenomenal. Like the iceberg that sank the Titanic (forgive me), her passion is deep and she isn't capable of keeping it submerged. The outcome is dramatic and over the top, as diva music must be.

The effect of a diva is paradoxical. They save our lives—always there for the break up and the bad hair days—but they also pull at *our* need to rescue *them*. We also secretly want her to crash, to crave the drama. We want to show her a real troublemaking stud of a husband (someone with bad habits beyond a minor addiction to gambling and the occasional flirtation). We are prepared, like her imaginary friend, Ziggy, to be her confidant and talk to her at four in the morning. And of course, we would be her fashion consultant—there's *no* way we would have let her wear that on-backwards blazer and fedora to the Oscars!

Determined and unique, Céline, like Jennifer Lopez or Tina Turner, knows where she comes from, and she is going to keep true to her version of success. She doesn't bat a false eyelash or sing a false note. Whatever is said about Céline, no one can deny that the girl can sing. To be successful she didn't marry the bad husband like Whitney or Tina (people hate her for playing it safe). Céline is a Michael Jackson–Edith Piaf hybrid, halted and gaudy. A beauty and the beast rolled into a tiny bomb. She is a Quebec soul with big-time American aspirations.

Divas mirror our sadness and shattered dreams, but they always survive. There are many Céline songs that mention love—"Love Can Move Mountains," "Because You Loved Me," and "One Heart"—to name just a few. Love from a singer like Céline is an offer of good fortune, a gesture of hope. She connects with us and her story inspires us to take risks and live a rich, adventurous life. And like the poets whom I most admire—Elizabeth Bishop, Lucie Brock-Broido, John Ashbery, and Henri Cole—Céline is a disciplined and focused artist.

Language and music are vehicles of transformation; they illuminate and inspire. A good song takes us away from our everyday responsibilities and worries. Céline's singing is sappy and saccharine but I'm thankful—her voice is the *luminous swell that rose from the deep,* her songs are the life rafts that keep my spirit from sinking.

Parker Posey

A Pocket Full of Posey

Michael J. Andrews

$\mathscr{I}$ am that guy who prefers chic to elegant whenever I rate my favorite *Project Runway* couture du jour. I mean, I might not be that guy in a tuxedo shirt and skinny black jeans, but I do pay some attention to what I wear and am a bit of a label whore (in that "pair it with those yard-sale corduroys" sort of way). I also must confess that when I run out of dress shirts for work, I will drag out that tuxedo shirt and tell my put-together Manhattanite coworkers, "Getovahit, I live in Brooklyn!" What I am trying to say is that fashion, in my eyes, should be more Parker Posey than, say, Nicole Kidman, or even Paris Hilton. I'm just over Hollywood glam,

L.A. club pics, tabloid cover girls. Though this is definitely not about me, or about fashion, but about ICON.

I want everyone to know: I make an UGLY woman and would never wear drag because I hate looking ugly. However, that does not mean I don't desire to emulate some of the most amazing people ever to grace the planet, and that those might happen to be women. AND I plan on emulating not only their intelligence (Hillary Clinton), their passion (Sojourner Truth), or their trashiness (Lindsay Lohan), but also their style. Hillary, Sojourner, and Lindsay all are very impressive women in one way or another, but GOD, they are so very much not my definition of cool.

When I imagine the perfect woman, the one I would "like to have a beer with," the irony is that it's not with anyone looking to be part of this big collective unconscious. And I would rather not have a beer, per se. I would rather not try to identify with Midwestern farmers (well, conjugally maybe). I want a goddamn vodka martini in some dungeon of a nightclub or a pitcher of Jack&Gingers stirred on some stranger's roof deck. And basically I want to be Parker Posey while doing it. Hell, she did get that studly falafel vendor in *Party Girl,* all while giving '90s America its first taste of anything "Fashion Forward."

See, this is what I'm talking about: sly, cool, abandoned, and unafraid. So, people were a little obsessed with individuality in the '90s. There was the tripped-out warehouse scene in NYC with all sorts of bizarre denizens as well as the plaid-clad rockers out in Seattle. Now, I know I'm being nostalgic, but there was a premium in the '90s on being different, on standing out, standing apart. But the alt rock world mated with NYC, giving birth to the downtown mall of models and lawyers, and the alt rock scene devolved in indie Williamsburg across the river, home of the unlaundered T-shirt, jeans, and designer sunglasses. Yet these are places I adore so much more than the plastic on the other coast! Why can't we have cool without being either disheveled or primped? Why can't chic go back to being a fire-engine-red thong from Bergdorf's? Isn't

Parker Posey

272

that just a little more acceptable than soiled H&M underwear? Parker Posey is the epitome of a man's thong. She's thin as a string, hides just the most vulgar of humor, and contains within herself something much bigger than she appears to. Whereas H&M is just the wrong idea of a European import. "Hello: Chanel!"

How is New York to compete with Britney if we don't take a gander at the Parker of the '90s?

I am a Brooklynite, and I am describing my peers just a little bit harshly, but we need to look to Parker Posey for style, not combine a love of Lindsay with the nostalgia for Courtney Love. Let's walk down Metropolitan Avenue like the cosmopolitan faggots we are. Let's bring LES *Party Girl* land to Brooklyn. Manhattan is full of middlebrow chains. Let's not rebel by being bums; let's rebel by showing them up.

What ever happened to combining fabulous with intelligent? Parker has played a role in which she campily explains that a folk group took her off the streets, and another as a bit-part Roller Blader cursing Steve Martin. Remember cool Steve Martin? Remember *L.A. Story*? Remember Shabby Chic? I am fed up with Shabby Trashy. What about Trashy Chic, like the entire cast of *Hurlyburly,* where '90s icon Ethan Hawke loses Parker to some less-famous actor and does tons of drugs. Parker was channeling Sigourney Weaver; and my generation—those caught between Winona Ryder and Paris Hilton—would do better to look to those slightly older than ourselves than to the plastic girls of the youth generation. Maybe it's that I'm turning thirty and am fed up, but I still strive for bony, cracked-out 4 a.m. glamour instead of the barfing mess I see others in every goddamn weekend. I don't see those vomiting Hollywood gals yelling at the nearest black drag queen "Nat-Tah-Sha" and doing some light vogueing before working the room. In fact, there are no drag queens *in* these L.A./Las Vegas nightclubs; and frankly, fashion and fame have become too stuck-up, or maybe too wannabe and too uneducated to even realize that they are not cool.

I mean, who doesn't want to be the adversary to Meg Ryan? We have to excuse some moneymakers like *You've Got Mail*, but she *is* resting on her laurels in that. Far better is this kind of priceless indie effect: "Well, there's something I've been meaning to ask you. There's this thing I've heard, and if I thought for one second it was true I'd probably kill myself. Does your fiancée work—in a doughnut shop?" Parker famously says as our sex kitten/Jackie-O in *House of Yes*. I mean the girl played Fay Grim in a Hal Hartley film. She was queen of 1990s "cinema." She got to say such illuminating lines as, "My aunt brought out her atlas that I look at a lot. This big blue book and opened up to New York and it's an island, is really what it is. It's this island full of people of different colors and different ideas and I can't—it sounds like a lot of fun to me. You know, we don't see much of that in Blaine. I'd like to maybe meet some guys, some Italian guys, you know . . . watch TV and stuff." So says the adorable Parker as Libby Mae Brown. And her humor really shined again in 1996 when she played the put-out sister in *Daytrippers*.

More than smart and fabulous, Parker Posey is fall-on-the-floor ridiculous. One thing I've always thought about Marilyn Monroe was that she was hysterically funny. My Posey gives that broad a run for her money. Her anal-retentive owner of a possible champion dog (in *Best of Show*) gives a line that I think sums up her height as an icon of the nineties: "We met at Starbucks. Not at the same Starbucks, but we saw each other at different Starbucks across the street from each other." Or even better, "We are *so* lucky. We are *so* lucky to have been raised amongst catalogs."

I might not vote Parker for president, but I definitely would buy her a drink and tell her that she's too old for that bump of coke. That I'd be delighted to pass her the spliff I just rolled and discuss how she would have voted if she was the final guest judge on season 2 or 3 or even 4 of *Project Runway*. I'd argue that she would wear Uli above the rest, hands down, and that she needs to make another movie, another *Party Girl*, and make it about being (as *Project Runway*'s Nina would say) "Chic, Modern, Contemporary" without being "Boring or Cheap." If anyone could do it, Parker Posey could.

Margaret Cho

How to Break Every Oriental Stereotype in the Book

Kenji Oshima

Chink!" . . . "Freak!" Ah, the verbal genius of junior high school taunting. Why do homophobic bullies never have anything clever to say? In the words of *my diva,* "Ooo, enchanté!"

The full details of those torturous years evade me now, but seared into my experience is Danny Fitzpatrick calling me (INSERT *any "Oriental" slur* HERE) wherever and whenever he pleased—in class, the halls, gym, and once even in front of a teacher who only laughed. Name-calling, threats, and punching weren't necessarily daily occurrences, but it *was* made crystal clear to me that as the single nonwhite kid in my school, I could be accosted anytime. Even the instructors were openly racist when it came to Asians (and you gotta assume I was the tip of the iceberg). "How *do* they do it in China?" one blonde teacher skewered me with when my friend Michael and I passed notes to one another. Don't ask me what she meant; to this day, I haven't a clue. And why "faggot" wasn't my harassers' slap of choice was never clear either, given that I was sensitive and long-haired with an obvious crush on the most popular boy.

Since racism and homophobia were de rigueur throughout my teenage years, who better then to inspire my spleen-venting adulthood than a kick-ass, foul-mouthed, bisexual, brilliant San Francisco Asian woman who has an "inner drag queen," and wouldn't think twice about telling someone to fuck off? Whose diva would win the prizefight diva-bitch-slap contest? Mine.

Margaret Cho is a fully enlightened fabulous diva who is utterly unabashed about sharing her struggles with addiction, racism, and an eating disorder. When a reporter once wondered aloud if her "Korean family was ashamed" of her, she shot back: "*Any* family would be ashamed of me." That's my mentor, of whom I am so proud.

Some of my adulthood has been given over to processing the gauntlet of childhood and rejecting all the lies punched into me: that as a biracial Asian gay man, I'm *not* unattractive, *not* second-class, *not* sexless, and *never* alone in struggles with my body issues and unfavorable internalized self-image. Luckily, I am off the rollercoaster self-esteem ride from hell. I have the "Notorious C.H.O." to thank for helping to rid my psyche of these ugly beliefs.

I've never been one of those gay boys who lined up for Barbra or paid two hundred dollars to see Céline fly around on wires (would someone please *cut* them already?). In fact I'd be really hard pressed to name who's on the cover of *People* magazine, because somewhere along the Fag-O-Matic DNA-dispensing conveyer belt, I didn't get the gossip gene.

Who wants a diva who can strut around in a twenty-thousand-dollar gown, when my diva posted on her Web site the deluge of racist, homophobic hate mail she received after saying that "George Bush is *not* Hitler . . . he would be if he *applied* himself"? The same ignorant masses who spammed her with "Dyke, chink, gook from Mongolia, go back to your country where you came from, you fat pig" unintentionally included their return e-mail addresses and "all their work information and their home email, and their home telephone number . . . and what kind of ice cream they liked . . . what they're [*sic*] second choice was." She confessed, "I didn't realize this, but there are people out there who *realllllly* like me, and they are pissed off to begin with . . . [so] in posting these emails I had inadvertently activated the terrorist sleeper cell Al-Gay-Da." And we all know what happens when you piss off a bunch of queens who love their divas? Particularly queens who vividly remember their junior high school years? I don't think most of the morons who e-mailed Margaret knew what hit them. Can you imagine? Five thousand gay men, at work, bored, remembering being called something evil when they were little gay boys, now granted the opportunity to tell some of these dunces what they thought? She joked, "I was getting apology emails so fast . . . flooding in . . . I'm sorry, I'm sorry I called you a chink . . . please make these gay people leave me alone! I'm sorry . . . hurry . . . I'm *afrrrrraid* . . . I think Cirque Du Soleil is warming up on my front lawn!!!"

I first met the full force of Ms. Cho in a living-room-sized theater in my current hometown of San Francisco, when a friend suggested we go see her stand-up comedy in her new movie *I'm the One That I Want*. Of course I knew of her, because how many famous Asian Americans have had a show called, get this, *All American Girl*? Seeing an Asian actress on television who wasn't "a prostitute" in a Vietnam War drama was an oddity. I mean, as Margaret says, we always have to "*be* something." The dealer, the broken-English Kwik-E-Mart owner, or the asexual dorky exchange student. We can't just be your neighbor or your coworker.

Remember: I grew up in the 1970s, when "Oriental" characters always had to be the buck-toothed laundry boys who pined for the sexy girl, never the hero or hunk (not that it's changed much). Ms. Cho points out that one of my favorite 1970s TV shows, *Kung Fu,* starring the Caucasian David Carradine, should have really been named, *Hey . . . That Guy's Not Chinese!* It's pretty much been that Asians, a.k.a. "Orientals," were the ching-chong version of the Village Idiot in just about every American drama. Needless to say, I've tired of this in my "old age."

My diva not only breaks all those stereotypes of the oh-so-polite eyelash-batting, teeth-covering Asian girl, but also manages to throw them out—the baby, the bathwater, the chopsticks, and the redneck. "So, Ms. Cho," said a Midwestern TV announcer, "we're changing our affiliate. Why don't you tell our audience in your *native* language?" Margaret made a "what-the-fuck?" face, turned to the camera, and said, "They're *changing* their affiliate."

The thing about being gay is that I could always sort of hide it, but being the son of a Japanese man, it's sometimes an unmistakable difference; technically, I'm "half" Asian—thank you, Cher: "Half-Breed, how I love to hate the word!"—no really, look it up. Cher *sang* that!

"What *are* you?" the bus driver, my date, or the kid sitting next to me in class would ask, puzzled by my "racial" features that defy categorization. I wish I could have been more like Margaret in these situations, and especially in junior high. I wanted to be the Action Hero for gay Asian boys who refuse to fit the stereotypes: the sexless bottom or the "mathlete" for that matter—man, I suck at math.

My internal change culminated in a warm, close, and lovingly bitchy relationship with my friend Peter, who's "foreign" born but from upstate New York. We would recite Margaret's best lines back and forth to each other in this rhythmic have-to-be-in-the-know secret decoder-ring banter. Why? Because like me, he grew up on the East Coast thinking that as a queer Asian boy he was a second-class citizen, never a brilliant hottie, worthy of love and attention.

Peter and I had a ritual of sorts, wordplay to reinforce our shared "We're tired of this racist shit," and the only person who came close to expressing how we've felt our whole lives was our hero Margaret. "Go back to where you came from!" A common request thrown at people who seemingly aren't born in America. Thankfully, Margaret made popular what we always thought but only occasionally said: "Well, I can't go *back* to where I came from . . . I think the only people who can say that are the Native Americans."

I grew, I learned, I helped organize gay Asian men's groups across the country. I found other mixed/Asian men, and I became a lot less bitter. While I no longer have a need to vent on every street corner, I still adore biting humor. I think it's the bitchy-queen gene that I did manage to get.

Divas reflect our sense of drama, tragedy, and love of the limelight. Or at least a wish to be seen and admired, not punched and insulted. The myriad of divas, and the boys and men who admired them in this collection, just goes to show that there's one for every one of us: some of them graceful, some tragic, and some who you'd want on your side in a bar fight.

I used to think that I could never identify with the Barbras or the Célines, but I suppose I do. I just needed mine to look more like me, to be the tomboy I wish I could have been, and to have a sailor's mouth like mine—but as brave, beautiful, and outspoken as I have learned to become, I'll never have the balls that Margaret has. She keeps me striving for more.

Mary J. Blige

I Take Shallowness Seriously

Jeffery Conway

Oddly enough, I rarely use the word "diva." It's just a personal quirk, but to me the word is clichéd, a little too sugary, because I always hear it used with a sense of sheer reverence, obsequiousness. Generally speaking, I want none of that. The word "diva," as once defined by Wikipedia, can be applied to great female opera singers (think Maria Callas), outstanding female performers of non-operatic works (such as Aretha Franklin), as well as "prominent women adored in gay male pop culture" (an always ambivalent adoration, I might add). Kathy Griffin (herself a woman beloved by gays) recently said about Oprah, "I worship her, AND I also think she is totally ridiculous!" Then there's the "negative connotation" of the word (a whole subsection of the Wikipedia definition): "a star who is a 'diva' is arrogant, difficult to work with, high-maintenance, manipulative, fussy, highly strung, and/ or demanding." Amen to that. It's not that I insist that the word have a pejorative meaning. Rather, the pleasure I take from divas comes from this interplay of the positive sense of the word with the negative—and every diva worth her salt, I contend, embodies both poles.

I discovered the music of Mary J. Blige in the mid- to late 1990s—though I didn't know her name until a few years later. The DJ at my gym would play her songs, and I always liked them, but I never knew who the singer was until "Dance for Me." When I heard that song I was immediately starved for it—the infectious rhythm and sexy lyrics (who doesn't, after all, want to get things "percolating"?)—and I couldn't rest until I bought the CD. Since that moment, it has been mostly about Mary. The last singer/diva who moved me in such a way was Stevie Nicks. Stevie's solo albums of the '80s hooked me in the early '90s, for some inexplicable reason—though if I reflect for half a second, I can see how her fragile, gravelly voice grabbed me viscerally, just as much as her impossibly fringy shawls, sky-high suede platform boots, and gauzy frocks made me gasp in delighted horror.

Mary spoke directly to me. This probably won't come as a shock, but there was this guy. Ripped my heart out, made me insane. In my despair, there she was. My sober black sister who, apparently, had had experience with the same type of man. Mary, who threw all reason and right thinking out the window for passion; who took tons of shit and abuse in the name of love; who found him cheating and stupidly took him back thinking she could change him, only to be lied to again. After shucking all friends, spiritual values, and any mode of healthy behavior for "this guy," I was alone. Enter Mary (via iPod and long, solitary walks along the Hudson). She could relate. Together we made it through.

This love for Mary has a dangerous edge. My various and multiform adulations of movie stars, singers, celebutantes, and their offspring are always accompanied by a slightly raised eyebrow. My fascination entails a certain degree of bemusement—especially when anyone takes themselves a tad-winkle too seriously. Is it wrong that I love reading tabloid accounts of Mary's toilet seat phobia (her infamous "35 Cities, 35 Toilet Seats" tour—she demanded new toilet seats in every dressing room bathroom at each concert hall), or that I like reading about the sordid details of Stevie Nicks trying to break out of a rehab in the middle of the night—her tattered shawl ensnaring her on a barbed wire fence? Is it wrong?

I take shallowness seriously. I want to know (and write about) the personality quirks, dirt, foibles, backstage hissy fits, and self-misconceptions of the famous, no matter how deeply I admire and enjoy their *art*. I've spent a lot of time writing about this, more than some might find the topics merit. *Phoebe 2002: An Essay in Verse* (New York: Turtle Point, 2003), the 650-page collaborative mock-epic deconstruction of the 1950 film *All About Eve* that I coauthored with David Trinidad and Lynn Crosbie, can be read as a paean to all the divas I have loved, especially Bette Davis. In that book, I wrote one section on the famous divas Jackie O., Joan Crawford, Anne Sexton, and Jackie Susann, and an exploration of what happens when their "celebrity" enters the realm of powder rooms, private bathrooms, and public restrooms, where rivals, smells, telltale sounds, and crazed fans may linger. I'm currently working on two new projects on movies, one on *Valley of the Dolls,* and one on *Showgirls.* My love of the dark side of divadom grows and grows.

But what is it about Mary J.? I ardently admire her soap opera of a life—overcoming a childhood of poverty, neglect, violence; struggling through relationships with lying, cheating men; triumphing over drugs and low self-esteem; getting over the betrayal of friends and the loss of family members—for having worked through all of these traumas and living to sing about it onstage in

Mary J. Blige

283

a platinum blonde bubble-cut wig and ginormous round white-frame sunglasses, working herself into a sweaty, disheveled, riveting frenzy. After all, only a diva would have to banish drama from her life. *That's* what it is about Mary. Well, that, and her toilet seat thing. Is nothing sacred? Probably not. I'm not sure if this personality defect, this desire to see and experience the underbelly of a diva's glamorous life, is decidedly "homosexual," though my gay friends are certainly more likely to get it than anyone else. Maybe it's just a Jeffery thing. This much I know is true: I heart, most sincerely, Mary J.

Princess Leia

Leia's Kiss

Christopher Hennessy

When *Star Wars* came to movie screens in 1977, I was only four years old. Even so, I found myself immersed in and obsessed with a story that would affect me in profound—and yet subtly felt, slowly realized—ways for a long, long time.

Star Wars held for me, among other things, the first woman-hero who captivated my imagination. My memory of her begins with the white, ghostlike flow of her robes as she slinks down dark corridors of a starship, fleeing Imperial Stormtroopers. Her "blaster" pistol is at the ready, slender with a long barrel, a black daggerlike shape against the white of her dress. As she fires energy blasts at her would-be captors, my child's brain must have thought, "What kind of girl is this?"

I had met my first diva.

In fact, only a few scenes later, Carrie Fisher as Princess Leia Organa delivers one of the most diva-laden lines in film history. Facing the man in charge of the monstrous Death Star space station, Governor Tarkin (played by Peter Cushing), she says, "Governor Tarkin, I should have expected to find you holding [Darth] Vader's leash. I recognized your foul stench when I was brought on board." The villainous Tarkin responds, "You don't know how hard I found it, signing the order to terminate your life." Brilliantly, she snaps back, "I'm surprised that you had the courage to take the responsibility yourself."

Leia is confident, quick to act, imperious, powerful, even downright bitchy at times, but more importantly her character allowed me to realize how I saw myself, and even more importantly offered me a lens of empathy through which I learned about my own desires.

I would grow up with Leia, seeing her as a kind of sister to my imagination, someone whom I looked up to, imagined myself as. In the first movie, as Leia and Luke make their escape from a jail cell on the Death Star, they come to a chasm they must swing across via a thin wire. She gives a quick kiss "for luck!" (drama queen!) to the astonished towhead, and they swing across, those white robes flowing behind her. It was the image of that quick kiss, hardly a blip on the screen, that reached into my four-year-old guts and turned a button, or flicked a switch . . . somehow sent a pulse throughout my body that awakened something I wouldn't understand until years later.

When she plants a forceful kiss on the recuperating Luke in *The Empire Strikes Back,* the little boy of seven was thrilled at the thought of kissing a handsome blond boy, forcing my lips onto his, of making his eyes pop open in surprise and excitement. Of feeling the electricity of desire.

The heart—and heat—of my reaction, of course, was clouded until years later, but in my imagination I would always take the place of the woman kissing the man. Not because I saw myself as feminine, but rather because it was a way to imagine, to access (subconsciously, no doubt) my own desire, my wish. How lucky she was to kiss Luke! And how terrified I was she would kiss the bad-boy loner Han Solo. That fear was also a terrible passion I tried to ignore.

But of course, though wanting to love the good-farm-boy-turned-solider Luke, she is pulled to Solo—who is then suddenly taken from her (by the order of her dark father Vader, no less!). She spends the last half of the second movie robed in a sexy, shimmering gown of maroons and pinks, her hair tightly and elegantly braided; she is the feminine epitomized. And even as she sheds tears as her man is taken from her, she emanates an austere willfulness.

In the third movie, *Return of the Jedi,* she appears clad in a (metal!) bikini as she lounges at the feet of an obscenely obese mob-boss slug, Jabba the Hut. And yet, enslaved as part of a plan to save her bad-boy love, she somehow maintains every inch of her dignity. Her eyes furtively dart for opportunity, her muscles tensed for the moment she must act. She is an Amazon queen as she leaps into action and strangles her mammoth captor with her own chains. *Oh, to be so strong, empowered, confident, and sexy—so perfect in one's own body,* lamented the chubby ten-year-old who felt so wrong in his own.

Just as I had stared longingly at the awkward, blond, and beautiful farm boy of Luke Skywalker, I was attracted in different (but powerful) ways to Leia. She was always regal, in control, athletic but feminine, graceful but emphatically official, sexy but unaware of her own sex appeal.

Somehow she fights wars in space and on hostile ice worlds, is enslaved in a dungeon, finds herself lost and alone on a strange forest planet—yet she remains, impossibly, perfectly coifed!

287

During those years of my childhood, from four to ten years old, Leia was a true princess, the stars' diva.

And the stars were where I learned about the imagination, where I discovered the epic power of the story of good and evil, of love versus power, of mysticism, of the Jungian archetypes (the princess, the hero, the dark king) that have followed me everywhere. Leia, Luke, Darth Vader, and even Han Solo helped me discover the possibilities that await those willing to consider the impossible.

Contributors

Michael J. Andrews works for a family-owned international advertising firm as a senior account manager working with fashion and electronics clients. A New School graduate in poetry in 2006, Andrews has been published in www.thundersandwich.com, *Cream City Review,* and *Yuan Yang.* He has read at Homo Text, a Dixon Place reading series, as well as Earshot out of Williamsburg, Brooklyn. He is currently the reader for *First Proof,* the literary supplement for *BOMB* magazine. He lives in Brooklyn with his partner, Craig.

Lawrence Applebaum, a native New Yorker, is an editor for *Mudfish,* a poetry and art journal. He has been nominated for three Pushcart Prizes, most recently for his poem in *Skidrow Penthouse.* His photography has been featured in *Playbill* and *TheaterWeek,* as well as on book covers. He is currently at work on his first novel.

David Bergman is the editor or author of over a dozen books. Most recently, he edited *Gay American Autobiography* (University of Wisconsin Press, 2009) and translated with Katia Sainson the selected poems of Jean Sénac (Sheep Meadow, 2009). He is the author of *The Violet Hour: The Violet Quill and the Making of Gay Culture* (Columbia University Press, 2004). His most recent book of poetry is *Heroic Measures* (Ohio State University Press, 1998) and he won the George Elliston Prize for *Cracking the Code* (Ohio State University Press, 1985). He lives in Baltimore and teaches at Towson University.

Mark Bibbins is the author of two books of poems: *Sky Lounge* (Graywolf, 2003), which received a Lambda Literary Award, and *The Dance of No Hard Feelings* (Copper Canyon, 2009). He teaches in the graduate writing program at the New School, where he also cofounded *LIT* magazine. He was a 2005 New York Foundation for the Arts poetry fellow. His poems have appeared in *Poetry, Paris Review, Boston Review, Tin House,* and *jubilat,* and in such anthologies as *The Best American Poetry 2004* (Scribner, 2004), *Great American Prose Poems* (Scribner, 2003), *Third Rail: The Poetry of Rock and Roll* (MTV Books, 2007), and *Legitimate Dangers: American Poets of the New Century* (Sarabande Books, 2006).

Richard Blanco was made in Cuba, assembled in Spain, and imported to the United States—meaning his mother, seven months pregnant, and the rest of the family arrived as exiles from Cuba to Madrid, where he was born. Only forty-five days later, the family emigrated once more and settled in New York City, then eventually in Miami, where he was raised and educated. His acclaimed first book, *City of a Hundred Fires* (University of Pittsburgh Press, 1998), explores the yearnings and negotiation of cultural identity as a Cuban American, and received the prestigious Agnes Starrett Poetry Prize from the University of Pittsburgh Press. His second book, *Directions to the Beach of the Dead* (University of Arizona Press, 2005) won the 2006 PEN/American Beyond Margins Award for its continued exploration of the universal themes of home and place. Blanco is currently working on a nonfiction collection of essays about growing up in Miami, where he now lives.

Michael Broder received his MFA from the Creative Writing Program at New York University in 2005. His work has appeared in *Court Green, Columbia Poetry Review, BLOOM, Painted Bride Quarterly,* and other journals, as well as in the anthology *This New Breed* (Windstorm Creative, 2004). He is working on a doctorate in classical studies at the Graduate Center of the City University of New York and is a City University of New York Writing Fellow.

Jericho Brown worked as speechwriter for the mayor of New Orleans before receiving his PhD in creative writing and literature from the University of Houston. He also holds an MFA from the University of New Orleans and a BA from Dillard University. His poems have appeared or are forthcoming in *The Iowa Review, jubilat, New England Review, Prairie Schooner,* and several other journals and anthologies. The recipient of a Cave Canem Fellowship, two scholarships to the Bread Loaf Writer's Conference, and two travel fellowships to

290

the Krakow Poetry Seminar in Poland, Brown now serves as assistant editor at *Callaloo* and teaches creative writing as assistant professor of English at the University of San Diego. His first book, *Please,* was published by New Issues in 2008.

Regie Cabico is a spoken-word pioneer, having won the 1993 Nuyorican Poets Cafe Grand Slam Championship, and has appeared on two seasons of HBO's *Def Poetry Jam.* His most recent solo play, *Unbuckled, Uncensored,* was presented at the Asian Arts Initiative. He received three fellowships for poetry and performance art from the New York Foundation for the Arts and a poetry fellowship from the DC Commission for the Arts. His short plays with Nina Simone's music were used in the New York production of *Too Much Light Makes Baby Go Blind,* which received three NY Innovative Theater Award Nominations and a 2006 Award for Best Performance Art Production. He is the artistic director of Sol & Soul and resides in Washington, D.C.

Joseph Campana is a poet and a scholar of Renaissance literature with essays on Spenser, Shakespeare, early modern poetics, and the history of sexuality in or forthcoming in *PMLA, Modern Philology,* and elsewhere. He is the author of poetic iconography of Audrey Hepburn, *The Book of Faces* (Graywolf, 2005). His poems have appeared or will appear in *Colorado Review, Hotel Amerika, New England Review, Michigan Quarterly Review, Prairie Schooner, Poetry, Triquarterly, Conjunctions, Kenyon Review, Field, Cincinnati Review, Post Road, Ninth Letter,* and elsewhere. He is the recipient of a 2007 Creative Writing Fellowship from the NEA. Current poetry projects include a recently finished manuscript, "Sheltering Bough," and a new collection in progress, "Seraphic Monologues."

Cyrus Cassells is the author of four acclaimed books of poetry: *The Mud Actor* (Holt, 1982; Carnegie Mellon, 2000), *Soul Make a Path through Shouting* (Copper Canyon, 1994), *Beautiful Signor* (Copper Canyon, 1997), and *More Than Peace and Cypresses* (Copper Canyon, 2004). His fifth book of poems and his translation of a selection of poems by Francesc Parcerisas are forthcoming. Among his honors are a Lannan Literary Award, a William Carlos Williams Award, a Pushcart Prize, two NEA grants, and a Lambda Literary Award. He teaches at Texas State University–San Marcos, and lives in Austin and Paris.

Guillermo Castro is a poet and translator. His work appears in *Nthposition, Eyewear, EOAGH, The Recluse, BLOOM, Barrow Street, Lapetitezine, Frigatezine,* and *Margin,* among others, and in anthologies including *This Full Green Hour* (Sonopo, 2008) and *Saints of Hysteria: A Half Century of Collaborative American Poetry* (Soft Skull, 2007). His prose is represented in the anthology *Latin Lovers* (Painted Leaf, 1999). His translations of Argentine poet Olga Orozco, in collaboration with Ron Drummond, are featured in *Guernica, Terra Incognita, Visions,* and the *U.S. Latino Review.* He's also collaborated on a musical with composer Doug Geers, *How I Learned to Draw a Sheep,* providing book and lyrics. Castro is the author of a chapbook, *Toy Storm* (Big Fat Press, 1997). He lives in New York City and is a native of Argentina.

Jeffery Conway's most recent book is *The Album That Changed My Life* (Cold Calm, 2006). He is also the author of two collaborations with David Trinidad and Lynn Crosbie, *Phoebe 2002: An Essay in Verse* (Turtle Point, 2003) and *Chain Chain Chain* (Ignition, 2000). His work is included in the anthology *Saints of Hysteria: A Half Century of Collaborative American Poetry* (Soft Skull, 2007), and recent poems can be found in *Painted Bride Quarterly, Electronic Poetry Review,* and *Softblow.* He lives in New York City.

Steven Cordova's first collection of poetry, *Long Distance,* is forthcoming from Bilingual Press. He is the author of the chapbook *Slow Dissolve* (Momotombo, 2003), and his poems have appeared in various journals and anthologies, including *The Wind Shifts: New Latino Poetry* (University of Arizona Press, 2007), *Barrow Street, Calalloo, Cimarron Review, The Journal,* and *Northwest Review.* He lives in Brooklyn, New York.

Alfred Corn is the author of nine books of poems, the most recent titled *Contradictions* (Copper Canyon, 2002). He has published a collection of essays, *The Metamorphoses of Metaphor* (Viking, 1987), and a novel, *Part of His Story* (Mid-List, 1997). In 2001 Abrams brought out *Aaron Rose Photographs,* for which he supplied the introduction. Fellowships and prizes awarded for his poetry include a Guggenheim, an NEA, an Award in Literature from the Academy and Institute of Arts and Letters, and one from the Academy of American Poets. For 2004–5, he held the Amy Clampitt residency in Lenox, Massachusetts. In 2005–6, he taught for the Poetry School in London. He lives in Hudson, New York.

Peter Covino is assistant professor of English and creative writing at the University of Rhode Island. He is the author of the poetry collection *Cut Off the Ears of Winter* (New Issues, 2005), winner of the PEN/Osterweil Award, and a finalist for the Thom Gunn Award and the Paterson Poetry Prize. His chapbook, *Straight Boyfriend* (Thorngate Road, 2001), won the Frank O'Hara Poetry Prize. He received his PhD from the University of Utah and an MS from the Columbia University School of Social Work. His poems have appeared or are forthcoming in *Colorado Review, Columbia, Gulf Coast, Interim, Paris Review, Verse, The Penguin Anthology of Italian-American Writing* (Penguin, 2002), and *European Poets* (Graywolf, 2008), among others.

C. Cleo Creech, an Atlanta writer and poet, is originally from the small rural tobacco community of Stancil's Chapel, North Carolina. In addition to having once been editor for the Georgia Poetry Society, he has published a number of chapbooks of his own and edited others. His work has appeared in such publications as *White Crane Journal, Pedestal Magazine, Phoenix Feathers, Outside the Green Zone,* and *Di-verse-city.* He is active in the local poetry, intown neighborhood, and activist community.

Lewis DeSimone is the author of the novel *Chemistry* (Lethe, 2008). His work has appeared in *Christopher Street, James White Review,* and *Harrington Gay Men's Fiction Quarterly,* as well as in the anthologies *Beyond Definition: New Writing from Gay and Lesbian San Francisco* (Manic, 1994), *Charmed Lives: Gay Spirit in Storytelling* (Lethe, 2006), and *Best Gay Love Stories: Summer Flings* (Alyson Books, 2007). He lives in San Francisco, where he is currently working on a new novel. He can be reached through www.lewisdesimone.com.

John Dimes, a District of Columbia native, is a professional illustrator and writer—and former standup comic—whose works have appeared in *BENT Magazine* and in the anthologies *The Sound of Horror* (Magus, 2007) and *Diabolic Tales: An Anthology of Dark Minds* (Diabolic Publications, 2007). He is the author of the novels *Intractions* (DarkHart, 2007) and *The Rites of Pretending Tribe* (Zumaya Otherworlds, 2007). You can find out more about him on his official Web page at www.johndimes.com.

Mark Doty is the author of eight books of poetry, including *Fire to Fire: New and Selected Poems* (HarperCollins, 2008). He's also published four volumes of nonfiction prose, most recently *Dog Years* (HarperCollins, 2007), which won the Stonewall Book Award from the American Library Association for the best GLBT nonfiction book of 2007. He's received the National Book Critics Circle Award, the L.A. Times Book Prize, the T. S. Eliot Prize in the U.K., and two Lambda Literary Awards. He lives in New York

City and on Fire Island, and will soon join the faculty at Rutgers University.

Peter Dubé is the author of the chapbook *Vortex Faction Manifesto* (Vortex Editions, 2001), the novel *Hovering World* (DC Books, 2002), and *At the Bottom of the Sky* (DC Books, 2007), a collection of linked short fiction. He is also the editor of the anthology *Madder Love: Queer Men and the Precincts of Surrealism* (Rebel Satori, 2008). In addition to writing fiction, he is a widely published cultural critic with essays on books and the visual arts appearing in journals such as *CV Photo, ESSE,* and *Spirale,* and in exhibition publications for various galleries, among them SKOL, Mercer Union, and the Leonard and Bina Ellen Gallery of Concordia University. Dubé lives and works in Montreal.

Jim Elledge's most recent book, *A History of My Tattoo: A Poem* (Stonewall, 2006), earned him the Lambda Literary Award for gay male poetry as well as the Georgia Author of the Year Award in poetry. It was also a finalist for the Thom Gunn Award for gay male poetry. His chapbook, *The Book of the Heart Taken by Love,* was recently issued by Woodland Editions. His work has appeared in *Paris Review, jubilat, Five Fingers Review, Eleven Eleven, Court Green,* and other journals. He directs the MA in Professional Writing Program at Kennesaw State University, where he also directs both the Writers Workshop of Puerto Rico and Thorngate Road, a press for queer poets.

Edward Field lives in New York City's Greenwich Village with his partner, Neil Derrick, with whom he wrote *The Villagers* (Painted Leaf, 2000), a historical novel about the Village. He is the author of more than ten books of poetry, his most recent being *After the Fall: Poems Old and New* (University of Pittsburgh Press, 2007). His memoir, *The Man Who Would Marry Susan Sontag: And Other Intimate Literary Portraits of the Bohemian Era,* was published by the University of Wisconsin Press in 2005. His awards include the W. H. Auden Award, the Bill Whitehead Lifetime Achievement Award, and the Lambda Literary Award, among others.

Bill Fogle is a contributor to *Walking Higher: Gay Men Write about the Deaths of Their Mothers* (Xlibris, 2004), edited by Alexander Renault. He is the brother of the 1970s rock legend Jobriath. An artist and writer living in Washington, D.C., he shares a house with five dogs and three cats. He is a very good cook.

RJ Gibson is a poet, designer, and landscaper splitting his time between north central West Virginia and Baltimore. He has studied literature and creative writing at West Virginia Wesleyan College and West Virginia University. His work has appeared in *BLOOM, Knockout, qarrtsiluni,* and *Six Sentences.* He is currently on his fifth copy of Eurythmics' *Savage* and is entering Warren Wilson's MFA program.

Rigoberto González is the author of seven books, most recently the memoir *Butterfly Boy: Memories of a Chicano Mariposa* (University of Wisconsin Press, 2006), winner of the American Book Award from the Before Columbus Foundation; and a story collection, *Men without Bliss* (University of Oklahoma Press, 2008). The recipient of Guggenheim and NEA fellowships, and of various international artist residencies, he writes a semimonthly Latino book column, now entering its seventh year, for the *El Paso Times.* He is contributing editor for *Poets and Writers Magazine,* on the board of directors of the National Book Critics Circle, on the board of directors of Fishouse Poems: A Poetry Archive, and on the advisory circle of Con Tinta, a collective of Chicano/Latino activist writers. He lives in New York City and is associate professor of English at Rutgers University–Newark.

Forrest Hamer is the author of *Call & Response* (Alice James, 1995), winner of the Beatrice Hawley Award; *Middle Ear* (Roundhouse, 2000), winner of the Northern California Book Award; and *Rift* (Four Way Books, 2007). His work is widely anthologized and appears in three editions of *The Best American Poetry.* He has received fellowships from the California Arts Council and the Bread Loaf Writer's Conference, and he has taught on the poetry faculty of the Callaloo Creative Writing Workshops.

Benjamin Harper is a graduate of Warren Wilson College in Asheville, North Carolina. He has been employed as a garbage collector, as an oral surgery assistant, and in various positions in the world of children's publishing. He currently works as a planning manager for Scholastic, Inc. in Manhattan. Harper has published twenty-seven books, including *Obsessed with Star Wars* (Chronicle Books, 2008) and a toddler favorite, *Thank You, Superman!* (Meredith Books, 2006). He lives in Brooklyn.

Christopher Hennessy is the author of *Outside the Lines: Talking with Contemporary Gay Poets* (University of Michigan Press, 2005). His poetry appeared in *Ploughshares'* special "Emerging Writers" edition and was anthologized in *This New Breed* (Windstorm Creative, 2004), a collection of emerging gay poets. His writing has been published in *American Poetry Review, Verse, Cimarron Review, Writer's Chronicle, Crab Orchard Review, Natural Bridge, Wisconsin Review, Brooklyn Review, Knockout,* and elsewhere. He is associate editor of the *Gay and Lesbian Review Worldwide* and maintains the blog areyououtsidethelines.blogspot.com.

Scott Hightower is the author of three books of poetry. His third book, *Part of the Bargain* (Copper Canyon, 2005), won Copper Canyon Press's Hayden Carruth Book Prize. He is also a former fellow of the Valparaiso Artist Center in Mojácar and the recipient of a 2008 Willis Barnstone Translation Prize. Hightower is a contributing editor to *The Journal.* A native of central Texas, he lives and works in New York City.

Walter Holland, PhD, is the author of two books of poetry, *A Journal of the Plague Years: Poems 1979–1992* (Magic City, 1992) and *Transatlantic* (Painted Leaf, 2001), as well as a novel, *The March* (Masquerade Books, 1996). His short stories have been published in *Art and Understanding, Harrington Gay Men's Fiction Quarterly,* and in the anthologies *Rebel Yell* (Haworth, 2001) and *Mama's Boy: Gay Men Writing about Their Mothers* (Painted Leaf, 2000). Some of his poetry credits include *Antioch Review, Art and Understanding, Barrow Street, Bay Windows, Body Positive, Christopher Street, Chiron Review, The Cream City Review, Found Object, Men's Style, Pegasus, Phoebe,* and the anthology *Poets for Life: Seventy-Six Poets Respond to AIDS* (Crown, 1989). He lives in New York City and teaches poetry and literature at the New School as well as working as a physical therapist.

Jonathan Howle earned an MFA in playwriting from the New School University School of Drama in 2004. His play *The Great American Horror Movie Musical* debuted at the Minneapolis Fringe Festival during the summer of 2008. He teaches at Plaza College in Jackson Heights, New York, and is currently writing a new full-length play entitled "The Trembling."

Collin Kelley is an Atlanta native and award-winning poet, playwright, and journalist. He is the author of *After the Poison* (Finishing Line, 2008), *Slow to Burn* (Metro Mania, 2006), *Better to Travel* (iUniverse, 2003), and a spoken-word album, *HalfLife Crisis* (Perry Playhouse Productions, 2004). He is the recipient of a Georgia Author of the Year Award and a nominee for the Kate Tufts Discovery Award, Lambda Literary Award, and the Pushcart Prize. Kelley's poetry has appeared or is forthcoming in *Atlanta Review, MiPOesias,*

LocusPoint, Terminus, In Posse Review, Blue Fifth Review, New Delta Review, Chiron Review, poeticdiversity, The Pedestal, Lily, Welter, SubtleTea, and the critically acclaimed anthologies *Red Light: Superheroes, Saints, and Sluts* (Arsenal Pulp, 2005) and *We Don't Stop Here* (Private Press, 2008). He is also coeditor of the award-winning *Java Monkey Speaks* anthology series (Poetry Atlanta Press). For more information, visit www.collinkelley.com.

Michael Klein is the author of the memoirs *Track Conditions* (Persea Books, 1997; University of Wisconsin Press, 2003) and *The End of Being Known* (University of Wisconsin Press, 2003), and a book of poems, *1990* (Provincetown Arts, 1993), which tied with James Schuyler to win a Lambda Literary Award in 1993. He also won a Lambda Literary Award in 1990 for editing *Poets for Life: Seventy-Six Poets Respond to AIDS* (Crown, 1989). He has taught at Sarah Lawrence College, City College of New York, and, for the past decade, in the MFA program at Goddard College in Port Townsend, Washington. He is currently working on a book of poems called "Then, We Were Still Living" and a memoir called "When I Was a Twin."

Wayne Koestenbaum has published five books of poetry: *Best-Selling Jewish Porn Films* (Turtle Point, 2006), *Model Homes* (BOA Editions, 2004), *The Milk of Inquiry* (Persea Books, 1999), *Rhapsodies of a Repeat Offender* (Persea Books, 1994), and *Ode to Anna Moffo and Other Poems* (Persea Books, 1990). He has also published a novel, *Moira Orfei in Aigues-Mortes* (Soft Skull, 2004), and five books of nonfiction: *Andy Warhol* (Lipper/Viking, 2001); *Cleavage* (Ballantine Books, 2000); *Jackie Under My Skin* (Farrar, Straus & Giroux, 1995); *The Queen's Throat* (Poseidon, 1993), a National Book Critics Circle Award finalist; and *Double Talk* (Routledge, 1989). His newest book, *Hotel Theory* (Soft Skull, 2007), is a hybrid of fiction and nonfiction. He is a Distinguished Professor of English at the City University of New York Graduate Center, and currently also a visiting professor in the painting department of the Yale School of Art.

Patrick Letellier, a writer living in San Francisco, has won three national journalism awards, including the 2003 Sarah Pettit Award for Excellence in LGBT Media, a 2006 Excellence in Online Journalism Award, and a 2007 AEPOCH Award. His work has appeared in the *San Francisco Chronicle, Journal of the American Medical Association,* and gay publications nationwide including *Advocate, POZ* magazine, and gay.com. Though not transgender or a lesbian, Patrick writes a monthly column on transgender rights for *Lesbian News,* a

297

Los Angeles–based magazine. He is a 2007 Lambda Literary Foundation Retreat fellow as well as coauthor of the first book on gay domestic violence, *Men Who Beat the Men Who Love Them* (Haworth, 1991). Besides Queen Elizabeth I, his obsessions include *The Simpsons,* insects, Rome, and marathon running.

Vince A. Liaguno is a writer, editor, and founder of the small publisher Dark Scribe Press. As a longtime contributing editor at *Autograph Collector,* a national specialty-niche magazine for enthusiasts of the titular hobby, his many celebrity interviews and profiles have included a healthy dose of divas, including Kathy Bates, Meg Tilly, Olympia Dukakis, the late Janet Leigh, and Jamie Lee Curtis—with whom he jokingly claims to have developed a "lifelong obsession" and to whom he dedicated his debut novel, *The Literary Six* (Outskirts, 2006). He currently resides on the eastern end of Long Island, New York, with his partner of twenty years, their two cocker spaniels, and a cat named Moyet—after British chanteuse Alison Moyet. He is a member of the Horror Writers Association (HWA) and the National Book Critics Circle (NBCC). He can be reached at www.VinceLiaguno.com.

Paul Lisicky is the author of *Lawnboy* (2006) and *Famous Builder* (2002), both published by Graywolf Press. His recent work appears in *Five Points, Conjunctions, Gulf Coast, Subtropics, The Seattle Review, The Literary Review,* and in the anthologies *Truth in Nonfiction* (University of Iowa Press, 2008) and *Naming the World* (Random House, 2008). He has taught in the graduate writing programs at Cornell, Sarah Lawrence, and Antioch Los Angeles. He lives in New York City and teaches at New York University and in the low-residency MFA program at Fairfield University. A novel and a collection of short prose pieces are forthcoming.

Timothy Liu is the author of eight books of poems, most recently *Of Thee I Sing* (University of Georgia Press, 2004), *Bending the Mind around the Dream's Blown Fuse* (Talisman House, 2008), and *Polytheogamy* (Saturnalia Books, 2009). His journals and papers are archived in the Berg Collection at the New York Public Library. Liu, who lives in Manhattan, is associate professor of English at William Paterson University and a member of the Core Faculty in Bennington College's Graduate Writing Seminars.

Gary Ljungquist is Hixson Professor of Humanities and Coordinator of Women's Studies at Salem College, a small women's college in Winston-Salem, North Carolina, where he teaches French, Spanish, women's studies, and GLBTQ studies. He earned a doctorate in French literature from Cornell University. He lives in Lewisville, North Carolina, with his partner, Billy McClain, and his cat, Lulu. He is currently working on a collection of poems inspired by Alfred Hitchcock films and another inspired by childhood memories of penny candy.

Jack Lynch holds an MFA from Hunter College and a BFA from the New School. His poetry has appeared in *Ology, POZ* magazine, *Paterson Literary Review,* and various online literary journals. Lynch's work can also be seen in a forthcoming anthology about "Poets on Loss." He lives in New York City.

Dante Micheaux is an emerging poet whose work has appeared in various journals and anthologies, including *BLOOM* and *Callaloo.* He has been a guest poet of the Poetry Project and the Cathedral Church of Saint John the Divine, among others. His honors include a prize in poetry from the Vera List Center for Art & Politics, the Oscar Wilde Award, and fellowships from Cave Canem Foundation and the New York Times Foundation. He has served on the faculty of foreign languages at the New School and has taught numerous poetry workshops. He resides in New York City.

Sam J. Miller is a writer and a community organizer. His work has appeared in literary magazines such as *Fourteen Hills, Fiction International, Permafrost, Pindeldyboz, other, SMUT!* and *Velvet Mafia,* as well as numerous zines and anthologies. He lives in the Bronx with his partner of seven years. Visit him at www.samjmiller.com, and/or drop him a line at samjmiller79@yahoo.com.

Michael Montlack has two chapbooks: *Cover Charge* (Gertrude Press, 2008), winner of the 2007 Gertrude Prize; and *Girls, Girls, Girls* (Pudding House, 2008). His work has appeared in *Cimarron Review, New York Quarterly, BLOOM, 5 AM, Swink* (online), *Cream City Review, Court Green, MiPOesias, Poet Lore,* and other journals. A resident of New York City, where he graduated from New School's MFA program, Montlack teaches at Berkeley College and acts as an associate editor for *Mudfish.* In 2007 he was a Lambda Literary Fellow, a Ucross writing resident, and a finalist for the Brittingham/Pollak Poetry Prize. He can be reached at mikemont17@hotmail.com.

Christopher Murray is a Brooklyn-based writer whose work has appeared in *BLOOM, The Advocate, POZ* magazine, *New York Blade,* and the award-winning anthology *Bend, Don't Shatter* (Soft Skull, 2004), among others. He is a contributing writer at New York City's

299

Gay City News and has had his poems read by Garrison Keillor on NPR. He was a 2006–7 Charles H. Revson Fellow at Columbia University, is a psychotherapist in private practice in New York, and blogs at http://christophertmurray.blogspot.com.

Jim Nason has published two books of poetry, *If Lips Were as Red* (Palmerston, 1991) and *The Fist of Remembering* (Wolsak and Wynn, 2006). He has recently completed a new collection of poetry, "Chardin's Rabbit," and is presently working on a collection of short stories, "The Girl on the Escalator." His novel *The Housekeeping Journals* (2007) was published by Turnstone Press. He lives in Toronto.

Christopher Lee Nutter is coauthor of *Ignite the Genius Within* (Penguin, 2009) and *The Way Out: The Gay Man's Guide to Freedom* (HCI, 2006). He has also written about cultural trends, spirituality, and gay life for publications such as the *New York Times, Village Voice, Time Out New York, Vibe,* and *Details.* He lives in New York City.

Jeff Oaks is the author of two chapbooks, *The Unknown Country* (State Street, 1992) and *The Moon of Books* (Ultima Obscura, 2000). He has published poems in *Ploughshares, BLOOM, Seneca Review, 5 AM, Southern Poetry Review,* and other literary magazines. A recipient of three Pennsylvania Council of the Arts fellowships and a Pittsburgh Foundation fellowship, he teaches creative writing at the University of Pittsburgh, where he is the managing director for the Pittsburgh Contemporary Writers Series.

Kenji Oshima grew up in the suburbs of Boston during the 1970s but is now based in San Francisco. He was inspired by his social-worker parents to take on activism issues related to gay rights and HIV prevention, and in 1994 he moved to the Bay Area to become a national community organizer for gay Asian men's groups. He has subsequently spent his time as a mentor, consultant, writer, and educator. Currently his primary focus is life coaching others with ADHD and consulting with private industry representatives and individuals facing disability or oppression. In his spare time he breaks and builds things, writes for sfgam.com, and volunteers repairing wheelchairs for the homeless.

Ron Palmer is the author of *Logicalogics,* published in 2005 by Soft Skull Press. After teaching English at New York University, Binghamton University, Framingham State College, and the New School, he made a transition into a corporate career in sales. He lives in San Francisco with his boyfriend, Kevin Rolston.

D. A. Powell is the author of four books of poems. Recipient of the Pushcart Prize, an Academy of American Poets' Prize, and a fellowship from the National Endowment for the Arts, Powell's work has appeared in numerous magazines and anthologies, including *Boston Review, Kenyon Review, Best American Poetry 2008,* and the *Washington Post.* He teaches at the University of San Francisco.

Steven Riel's two chapbooks, *How to Dream* (1992) and *The Spirit Can Crest* (2003), were published by Amherst Writers & Artists Press. Christopher Bursk named Riel the 2005 Robert Fraser Distinguished Visiting Poet at Bucks County Community College. In 1987 one of Steven's poems was selected by Denise Levertov as runner-up for the Grolier Poetry Peace Prize. From 1987 to 1995 he served as poetry editor of *RFD.* Riel's poems have appeared in several anthologies, including *Lives in Translation* (Soleil, 1990) and *The Badboy Book of Erotic Poetry* (Masquerade Books, 1995), and in numerous periodicals, including *The Minnesota Review* and *Christopher Street.*

Michael Schiavi is associate professor of English and coordinator of English as a Second Language at New York Institute of Technology's Manhattan Campus. He received his PhD in English from New York University. His articles have appeared recently in *Cinema Journal, Theatre Journal, Modern Drama, College Literature,* and *Modern Language Studies.* He is currently working on a biography of Vito Russo.

Christopher Schmidt's first book of poems, *The Next in Line* (Slope Editions, 2008), was selected by Timothy Liu for the Slope Edition Book Prize. A PhD candidate at City University of New York Graduate Center, Schmidt's poems and essays have appeared in *Tin House, Court Green, SubStance,* and *Canadian Poetry,* and his journalism has appeared in *The New Yorker, New York Observer,* and *Village Voice.* He blogs at www.thenextinline.com.

Jason Schneiderman is the author of *Sublimation Point* (2004), a Stahlecker Selection from Four Way Books. His poems and essays have appeared in numerous journals and anthologies, including *Best American Poetry* (Scribner, 2005), *Tin House, Virginia Quarterly Review, Poetry London, American Poetry Review,* and *The Penguin Book of the Sonnet* (Penguin, 2001). He has received fellowships from the Bread Loaf Writers' Conference, the Corporation of Yaddo, and the Fine Arts Work Center in Provincetown. He has received the Emily Dickinson Award from the Poetry Society of America. A doctoral candidate at the Graduate Center of City University of New York, he teaches literature at Hunter College.

Lloyd Schwartz is Frederick S. Troy Professor of English at the University of Massachusetts–Boston, classical music editor of *The Boston Phoenix,* and a regular commentator for NPR's *Fresh Air.* His most recent book of poems is *Cairo Traffic* (University of Chicago Press, 2000), and he is coeditor of Library of America's collected works of Elizabeth Bishop, *Bishop: Poems, Prose, and Letters* (2008). His poems, articles, and reviews have appeared in *The New Yorker, The Atlantic, Vanity Fair, The New Republic, The Paris Review, The Pushcart Prize XII* (1987), and *Best American Poetry* (Scribner, 1991 and 1994). In 1994 he was awarded the Pulitzer Prize for criticism.

Reginald Shepherd (1963–2008) was the editor of *The Iowa Anthology of New American Poetries* (University of Iowa Press, 2004) and *Lyric Postmodernisms* (Counterpath, 2008). His five volumes of poetry, all published by the University of Pittsburgh Press, are *Fata Morgana* (2007); *Otherhood* (2003), a finalist for the 2004 Lenore Marshall Poetry Prize; *Wrong* (1999); *Angel, Interrupted* (1996); and *Some Are Drowning* (1994), winner of the 1993 Associated Writing Programs' Award in Poetry. He was also the author of *Orpheus in the Bronx: Essays on Identity, Politics, and the Freedom of Poetry* (University of Michigan Press, 2008), a National Book Critics Circle Award finalist. A widely anthologized recipient of many awards and honors, including fellowships from the National Endowment for the Arts and the Guggenheim Foundation, he lived with his partner, a cultural anthropologist, in Pensacola, Florida.

Aaron Smith is the author of *Blue on Blue Ground* (University of Pittsburgh Press, 2005), winner of the Agnes Lynch Starrett Poetry Prize. His chapbook, *What's Required* (Thorngate Road, 2003), won the Frank O'Hara Award. His work has appeared in various publications including *Barrow Street, Court Green, 5 AM, Gulf Coast, Pleiades,* and *Prairie Schooner.* He is a 2007 Fellow in Poetry from the New York Foundation for the Arts.

Allen Smith has had poems appear in such literary publications as *Asheville Poetry Review, Bay Leaves, Broad River Review, Crucible, Maryland Poetry Review,* and *Off the Rocks.* Pudding House Publications will be publishing his chapbook *Unfolding Maps.* The coauthor of Thompson Publishing Group's *Accommodating Employees with Psychiatric Disabilities: A Practical Guide to ADA Compliance* (2008), he has been a writer in the business-to-business legal publishing industry for seventeen years and written numerous newsletter and trade magazine articles. Originally from Durham, North Carolina, Allen has lived in Alexandria, Virginia, for more than a decade with his partner, Andrew Wilson.

Scott F. Stoddart, PhD, is dean of the School of Liberal Arts at the Fashion Institute of Technology, State University of New York. Prior to this, he was associate professor of liberal arts at Nova Southeastern University, where he taught courses in American literature, cinema studies, and musical theater history. He has published on the fiction of Henry James, E. M. Forster, and F. Scott Fitzgerald; the musical plays of Stephen Sondheim; and the films of the Coen Brothers, Jane Campion, Jack Clayton, John Ford, Oliver Stone, and Martin Scorsese. He has also published on the image of the president in Hollywood film and television. His first book, *The 1980s* (Greenwood Press, 2007), is in the series American Popular Culture Through History; he is at work on his second book, "'Queer Eye' for a 'Straight Dick': Contextualizing the Queer Villain in Film Noir."

Richard Tayson's books of poetry, both published by Kent State University Press, are *The World Underneath* (2008) and *The Apprentice of Fever* (1998), the 1997 Stan and Tom Wick Poetry Prize winner. Tayson's other awards include a New York Foundation for the Arts Fellowship, *Prairie Schooner*'s Edward Stanley Award, and a Pushcart Prize. His reviews, poems, and essays appear in *The Advocate, I Do / I Don't: Queers on Marriage* (Soft Skull, 2004), *Paris Review, Velvet Avalanche: A Collection of Erotic Poetry* (Satjah, 2006), *Jugular Defences* (Oscars, 1994), *Virginia Quarterly Review,* and *Lambda Book Report.* His coauthored book of nonfiction, *Look Up for Yes* (Viking-Penguin, 1998), appeared on bestseller lists in Germany and has been included in *Reader's Digest*'s *Today's Best Nonfiction* in the United States and Australia. Tayson is a Chancellor's Fellow in the PhD program in English at City University of New York's Graduate Center, where he is writing about William Blake's influence on American pop culture.

Brian Teare, the recipient of poetry fellowships from Stegner, National Endowment for the Arts, and MacDowell Colony, is the author of the award-winning debut *The Room Where I Was Born* (University of Wisconsin Press, 2003) and the chapbooks *Pilgrim* (palOmine, 2004) and *Transcendental Grammar Crown* (Woodland Editions, 2006). Two new books are forthcoming: *Sight Map* (University of California Press, 2009) and *Pleasure* (Ahsahta, 2010). He lives and teaches in San Francisco.

David Trinidad's most recent book of poetry, *The Late Show,* was published in 2007 by Turtle Point Press. His anthology *Saints of Hysteria: A Half-Century of Collaborative American Poetry* (coedited with Denise Duhamel and Maureen Seaton) was also published in 2007 by Soft Skull Press. His other books include *Plasticville* (Turtle Point, 2000) and *Phoebe 2002: An Essay in Verse* (Turtle Point, 2003). Trinidad teaches poetry at Columbia College in Chicago, where he coedits the journal *Court Green.*

Jim Van Buskirk's essays have been featured in various books, newspapers, magazines, radio broadcasts, and Web sites. He coauthored *Gay by the Bay: A History of Queer Culture in the San Francisco Bay Area* (Chronicle Books, 1996) and *Celluloid San Francisco: The Film Lover's Guide to Bay Area Movie Locations* (Chicago Review Press, 2006), and he coedited the nonfiction anthologies *Identity Envy: Wanting to Be Who We're Not* (Harrington Park, 2007) and *Love, Castro Street: Reflections of San Francisco* (Alyson Books, 2007). After working as program manager of the James C. Hormel Gay and Lesbian Center at the San Francisco Public Library from 1992 to 2007, Van Buskirk is currently at work on a family memoir to be entitled "My Grandmother's Suitcase."

Gregory Woods is professor of gay and lesbian studies at Nottingham Trent University, U.K. His critical books include *Articulate Flesh: Male Homo-eroticism and Modern Poetry* (1987) and *A History of Gay Literature: The Male Tradition* (1998), both from Yale University Press. His poetry collections are *We Have the Melon* (1992), *May I Say Nothing* (1998), *The District Commissioner's Dreams* (2002), and *Quidnunc* (2007), all from Carcanet Press.

Mark Wunderlich's first volume of poetry, *The Anchorage,* was published by the University of Massachusetts Press in 1999 and received the Lambda Literary Award. His second volume, *Voluntary Servitude,* was published by Graywolf Press in 2004. He is the recipient of fellowships from Stanford University, the NEA, the Fine Arts Work Center in Provincetown, the Massachusetts Cultural Council, and the Amy Lowell Trust. His work has appeared in such journals as the *Paris Review, Yale Review, Slate, Poetry,* and *Ploughshares,* among others, and his poems have been widely anthologized. He has taught at Stanford and Barnard College and in the graduate writing programs at Columbia University, Sarah Lawrence College, San Francisco State University, and Ohio University. He is currently a member of the Literature Faculty at Bennington College in Vermont and lives in New York's Hudson River Valley.